DESIGNING & BUILDING A SOLAR HOUSE

The Sun Stone. *The Aztec Calendar, drawing based on stone relief, approximately 11 feet 9 inches in diameter. The stone depicts the Aztec universe, with the sun at the center. Various markings indicate the time of year, which in Aztec culture was subdivided by 18 months of 20 days each.*

Four years the sacred oven
Had burned. . .
And the god of life
And the god of time
Called the one full of sores
And told him:
You must now support
The sky and the earth!

(Cuauhtitlán Codex)

DESIGNING & BUILDING A SOLAR HOUSE

YOUR PLACE IN THE SUN

BY DONALD WATSON

GARDEN WAY PUBLISHING
CHARLOTTE, VERMONT 05445

To Elise and Petrik

Copyright © 1977 by Donald Watson

Designed by David Robinson

Cover design by Trezzo/Braren Studio

Printed in the United States by The Village Press, Inc.

Library of Congress Cataloging in Publication Data

Watson, Donald, 1937-
  Designing & building a solar house.

  Bibliography: p.
  Includes index.
  1. Solar heating. 2. Solar houses—Design and construction. I. Title.
TH7413.W37   697'.78   76-53830
ISBN 0-88266-086-1
ISBN 0-88266-085-3 pbk.

CONTENTS

CHAPTER 1

SOLAR HEATING NOW

A solar house is designed to obtain part or all of its heating from the sun. Facing a window to the sun to directly trap solar heat is one of the simplest methods of solar heating, while placing solar collector panels on a house is typical of more advanced solar heating systems now being installed throughout the United States. Most houses built in the future probably will use similar solar methods because—as conventional fuels cost more and their supply becomes more uncertain—solar energy now has become economically practical and environmentally desirable.

Once one sees how easily house heating can be obtained from the sun, this forecast will not seem unrealistic. Many solar heating techniques can be made part of house design and construction without adding to the building costs. Other methods require an additional investment for the solar equipment, but they return that investment in fuel savings well within typical mortgage periods.

Solar heating is an essential part of house design because the proper planning and construction of the building itself can result in major energy savings. In addition to windows oriented to obtain winter solar heat, for instance, masonry surfaces on the interior can help store the heat that is gained. The house plan can be made compact and with separate zones, to reduce the volume of space that must be fully heated at one time. Such techniques—which use the conventional parts of a building to collect, store and distribute solar heat without energy-using pumps or fans—are examples of "passive" solar heating.

Specially designed equipment, solar collectors and heat-storage units for domestic water heating or for space heating and cooling require additional energy to operate pumps and fans to control the movement of heat, and thus are referred to as "active" solar heating methods.

Passive solar techniques are age-old, having been used with great ingenuity in traditional buildings throughout the world. Active solar heating has been developed in experimental houses in the United States since the late 1930's. These two approaches are often argued to be mutually exclusive of one another, but in fact are complementary, and can produce better results in combination than by being used independent of one another.

Buying or building a house is, for most people, a major investment of money and time—often the largest investment that one makes in a lifetime. With careful design and planning, what otherwise would be an ordinary house-building project can become a rich and satisfying experience, which contributes to the life of the family much more than can be measured in monetary terms. A solar house, in its relation to the land and the surrounding community, can embody our most profound feelings about living with nature and with society. And through the intelligence of the design, it can bring into form the ideals by which we hope to live. This book is written for those who wish to bring these ideals into reality.

1.1
From Indian to Astronaut: The Development of Solar Houses

Figure 1.1 *An engraving of Pueblo Bonito.*

Scientific research in solar energy began less than a century ago and was applied to house heating first in the 1930's. However, the early buildings of some native American Indians applied basic solar heating principles with great sophistication.

Pueblo Bonito in Chaco Canyon, New Mexico, is one of several extraordinary examples of early Southwest Indian settlements, (Figure 1.1). Built from 919 to 1180 A.D., and now in ruins, the pueblo once housed 1200 inhabitants within its semicircular structure—which measures about 520 feet in diameter and stood in tiers up to four stories. The determining points of the plan's geometry were based on the position of the sun at the summer and winter solstices. Mathematical analyses by Professor Ralph Knowles and students at the University of Southern California have revealed that the pueblo in its various stages of growth was so dimensioned that its surfaces were exposed to more solar radiation in winter than in summer. The effect was that the temperature maintained within the building's interior remained as evenly balanced as possible despite the outside seasonal and daily temperature variations. Wall and roof construction was varied in thickness and composition to store the sun's heat and to permit the proper time lag of the day's heating effect into the interior at night. In the winter, when the sun's heat was welcomed, it reached into the interior through door and window openings dimensioned to shade the higher summer sun. The outside public spaces enjoyed a higher daytime temperature because they were protected from the winter wind by the structure's arcing plan.

The Acoma Pueblo near Albuquerque provides a similar illustration of design in response to the daily and annual movement of the sun, (Figure 1.2). Positioned high on a protected mesa, the settlement has remained in continued use for 400 years. The horizontal terraces outside each dwelling, used throughout the year for food preparation and drying, are never in shadow.

Even in December, when the sun is lowest on the horizon but its daily warmth is needed, no part of the south-facing wall of the houses is shaded by adjacent buildings—thus providing an early example of how "sun rights" can in fact be respected within a dense urban settlement, (Figure 1.3).

Colonial American home builders, too, responded to the particular conditions of the climates in which they settled. The orientation of the New England "saltbox" demonstrated good "climatic" sense by exposing the high wall (and thus most of the windows) towards the south, capturing the maximum amount of winter heat and drying effect from the sun. The low, sloping roof faced the prevailing winter winds, while the front door and windows were on the protected side (Figure 1.4). The plan of the house was oriented around the fireplaces and ovens, and parts of the house could be closed off to reduce heating space in winter months.

Figure 1.2. *Aerial view of Acoma Pueblo.*

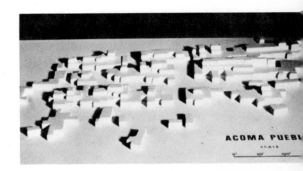

Figure 1.3. *Sun Study Model of Acoma Pueblo. View shows sun's position 10 AM, December 21. No south walls are shaded by adjacent rows of houses. (Source: Ralph Knowles, University of Southern California)*

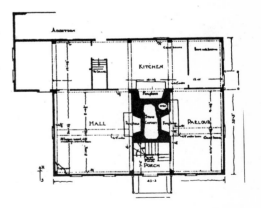

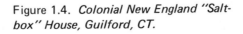

Figure 1.4. *Colonial New England "Saltbox" House, Guilford, CT.*

3

Early Solar Energy Applications. *In 213 B.C., Archimedes reportedly set fire to an attacking Roman fleet. "With burning glasses," says Galen, "he fired the ships of the enemies of Syracuse."*

In the 1700s an optician named Vilette of Lyons, France was producing polished-iron solar furnaces capable of smelting metals, and was exporting these solar devices to Persia and Denmark. Napoleon III backed August Mouchot in the development of a solar-powered steam engine which proved to be a success by 1872. Swedish inventor John Ericsson earned an honorary Ph.D. from the University of Lund for his work on solar hot air engines prior to 1868. Abel Pifre built the world's first solar-powered printing press back in 1880 and called his publication Le Journal Soleil *("The Sunshine Journal"). The first work on solar batteries was noted in 1839, though it wasn't till 1931 that Dr. Bruno Lange began to demonstrate photovoltaic solar power to the world.*

Solar Energy research in America began before the 20th century. In 1885 Scientific American *proposed a system in which flat-plate solar collectors would serve as both the metal roof of a factory building and the power source for various production machines within.*

At the end of the 19th century and the early 20th century, heating devices were patented, one by Charles Davis (1899), another by Robert McIntyre (1911).

By 1908, Frank Shuman of Tacony, Pennsylvania had formed the Sun Power Company to build a 55 horsepower solar irrigation pump on the outskirts of Cairo, Egypt. By 1912 his experimental unit was a complete success. Famous American scientists like Drs. Charles G. Abbot and R. H. Goddard were working in solar development as early as 1916.

In the late 1920's, several solar heating applications to house heating have been reported in Scottys Castle, Death Valley, California and Phoenix, Arizona. (Source: Joel Wasserman)

Printing Press of Le Journal Soleil *(1882).*

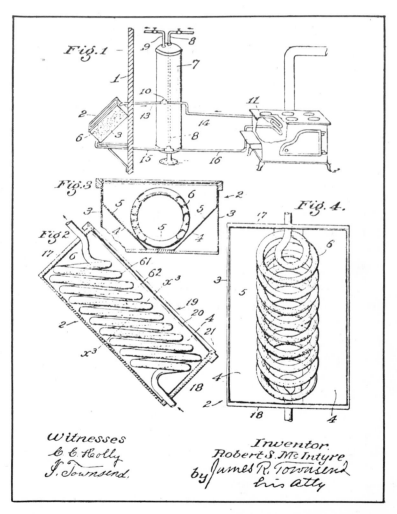

Robert McIntyre's solar water heater, assisted by wood burning stove (1911).

In the hot, humid climates of the United States South and Gulf states, colonial house plans—from the modest "dogtrot" house to plantation villas—display an equal amount of ingenuity to maximize natural cross-ventilation. They were raised from the ground, and open corridors and verandas were placed so that every room had at least two sides exposed to outside air flow (Figure 1.5).

To design houses that work in balance with their natural environment, we now can add to these traditional building solutions the modern advances in active solar-heating methods—recently developed to the point that they were used to energize the Skylab space station.

Since the 1700's, numerous inventions had been proposed to use solar energy for heating, and it actually was applied to houses in several areas of the United States in the 1920's. The term "solar house" was first used in Chicago newspaper articles to describe houses with large south-facing windows designed to obtain heat directly from the sun's rays. Pioneered by architects George and William Keck, these houses began when the architects observed the sun's direct heating effect in the 1932 House of Tomorrow exhibit and the 1933 Crystal House at the Chicago World's Fair, which they had designed with walls of glass. Intrigued by this unexpected but convincing example of how the sun could heat a building during the day without any additional heating, the Kecks built many residences with extensive glass areas to the south expressly to take advantage of direct solar heat in winter (Figure 1.6). An overhang over the glass was dimensioned to shade the glass against overheating in summer. Masonry surfaces were located in the interior—in the fireplace wall and the floor—to help absorb the heat on sunny days and to carry some heating effect into the evening.

This straightforward method of solar heating is effective if used in combination with insulating draperies. However, without more efficient means of storing the heat gained during sunny days for carry-over into periods of sunless weather, solar windows alone provide only supplementary heat for buildings in northern climates.

In the meantime, beginning in 1938, research

Figure 1.5. *Southern "Dogtrot" House.*

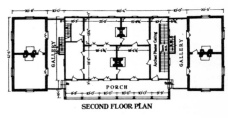

SECOND FLOOR PLAN

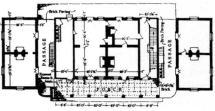

FIRST FLOOR PLAN

Plan of Ormond Plantation, *near New Orleans. Rooms arranged to give greatest possible cross ventilation. (Riciuti)*

Hedrich-Blessing
Crystal House *(1933)*

5

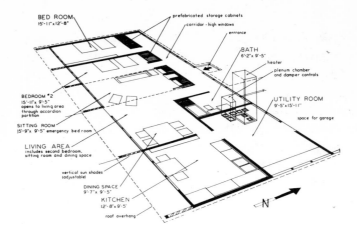

Figure 1.6. *Solar-Oriented Window Design. George and William Keck's prototype house design for Green's Ready-Built Homes (1940) based on direct solar heating through windows with massive interior masonry to act as a heat sink.*

Figure 1.7. *MIT Solar House IV, Lexington, Massachusetts. The last of four experimental solar heating installations undertaken by MIT Cabot Foundation Research Program (1939-1950). (Courtesy Dr. Hoyt Hottel)*

began with solar collector panels to trap the sun's heat at a high enough temperature so that it could be stored for several days and thus become available as needed for space heating. From 1938 to 1961, four solar houses were built and documented at the Massachusetts Institute of Technology. The first three projects, built on the MIT campus, were among the first to demonstrate liquid-type solar collector and storage—in which a water and anti-freeze solution is used to transfer heat from the solar collectors to the house. The MIT Solar House IV, built in Lexington, Mass. in 1958 (Figure 1.7), was inhabited and its solar heating fully monitored for two years. After this time the solar equipment was removed, the house converted to conventional heating and was sold.

In 1949, a house was built in Dover, Massachusetts with a solar system designed to supply all of its heating requirements (Figure 1.8). Architect Eleanor Raymond and Solar Engineer Maria Telkes designed this as one of the first to use air-type solar collectors—air instead of liquid used to remove heat from the collectors and transfer it to the house. An experimental heat-storage system, also first demonstrated here, used chemical compounds that absorb or give off heat as needed by being changed from a solid to a liquid state.

In the mid 1950's several solar installations were completed in Arizona by the husband-and-wife engineer team, Ray W. Bliss and Mary K. Donovan. The 1950's also saw the pioneering solar installations of George Löf of Denver and Harry Thomason in Washington D.C. These early solar houses, some of them described in detail in Chapter 5, provided the basis of subsequent research and development.

6

Beginning early in the 1970's, the economic and environmental cost of using conventional fossil fuels for heat brought public attention back to these early projects which had proven, many years before, the technical—if not the economic—feasibility of solar collector and storage systems. Early experimental solar houses at MIT, Dover, Arizona and Princeton have since met varied fates. They are either demolished or remain standing with their solar equipment removed—but not without first demonstrating that, even in cold and cloudy climates such as New England, solar house heating could work, and deserved sustained technical development.

These interests have been taken up again now and solar equipment begins to be commercially available for applications which, in many instances, are more economical than other energy sources.

Today the questions about solar heating are practical ones—relating to appearance, construction method and cost—in contrast to theoretical work that occupied earlier solar researchers. In the last few years, the examples of operating solar houses in the United States increased from less than a dozen in 1972 to more than 1000 built or under construction at the beginning of 1977. For the first time, solar houses are being built and sold in competition with conventionally fueled houses (Figures 1.9 and 1.11).

Figure 1.8. *Dover House, an early solar heating installation, in which heat of fusion type of heat storage was used. About 80% of heat load was provided by solar heat from 1949 to 1953. (Courtesy Dr. Maria Telkes)*

Figure 1.9. *Solar House, Westbrook, CT. (1974). One of the first solar houses in New England built for the private housing market. Donald Watson, AIA Architect.*

Robert Perron

1.2
Solar Heating in Your Future: How To Use This Book

Figure 1.10. *Colorado State University Solar Experimental House (1974-1977). One of three identical houses funded in part by the National Science Foundation to test various solar collector and storage systems.*

Figure 1.11. *New Century Townhouses, Vernon Hills, IL (1976). Solar heating on for-sale housing.*

There are many alternative methods of solar heating, each with its own effect on the appearance of a house, its heating fuel requirement and the cost of construction. These three factors—appearance, performance, and cost—are discussed throughout this book, so that comparisons of solar heating methods can be made as applicable to individual circumstances.

In Chapters 2 through 5, the basic methods and principles of operation of passive and active solar heating are presented. The purpose there is to describe how particular types of solar equipment fit into the overall heating-system design. The operation of a solar heating system is presented as a series of three steps: solar heat collection, its storage, and its distribution to the house interior. While solar collectors are the most noticeable feature of a solar installation, the ways in which the solar heat is stored and distributed are equally important and directly affect decisions in the house design and construction process. In Chapter 5, these individual steps are illustrated as used in some of the early solar house prototype systems on which current developments have been based.

In Chapter 6, solar heating is shown to be part of a total approach to energy conservation in building. We give this the term "ecodesign," to describe the many techniques of house-planning and construction that can be used to reduce fuel consumption. While solar heating is a major part of energy conservation design, it cannot be separated from other equally effective methods, each appropriate to particular climates. As shown by the review of ecodesign principles in Chapter 6, any building exposed to wind and sun can be designed to use them beneficially. By identifying at the beginning all the ways by which a building can be designed to fit its particular site and climate location, house planning decisions can have the greatest impact in reducing energy needs in a practical and economical way.

The first six chapters thus present basic solar equipment and house-design principles on how solar heating is being developed and applied to today's houses. The remaining Chapters 7 and 8 and the Appendices are expressly for the reader who wishes to apply these principles to design and build a solar house. Chapter 7 compares six alternative approaches to solar house heating, each with different installation costs and heating energy results. These alternatives—ranging from a small solar installation (for domestic water heating or auxiliary solar heating only) to a large-capacity solar space heating system—are compared in terms of economic payback in four northern climates. The methods of calculation are described in an Appendix by which readers can evaluate their own choices in terms of local climate, installation cost and financing charges. As we will discuss further, current costs of a solar installation vary widely, due to its relatively recent introduction to the home building market. Climate differences and local fuel cost variations also greatly affect the relative economic merit of solar heating alternatives. Thus such calculations are necessary to evaluate circumstances that are unique to a particular project.

The basic steps in planning a solar house project are described in Chapter 8, from site planning and design to construction, and checklists are provided of important points to consider under each of these topics. The many ways by which to proceed toward realizing a solar project are discussed. These include working with solar design consultants, equipment suppliers and builders.

In Chapter 8 the construction of a solar house is described with the owner-builder in mind. Building one's own house has its own challenges, and is often the choice of families who want to maximize their involvement in the creation of their homes. The potential problems in building one's own solar house, therefore, are discussed in order to make that choice a less risky one.

Many of the houses that illustrate the text have been constructed by owner-builders who had no previous solar experience, but who were able to realize good ideas that often had been untried and not yet proven in use. Their success has been the basis of many of the recommendations set forth in this book.

Percent of Total U. S. Energy Consumption used in Housing: Residential Space heating represents more than 10% of U.S. energy demand. Source: Office of Energy Conservation, U.S. Department of Interior (1973)

	% Total	Annual Rate of Growth (1960-1968)
Space Heating	10.6%	4.1%
Hot Water	2.9	5.2
Cooking	0.9	1.7
Clothes Drying	0.4	10.6
Refrigeration	1.3	8.2
Air-conditioning	1.2	15.6
Other	2.1	5.5
Total Residential Use	19.5%	4.8%

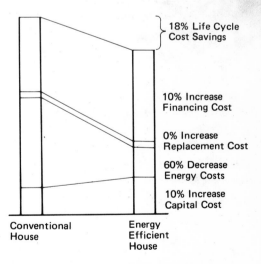

18% Life Cycle Cost Savings

10% Increase Financing Cost

0% Increase Replacement Cost

60% Decrease Energy Costs

10% Increase Capital Cost

Conventional House   Energy Efficient House

Figure 1.12. *Total Twenty-Year Owning Costs—One-Family Residence. Solar heating requires added cost of construction and financing, but achieves net savings over the life of the conventional house construction mortgage.*

CHAPTER 2

HOW SOLAR HEATING WORKS

2.1

From Sun to Building

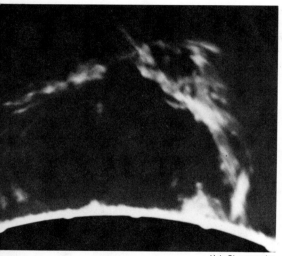

Hale Observatories

Figure 2.1. *Solar Flare (with a prominence approximately 205,000 miles high): The electromagnetic radiation produced by the sun reaches the earth's atmosphere approximately 6 minutes later to provide the basic energy for life on our planet.*

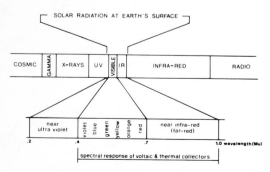

Figure 2.2. *The Spectrum of Total Solar Radiation at the Earth's Atmosphere.*

More than 90 million miles away from earth, the sun generates the energy that drives the entire solar system. The earth's atmosphere, the layer of dust, moisture and clouds held close to the earth's surface by its force of gravity, shields us from the full effect of this direct solar radiation.

All of the energy that we use on earth began with the sun. The sun gives life to the process of photosynthesis from which all of the fossil fuels derive. Prevailing winds, which for centuries have powered ships and windmills, are set in motion by the earth's rotation and by the rise and fall of air masses heated by the sun. Wind and sun drive the cycle of evaporation and rainfall, which creates the basis of hydropower.

New developments of solar energy include photoelectric conversion, which uses solar cells to convert sunlight to electricity (such as used to power the controls of the NASA Skylab), and ocean thermal power, which relies upon the difference in temperature at various depths of the sea to drive a turbine. And, through the techniques described in this book, solar radiation at the earth's surface now is being used to provide heating for buildings.

Solar energy is received in various wavelengths, of which the light that we see is only one part (Figure 2.2). The ultraviolet wavelength portion provides energy for plant growth by photosynthesis. Radiation in the infrared wavelength heats the earth's surface.

Of the total solar radiation that reaches the outer earth atmosphere, only one half penetrates to the earth's surface (Figure 2.3). The other half is reflected away from the earth by clouds or is absorbed within the atmosphere itself. Part of the radiation received at the earth's surface is that which has been reflected by clouds, so that it falls on the earth's surface as scattered or diffuse radiation (that is, it comes from all directions of the sky). Only about a quarter of the total solar radiation at the earth's outer atmosphere ever reaches the ground directly.

To maintain its thermal balance, the earth must lose the same amount of heat that it receives—by re-radiation or cooling to the night sky, by evaporation, and by wind cooling. The solar energy received by the earth is held for a time in the atmosphere, in land and ocean masses, and given back to outer space as re-radiated heat. The earth itself is thus a system by which solar energy maintains climate and seasonal temperature balance (Figure 2.4).

The amount of solar heat received at a particular point on the earth's surface depends first on its relative position with respect to sun, as indicated by latitude. Thus, on an annual average, the portion of earth along the equator— 0° latitude —receives the greatest amount of solar radiation. As one goes farther north or south from the equator, there are fewer hours of annual sunlight, the path that the

Total radiation arriving (solar constant) = 100%

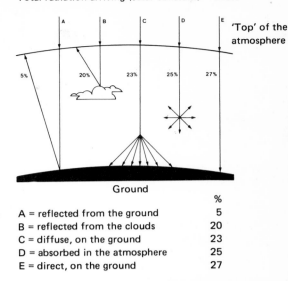

	%
A = reflected from the ground	5
B = reflected from the clouds	20
C = diffuse, on the ground	23
D = absorbed in the atmosphere	25
E = direct, on the ground	27

Figure 2.3 *Solar Radiation received at the Earth's surface.*

Figure 2.4. *The Earth's Weather System. The position of the earth in relation to the sun, the earth's motion and the effect of land and water bodies establishes the prevailing weather patterns in different parts of the world. (Source: Lt. Col. H. W. Brandli, Satellite Meteorologist)*

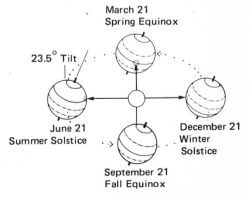

The Earth's Path Around the Sun.

11

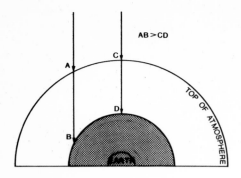

Figure 2.5. *Path of Solar Radiation through the Earth's Atmosphere.*

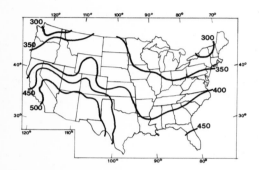

Figure 2.6A. *Average Annual Solar Radiation (in Langleys per day) on a horizontal surface influenced by prevailing cloud conditions and altitude. (1 Langley = 3.687 Btu/SF)*

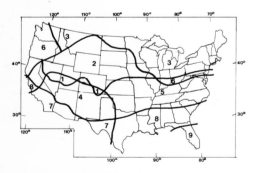

2.6B. *Areas where solar heating of buildings is most practical, relative to available solar radiation and winter heating requirement.*

1. *High Heat Demand—excellent sunshine.*
2. *High Heat Demand—good sunshine*
3. *High Heat Demand—fair sunshine*
4. *Moderate Heat Demand—excellent sunshine*
5. *Moderate Heat Demand—good sunshine*
6. *Moderate Heat Demand—fair sunshine*
7. *Low Heat Demand—excellent sunshine*
8. *Low Heat Demand—good sunshine*
9. *Low Heat Demand—fair sunshine*

sun's rays traverse through the atmosphere is longer and less solar radiation is received (Figure 2.5).

But the latitude position in and of itself doesn't account for the actual amount of solar radiation available at a given location. Due to climate conditions caused by oceans, land forms and local cloud formations, a great range in the actual amount of solar radiation is received at different locations along the same latitude, due to altitude and average sky conditions.

For example, Denver, Indianapolis and Pittsburgh are all close to 40° N latitude, yet Indianapolis receives 8 percent more sunshine in an average year than Pittsburgh and Denver 16 percent more than Pittsburgh. Figure 2.6A shows how annual cloud cover affects the amount of solar radiation received in different parts of the United States. However, because it does not include the additional factor of different seasonal heating needs (or local fuel costs), Figure 2.6A cannot be read by itself as an indicator of where solar heating for buildings is most practical, as shown in Figures 2.6B and 2.6C.

As the earth journeys through its annual orbit around the sun, the tilt of the earth's polar axis with respect to the sun establishes the basic geometry of solar orientation around which buildings can be designed (Figure 2.7). Seen from the earth, the sun's noon position in the sky changes each day from its lowest altitude on December 21st (the winter solstice north of the equator) to its highest position on June 21st (the summer solstice). The difference in the sun's altitude between June 21 and December 21 is 47°.

The location of the sunrise and sunset also varies each day with respect to east and west. The sun rises from true east and sets in the true west only twice each year (the spring and fall equinoxes). In summer, it rises and sets well to the north of the east-west line, and in winter well to the south. These facts of solar geometry become important in designing

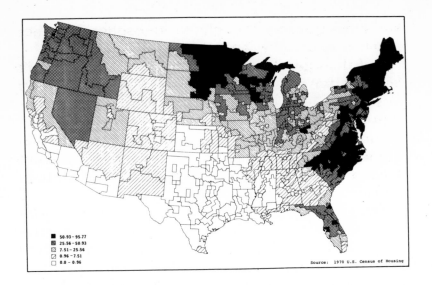

2.6C. Percentage of Housing using Oil for Space Heating (1970). Local differences in fuel types and costs are an additional factor that determines the economic attractiveness of solar heating. (Source: ADL, Inc. and U.S. Dept. H.U.D.)

buildings which take advantage of the sun's heat in winter while avoiding overheating in summer.

The beneficial effect of the sun for winter heating is known to everyone. The south side of a building is warmed by the sun even in the coldest climates, and more so if there is reflection from snow and protection from the wind. Using the sun's energy for winter heating is not much more complicated. Solar radiation passes through glass and heats the surfaces that it strikes—whether they are inside the house rooms or inside of a solar collector. The heat is trapped inside by window glass, where it contributes to space heating directly, as through the windshield of a car or through the glass walls of a sunporch, or indirectly, by a solar collector, where it can be removed by pumps or fans to a building interior.

Solar house design uses the sun's radiation that falls upon a building during sunny days to heat the house interior over one or several days, based on simple mechanisms to transfer heat from the outer building surface to a heat storage device and then to the building interior itself.

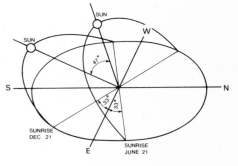

Figure 2.7. *Winter and Summer solar positions in relation to a location on the 40 degrees North latitude. (The position of the sun for each hour and day is given in Appendix II, Table II.5.)*

2.2
From Building to People

In collecting, storing and distributing solar heat, the earth itself demonstrates the basic mechanics used in solar house heating. The earth's surface is heated by exposure to the sun. The atmosphere acts as a protective cover that holds the heat near the earth's surface. Heat is stored within the land and water

13

masses and is transported to different parts of the planet by wind and water currents.

At the scale of an individual building, a solar heating system performs the same functions. An absorbent material (a building or an absorber attached to a building) is exposed to the sun. The absorber is covered by a glass or plastic cover sheet to minimize outward re-radiation and cooling. Heat is removed from the absorber by the passage of air or liquid to the building, where it is stored or distributed to maintain the temperature equilibrium in the building interior.

There are many types of solar heating methods and systems and even more collector designs. The basic systems of using the sun's heat for buildings begin with extremely simple methods such as solar-oriented windows that can be used with most any home. Other solar heating systems require special equipment or a design that is carefully organized around solar heat collection and storage principles. More sophisticated solar-powered heating and cooling equipment and solar-powered electrical energy is under development and may become available to the homeowner in the near future.

In the chapters that follow, these ways of using solar heat for buildings are detailed and illustrated, with examples of the various types of solar equipment and house plans. All methods of solar heating follow similar principles that are briefly introduced in the remainder of this chapter.

Any part of a building that is exposed to the sun will be heated by **solar radiation,** which may arrive at the building's surface in three ways—as **direct, diffuse** or **reflected radiation.**

Direct radiation is in the form of parallel rays, undeflected by the earth's atmosphere.

Diffuse radiation is multi-directional in its source, having been reflected from clouds, atmospheric dust and moisture particles.

Reflected radiation is that which bounces onto a building from nearby ground areas or other building surfaces.

Each of these sources of solar radiation is considered in solar house design.

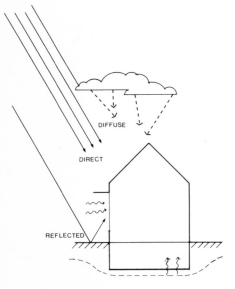

Figure 2.8. *Solar Heat Gain to a Building.*

14

Of the total solar radiation available in a given location, the amount that is direct, diffuse or reflected varies, according to the average cloud and moisture conditions of the climate. In a hot-dry climate, for example, where clear skies prevail, the solar radiation received is mainly direct (parallel ray).

In temperate or humid zones, 50 percent or more of the total solar radiation received by a building may be diffuse, due to generally cloudy conditions. Diffuse radiation, in being reflected from the entire sky, arrives from all directions, so that even those building surfaces that are not directly facing the sun experience some heat gain.

In far northern climates, low winter sun reflected from snow may account for a large portion of the total winter radiation input. This reflected radiation can effectively double the amount of solar heat that falls on a building surface.

Because the nature of solar radiation differs in various locations, the solar collector methods best suited to a particular use may vary, to take advantage of the prevailing sky conditions when solar heat is used, such as for winter space heating, summer cooling, or summer pool heating.

The sun's heating energy reaches a building in still other less direct but important ways. It heats the air that stands close to a building and it heats the nearby ground, both of which then make their own heating contribution to the building by **convection** (air movement) and by **conduction** (direct contact).

The temperature of the air near a building, of course, is affected by the amount of wind to which it is exposed, and the outside air will be considerably warmer if building surfaces are protected from the wind. Thus outdoor wind-protected courtyards can be pleasantly warm in winter. Conversely, building surfaces that are exposed directly to the wind will be comparatively colder and lose more heat in winter.

In addition, there can be a benefit of heat from the ground, for underground portions of a building will be warmed by direct contact with the earth. At 6 feet or more below the surface, the earth is considerably warmer than the winter air temperature on the surface, since the sub-surface earth retains the heat gained from previous months. The temperature of the earth below 8 to 12 feet remains

Sky	Sky Clearness	Diffuse Radiation
Clear	1.0	12%
Slightly Hazy	0.8	25%
Hazy	0.6	35%
Overcast	0.4	55%

Direct and Diffuse Radiation. The relative proportion of diffuse (multi-directional source) radiation compared to direct (solar beam) radiation increases with cloudiness and with lower solar altitudes. Northern climates thus have a higher percentage of diffuse radiation (30 to 40% of the total) than in dry arid regions (10 to 15% of the total). (Source: B. Givoni, Man, Climate and Architecture, *Elsevier Publishing, 1969)*

15

close to the average annual temperature of that particular location at the surface. In climates where humidity and ground moisture are not a problem, an underground building therefore can take advantage of the natural insulation given by the earth.

The most effective way to trap the sun's heat that falls on a building is with some type of a solar collector. The collectors used in homes today trap the sun's thermal radiation or heat. (Another type of solar energy collector now under development does not produce heat but instead uses sunshine to produce electricity by a photovoltaic solar cell.)

From a collector the heat can be used directly and immediately to heat the interior spaces (as in the case of a window oriented to the winter sun), or it can be used indirectly to heat a heat storage element, which retains the heat for use over a longer period of time.

A solar house could be said to be different from the conventionally heated house in the way that four basic objectives are achieved:

1. **It collects** the sun's heat that falls upon the building's surfaces during the winter days.

2. **It stores** that heat so that it can be used during the night or during sunless days.

3. **It distributes** the stored heat throughout the house for comfort and energy efficiency.

4. **It retains** the heat in the building by reducing or eliminating usual sources of heat loss.

In northern climates, solar heating systems that supply a major portion of house heating usually have separate parts to perform each of the above functions. Those that rely on pumps and fans to help transfer heat from collector to storage to house often are referred to as "active" systems.

There are, however, simple solar heating methods that rely on parts of the building itself to perform the functions of heat collection, storage, and distribution—often without mechanical means. These methods, often referred to as "passive" systems of solar heating, deserve careful attention because they can be easily built with little extra cost of construction.

For example, if the walls of a building facing the sun are painted dark, they will absorb the day's heat. They also can be made thick enough to delay the transfer of heat to the interior for eight or more hours after the sun has gone down. The thick walls of adobe, earth, or masonry—which create a time-lag in the heating impact of the sun—are particularly useful in hot-dry regions or in mountainous areas where days are warm but the nights are chilly. They are often found in traditional buildings in these climates.

The principles of solar heating—**to collect, to store** and **to distribute heat**—can be provided by any number of building plans and equipment designs, and, as discussed in Chapters 3, 4 and 5, they must be understood together as total heating systems.

The fourth objective—**to retain** heat within a building—is achieved by the design and construction of the building itself, rather than by any particular use of solar equipment.

Any building in a northern climate, whether solar heated or not, should be designed to minimize the amount of heating energy required. But this becomes particularly important with solar design, so that the size and cost of the collector and storage system can also be kept to the minimum.

To use solar heat efficiently once it is collected requires an efficient building enclosure, with good insulation and other provisions against heat loss—such as double doors ("air locks") at entry ways or by zoned planning of the house interior itself to reduce the amount of space fully heated. Design techniques such as these, aimed to reduce heat losses and to retain heat within a building, are described in Chapter 6.

Before continuing in a discussion which emphasizes the use of solar energy for winter heating, it should be mentioned that heating is just one aspect of solar house design. In some climates, cooling may be just as important, if not more so.

A building should be designed in any climate to prevent overheating in summer, and there are numerous ways of accomplishing this, such as shading by trees or sun screens, ventilating the building interior, and orienting the building plan to cool breezes.

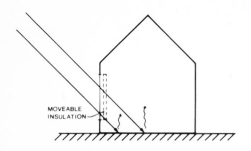

Figure 2.9. *Solar Windows oriented to the south used for direct solar heating.*

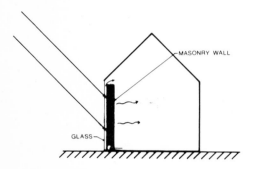

Figure 2.10. *Collector/Storage building elements (such as windows with a masonry wall behind).*

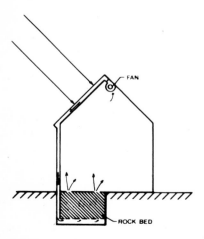

Figure 2.11A. *Active Solar Heating: air collector and rock storage system.*

In southern climates, the main requirement for comfort is for summer cooling rather than winter heating. In such locations, the size of a solar heating system can be much smaller than in the north, and therefore is easier to incorporate into a house design. Some solar equipment used for space heating also can be used for cooling, in ways that will be detailed in Chapters 3 and 5.

Solar collection, storage and heat distribution, as we have seen, are the three elements of a solar heating system for buildings. Each of the elements is designed according to principles of heat transfer, by which the sun's energy is converted to provide the heat required for maintaining comfortable house temperatures.

There are five basic system types by which solar energy is used for house heating—the first two generally considered as "passive" systems, the last three as "active." In any house design, it generally is desirable to combine both passive and active means for effective solar heating.

1. Solar windows. Windows are oriented to trap the sun's winter heat directly in the building interior. The window is the collector.

The temperature of the interior surfaces and the inside air is raised so that the mass of the building materials themselves serve as the heat storage.

The heat is distributed by natural air movement inside the building. To the extent that the interior surfaces have absorbed the heat, they act as heat storage and heat radiators after the sun is no longer available (Figure 2.9).

2. Collector/storage building elements. The sun's rays warm the absorbers (such as a masonry wall or a water container), and heat thus stored then radiates directly to the interior space. The natural movement of air in the building also may help distribute the heat to other areas (Figure 2.10).

3. Active collector, storage and distribution system. The sun's heat is trapped within a collector—usually a glass or plastic-covered metal absorber pan. The heat is drawn from the collector by liquid or by air passing through it, and is transferred

18

to a storage device. When the building requires heating, the stored heat then is distributed throughout the building interior via air ducts or water pipes and radiators (Figure 2.11).

4. Active systems with special heating (or cooling) equipment. This is a variant of the previous system, with the transfer of heat from collector to storage being accomplished in the same manner. But the stored heat then is used as a pre-heating source for mechanical heating or cooling equipment, rather than being used as heat distributed directly to the building spaces.

The most common example of such a system uses solar radiation to "preheat" a heat pump, whereby the temperature of water or of air is raised to a higher temperature. Then it can be distributed through the building in a conventional manner (Figure 2.12).

Several methods using solar heat to cool a building also fit into this category. In one method, solar heat is used to drive an absorption chiller or other refrigerant cooling device that is set into operation by heated water. Other methods use solar heat for drying—to help remove the moisture from hot-humid air—thus making it more comfortable.

5. Photovoltaic cells for electric conversion. A fifth system uses photovoltaic cells, which create electricity when exposed to the sun. This process is fundamentally different from the heat trap principles described above. Although not economically practical for home energy needs at this time, solar cells are being actively developed for possible application in the future (Figure 2.13).

In the next chapter, the first two of the five solar heating types—the passive systems—are described in detail and examples of important applications are given. In Chapters 4 and 5, the active systems are discussed, with emphasis placed on those systems that are in use today or soon will become available to the homeowner.

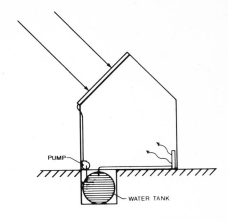

2.11B. *Active Solar Heating: liquid collector and storage system.*

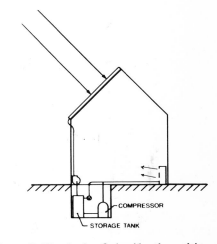

Figure 2.12. *Active Solar Heating with special equipment (such as a heat pump).*

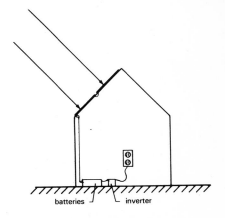

Figure 2.13. *Photovoltaic solar cells for electric conversion.*

CHAPTER 3

PASSIVE SYSTEMS

Windows (to collect the sun's heat directly) and masonry construction (to store the heat for a delayed heating effect) are examples of passive solar design which do not require any mechanical equipment to collect or to deliver the sun's heat to a building space.

These systems rely upon parts of the building design and construction for direct sun heating. In a strict sense such a system would use no energy other than the natural sources of sun and wind. In practice, however, fans to move air or motors to operate insulating panels are commonly used to make the passive solar designs much more effective.

3.1
Solar Windows

Components normally used in building construction—windows, greenhouses, sun rooms and skylights—can be used to capture heat directly from the sun and are particularly useful in solar house design because they are often part of the given building construction cost.

Properly designed windows can serve as solar collectors to add heat directly to the interior space with minimal cost. They illustrate an important point: contrary to common opinion, energy conservation **does** permit the full use of windows, glass structures and skylights, provided that they are designed to receive the sun's rays in winter and have some means of controlling heat loss in sunless hours and excessive heat gain in summer.

If windows are placed to face the sun (east, south, or west), the amount of heat gain received through the glass during the winter can contribute to the

20

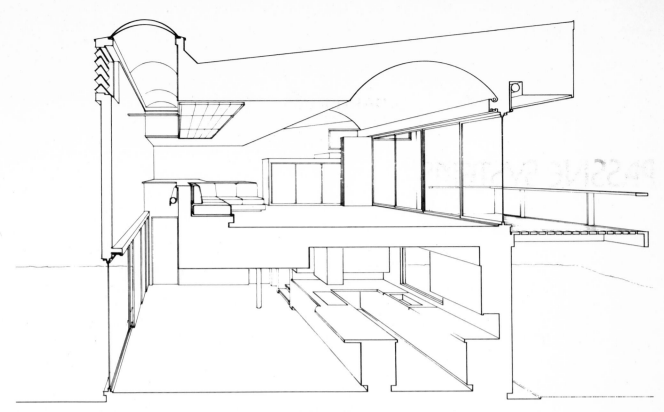

Wyden Residence. *Chester, CT (1974).*

A remodeling of a conventional house for energy conservation, including insulating panels on windows and skylight. The volume of heated space was reduced by lowering the ceiling. Summer ventilation was helped by the double-storied air shaft with a ventilator beneath the *skylight. The transparent insulating panel that slides under the skylight can be closed on summer days (to reduce over-heating) and on winter nights (to reduce heat loss). Donald Watson, AIA, Architect.*

house heating requirement. The exact amount of usable heat gained depends upon climate and the house design particulars, how well insulated it is and how the rooms are used. In temperate climates, from 20 to 50 percent of the annual heat for a home can be gained by heat from properly oriented windows with insulating controls.

This well-known building design technique was popular during the 1940's and '50's when houses with large glass areas facing south were frequently referred to as solar homes. In some parts of the United States—particularly the southwest—there is enough sunshine during the winter season to rely almost completely upon a solar-oriented window design for winter heating. Shading devices must be used over the windows in summer to exclude the sun when the heat is not wanted.

The two major drawbacks, in the use of both win-

21

dows and skylights for direct heating from the sun can be overcome. These are:

First, on cloudy days and at night the windows lose as much heat as they gain during sunny days—and this becomes quite critical in colder climates, since, compared to insulated walls and the roof, windows are also the major source of heat loss.

Second, heat can build up inside the window area, causing overheating on the sunny side of a building interior while the other side remains cold.

Even during winter days, the interior space near the solar window will become overheated. But the temperature must be allowed to climb if enough heat is to be trapped for any carry-over after sunset. This would seem to limit the use of the space, because it would be uncomfortably hot.

There also is a limit to the size of window walls and draperies, due to economics, aesthetics, and convenience. Furthermore, building materials, fabrics and furnishings have to be carefully selected to withstand fading and drying caused by the sun's intense rays.

However, by making provisions against nighttime heat loss and against heat imbalance, these disadvantages can be overcome. Designs for doing this—by insulating the glass area at night and distributing the heat evenly throughout a house—are discussed at the end of this chapter. The method of calculating the potential heat gain through south-facing windows for locations in the United States is described in Appendix II.

3.1.1 SOLAR-ORIENTED WINDOWS

The principal advantages of using windows to collect heat is that they are needed anyway—for ventilation, light and views. To use windows for winter heat therefore may add little to the construction cost, and simply will require careful planning and design of the window and day-use room locations to orient them to the sun.

In northern climates, the south-facing side of a building is ideal for solar windows. During the coldest winter months, the south side of a building gains more heat than a horizontal roof. And, because the sun is higher in summer, it is a simple matter to provide an overhang to shade these south-facing windows from undesired heat.

Glass on the north side gains some heat from diffuse sky radiation or reflecting surfaces. But the gain is negligible compared to the heat lost through the same glass area. In addition, cold winter winds usually come from the north. So in cold climates the north side is the least desirable location for windows and door openings.

Windows that face east or west also gain heat in winter, but the principal problem is with summer overheating: the horizontal window overhang that is so useful over the south-facing glass is not sufficient for shade against the sun from east or west, when it is so much lower in the sky.

However, if shutters are used to insulate against heat loss in winter, they also can be closed in summer to protect against overheating—provided there are other means of light and ventilation. Deciduous trees also are ideal sun shades. They grow their leaves in spring and lose them in the fall and thus coincide perfectly with the seasonal need for summer shading and winter sun on a building.

3.1.2 GREENHOUSES

Any glass structure can be attached to a house in order to trap heat directly, just as the solar windows described above. Such a structure, called a "greenhouse" here for convenience, exposes more glass (or plastic) surface area to solar heat gain than a vertical window. Conversely, more heat would be lost at night if no provision is made to use the heat during the day or to insulate the glass at night.

Because the greenhouse is attached to a house, however, it is a simple matter to close it off from the house proper at night, letting the temperature drop in the greenhouse without increasing the heating requirements of the house.

This is a normal function of glassed-in porches or sun rooms, which can be made part of solar house design so that they take advantage of free heat from the sun. Heat can be removed from the greenhouse to the house during the day by opening it to the

House Based on Greenhouse Heat Trap. *Project commissioned by American Wood Council uses greenhouse/sun room for direct solar heating. Main house is opened or closed to the greenhouse area to control heat gain and loss. Levinson, Legowitz and Zaprauskis, Architects.*

house interior or by drawing air by fan to the house or (as will be illustrated later) to thermal storage, permitting the heat of the day to be used at night.

Because the greenhouse is a separate zone from the house, the temperature can be allowed to drop at night below the house temperature. But an unheated greenhouse more or less would follow the same temperatures as the outside air, so if the greenhouse is used for gardening, insulating devices over the windows and some low-temperature heating should be included. The advantage of a south-facing greenhouse for growing vegetables is obvious—particularly in temperate climates where the winter heating requirement can be met largely by direct solar heating. The same provisions against overheating and for heat storage that are discussed below also can be used to maintain a healthy indoor garden.

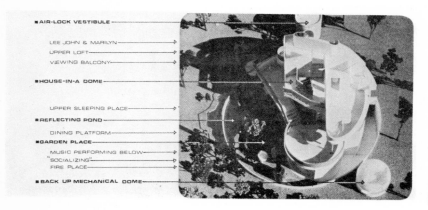

AIR-LOCK VESTIBULE

LEE JOHN & MARILYN
UPPER LOFT
VIEWING BALCONY

HOUSE-IN-A DOME

UPPER SLEEPING PLACE
REFLECTING POND
DINING PLATFORM
GARDEN PLACE
MUSIC PERFORMING BELOW
"SOCIALIZING"
FIRE PLACE
BACK UP MECHANICAL DOME

House Planned around Garden Greenhouse. *Joint Venture Architects.*

If not used at night and if otherwise unheated, a greenhouse enclosure still would be naturally heated during sunny days for use as a sunporch or family day room. It would have to be shaded and ventilated in warm seasons of the year.

A greenhouse structure is less expensive to build than a fully insulated structure, so that a glassed-in day room or sunporch adds additional area to a house at less cost than similar space that is to be maintained at house temperature. Greenhouse structures available as a manufacturers' stock item have both shading and ventilating controls as options. For the self-help builder, they also are available in kit form or can be built of recycled windows and doors.

Greenhouses are shown as parts of many of the house designs in this book, because they are indeed live-in solar collectors that provide living and garden space and, when properly designed, also can be used to provide heat, fresh air, and humidity to the sun-oriented house.

3.1.3 ROOF MONITORS

Roof monitors are cupolas, skylights or raised roof sheds with windows that are designed to provide natural lighting and ventilation in buildings. They also can serve as heat traps in winter by admitting the winter sun rays directly to the house interior. Like greenhouses, roof monitors are usefully incorporated into solar house designs because they work year-round by aiding natural ventilation and cooling in summer and by supplying direct solar heating in winter.

Because skylights are located high in the space to be heated, the sun's heat enters an area which is normally overheated anyway, due to the natural rise of heat within the building. It is advisable, therefore, to place a return air duct at the highest part of the space under the skylight in order to recirculate the warmed air back through the building's heating system. As with windows and greenhouses, shading or insulating the skylight against summer sun is essential.

Roof monitors are excellent sources of natural light, and in summer months they are ideal for natural ventilation, because heated air naturally rises to the top of a building. If there is an air exhaust located at the top of the space, a steady flow of air out of the building can be established even if there is no outside wind, thus permitting cooler air to enter at the bottom of the building.

In northern climates, ventilation by such natural methods usually is all that is required for summer cooling. With insulating and ventilating controls, roof monitors thus can be used to great advantage in any fuel-conserving approach to house design.

ELIMINATING HEAT LOSS
THROUGH WINDOWS AT NIGHT

Windows without some form of insulating draperies or shutters can lose as much heat during sunless hours as they can gain during sunny winter days. Window glass usually is the greatest source of heat loss in any building, in some climates accounting for 20 to 50 percent of the total loss. However, a shutter or drapery used to insulate the glass during sunless hours generally doubles the net heat gain efficiency of a window. The cost of adding insulating shutters over windows generally is repaid in fuel savings within two to four years.

Ideally one should be able to cover all large window glass areas with an efficient insulating material during sunless hours. To accomplish this, space is required on the inside walls for insulating draperies, shades or panels.

The insulating value of conventional draperies really is not adequate, due to the air leakage through the material and around the edges. However, they can be custom-fabricated and installed with windows to make an effective heat trap. Window shades are being developed, also, with very high insulating values, some of which are listed in Appendix I-D.

Insulating panels can be designed to operate like shutters or sliding pocket doors. For heat-retaining efficiency and for ease of operation, the panels should be located on the inside of a building space, rather than outside. If located on the outside of the window, heat still would be lost to the air space outside the glass.

Insulating shutters can be made from panels of rigid fiberglass or of expanded plastic foam (with masonite faces to reduce the fire hazards associated with exposed plastic foamboards). The edges should join to minimize air leakage, though some air change will control condensation which might form on cold window walls, particularly those with metal frames. Translucent fiberglass panels with an insulated airspace also can be used, with the advantage that they transmit light when closed.

26

Generally these panels must be opened and closed by hand, although electric controls are available and they can be set to operate automatically with the sun.

Two methods of automatically insulating a window or skylight area, according to details available from Zomeworks of New Mexico, are the **Beadwall** and the **Skylid** systems.

In the Beadwall system, developed by Dave Harrison, the window is composed of two layers of glass (or plastic) separated by an air space of about three inches (Figure 3.1). When adequate solar heat is not available during the day and at night, lightweight styrofoam plastic beads are blown automatically into the space between the two layers of glass. To remove the insulation, the beads are returned by vacuum pumps through pipes to a nearby storage bin.

Figure 3.1. *Beadwall Window Insulation System (left). Below, a Beadwall system in operation on a greenhouse structure. (Courtesy Zomeworks Corporation)*

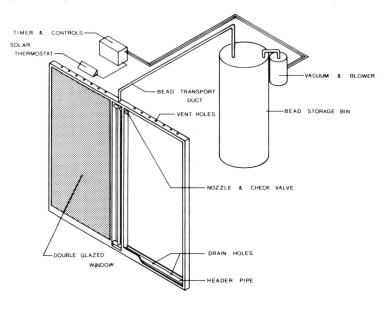

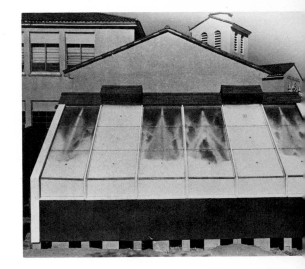

When the air space is filled with the styrofoam beads, the insulating value of the window area is increased about five times over a glass window without the insulation. This extremely effective system can be used in vertical windows and in sloping skylights that are steeper than 40 degrees from the horizontal.

The Skylid system, developed by Steve Baer, is composed of louvers placed on the underside of a skylight, which automatically open to let the sun

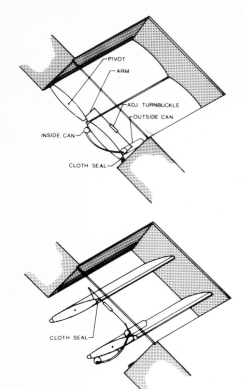

Figure 3.2. *Skylid insulating system.*

Skylid in a residential application. (Courtesy Zomeworks Corporation).

in (Figure 3.2). The ingenious control devised for the Skylid requires no electricity. It operates by controlling the cycle of evaporation and condensation of Freon, which, when heated by the sun, passes between two canisters that are attached to opposite edges of the insulating panel. When the interior space is warmer than that in the skylight above, the process is reversed and the louvers then shut.

CONTROLLING THE OVERHEATING EFFECT OF SUN-ORIENTED WINDOWS

Without some way of evenly distributing the heat that is trapped by a sun-oriented window, even during the winter months an overheating effect is created in the spaces next to the window. When that much heat builds up in a room, a homeowner might then wish to close the draperies to keep the sun out or even open the window to let the heat out. But in both cases the potential heat gain of the window is lost.

There are, however, several ways to lessen the overheating effect of sun-oriented windows and still use the heat to meet the comfort requirements of the home. The simplest is to plan the house so the heat can be easily removed from the areas near the solar windows and distributed to other parts of the building. This can be accomplished without fans if the solar windows are in a lower part of the house and if upper floors or rooms can be opened up to the sunny side—for example, by having rooms overlooking a sun room.

Orienting a large solar window area to the east of true south is also helpful by obtaining heat in the morning, when it is needed, and avoiding it in late afternoon, when the house is already up to comfortable temperatures.

Another means of reducing the overheating effect is to use exposed masonry surfaces on the **interior** of the space that has solar windows. Masonry, a good material for heat storage, can be heated directly by the sun (for example a brick or concrete floor) or if used in walls and ceiling it can absorb heat from the air itself. The masonry materials absorb heat and help to moderate the overheating ef-

28

fect, retaining the heat for a while after the sun is down.

In parts of the southwest, where adobe and other masonry construction is popular, their heat storage effect often is all that is needed to heat a home comfortably, as shown in several houses in Santa Fe, designed by architect Dave Wright (Figures 3.3 and 3.4). The sun's heat gained through solar windows during the day is absorbed by the interior masonry, which then offers a warm, radiant effect during the night.

A third means to prevent overheating employs fans to move the air. Where the heat build-up from solar windows cannot be distributed throughout a house by its natural upward flow, a small fan sometimes is sufficient to remove the heat from the sunny side of the house to colder areas. More effective than simply blowing the heated air is to duct it through a rock bin which picks up the heat and stores it for later use. This method is a combination of passive solar heat collection with an active means of re-recovering and storing solar heat, which will be described more fully in Chapter 5.

Figure 3.3. *Dave Wright's House in Santa Fe, NM (1974).*

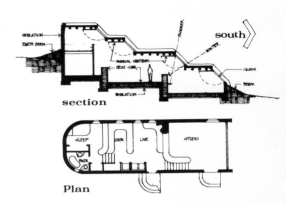

Figure 3.4. *Karen Terry Residence, Santa Fe, NM (1975). Dave Wright, Architect.*

Paul Koch

Other Window Collector Designs. *Various designs that combine a standard window with heat controls to either reflect heat back to the outside (to reduce summer cooling needs) or to syphon heat to the inside (sunny winter days).*

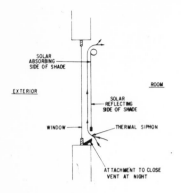

A. *Roll Shade for Heat Absorption. S. D. Silverstein, General Electric Company. The shade serves as a solar collector during winter daytime, provides added insulation comparable to vented storm windows during winter nighttime, and rejects solar heat gain during summer cooling periods.*

B. *Insealshaid, (patent pending). Ark-Tic-Seal Systems, Inc. Three roll shades in one valance. The outer shade is reflective (for reduced summer cooling needs); the middle shade is transparent (for increased insulation); the inner shade is heat absorbent. When the temperature between window and shade exceeds 80 degrees F., louvers open in the valance to permit the heat to enter.*

SOLAR HEAT GAIN FROM WINDOWS AS THE SOLAR HEATING SYSTEM: ADVANTAGES AND DISADVANTAGES

Even with below-freezing temperatures outside, solar energy can contribute directly to heating an inside space that has ample glass area oriented to the sun. In most northern climates, an insulating device over the windows to prevent heat loss at night is essential. An effective means is needed, too, for distributing the heat evenly throughout the building to take full advantage of the window-heat gain.

The analysis of solar heating systems, detailed later in the book, shows that solar-oriented windows and low-temperature heat distribution systems are among the most practical and cost effective alternatives available to the homeowner who wishes to minimize added construction costs. In cool but sunny locations such as Denver, a house with solar-oriented windows and good insulation can gain as much as half of the annual heating requirement from the sun. The conclusion is obvious—that the direct heat gain from windows should be used as part of any house design—to reduce the mechanical heating requirements. Solar window-heat is incorporated into the designs of all the solar houses shown in this book.

To summarize the advantages and disadvantages of solar window heating:

Disadvantages

- Glass areas also lose heat at night. An insulating system must be used to prevent a net heat loss.

- Masonry surfaces should be used in the interior to help control the overheating effect.

- Interior materials must be protected against sun bleaching and drying.

- A manually-controlled window insulating system requires operation by the building occupant at least twice daily.

- The heat contribution from windows alone cannot provide a major portion of the annual heating requirement of houses located in northern climates.

Advantages

- The insulating system also can serve to offer privacy at night, eliminating the need for a drapery installation and drapery cleaning.

- Moderately heated radiant masonry surfaces on the inside of a space help to balance temperature extremes between night and day and, therefore, add to the general feeling of comfort in a home.

- The normal cost of house construction includes windows. Thus the system usually can be built within normal construction budgets with no unusual building equipment needed.

- Solar windows can be used together with other solar heating systems in solar house designs.

C. *Clear-View Solar Collector. Environmental Research Laboratory, University of Arizona. Absorbent louvers between outer and inner window glazing can be opened or closed. In closed position, heat that is trapped is ducted to house heating system.*

3.2
Collector/Storage Building Elements

In the previous section, windows, greenhouses and skylights were shown to be usable for direct solar heating in winter. An extension of passive window heat designs is to add some heat storage (or "heat sink") device exposed directly to the sun's rays (behind a window or on a roof). It will help to control overheating by creating a time-lag in the house heating that will carry over into the night hours.

Examples of building elements used for combined collector/storage include glass-covered masonry walls, a wall of water containers, or the Skytherm System (developed by Harold Hay), in which a water container on the roof is alternately exposed to the sky or covered, depending on the need for heating or cooling.

In these cases, the collector, storage and distribution function is provided by one and the same element. In cases where the collector/storage element is also designed to serve as a radiator (to warm the space directly), no mechanical operation is required to distribute the heat to the interior. Insulating and reflecting panels can be added to such designs to improve their performance.

The principal advantages of these methods are that they are simple to build and—other than insulating panels which can be operated manually or automatically—they require no moving parts. Solar heating works best with some heat storage mechanism (for carry-over of daytime heat into the evening), and the passive collector/storage systems discussed in this section offer some of the simplest means of accomplishing it.

The principal disadvantage is that the heat effect from the collector/storage element is not easily controlled. This causes two problems: slow heat-up time and overheating. The response is slow between the time that heat is needed, say, on a winter morning, and the time that the heat is usable from the collector/storage element (several hours later). Also, by mid-afternoon, the solar heat that is by then available from the collector/storage may not be needed, and will thus cause overheating.

The problem of slow warm-up time is best met by adding to the house other heating methods which have quick response times. This can be done by providing an ample window area facing east to catch the morning sun directly. A wood stove also would provide quick space heating to overcome the morning chill while the collector/storage elements are being heated.

The carry-over effect of the solar heat stored in simple collector/storage systems is generally from three to six hours after the sun is off the collector area, although this varies depending upon the system and the climate. In areas with sunny days and only mildly cool nights, the time delay may extend to the early hours of the next morning before additional heating is needed.

If collector/storage walls can be oriented to the west rather than to the south, they can be heated by the afternoon sun which will extend their heating effect later into the evening, when outside temperatures drop rapidly. In this case the problem of overheating during sunny days is not such a problem. The wall itself is heated more efficiently because the sun is lower on the horizon. The greatest heat impact will be felt at sundown when the heat is most useful. Designs to obtain more control over the heat from the collector/storage element by adding insulating panels are shown in the specific examples that follow.

3.2.1 GLASS-COVERED MASONRY WALL

A dark-painted masonry wall, covered on the outside with glass or plastic, can be used as a collector/storage heating element, with the masonry storing the heat during sunny winter days. If the masonry is exposed directly to the building interior, the stored heat on the wall will radiate directly to the inside space, delayed by a time-lag of several hours or more (Figure 3.5).

This idea for a collector/storage wall combination was proposed in 1881 by E. L. Morse of Salem, Mass. It has been used since 1961 as part of the south wall design of a school in Wallasey, England. The entire heating of the school is obtained from a combination of south-facing windows, a masonry collector/storage wall system, plus the heat from the lighting fixtures and the occupants' body heat. A similar system has been installed in houses in Odeillo, France by the architect/engineer team of Michel-Trombe (Figure 3.6).

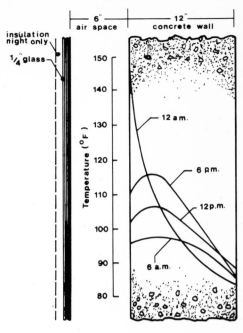

Figure 3.5. *Glass-covered masonry wall temperature as a function of time-lag calculated by computer simulation.* (*Source:* Other Homes and Garbage, *Sierra Club Books*)

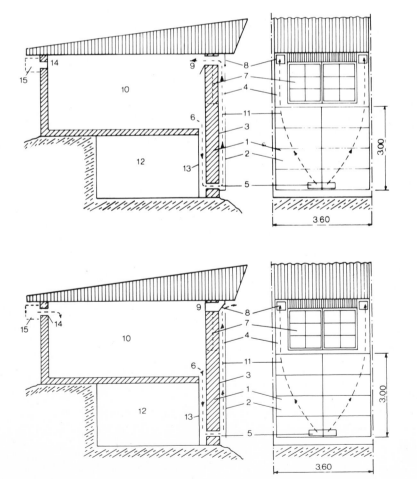

Figure 3.6. *Michel-Trombe Solar Wall (dimensions are in meters).*

1. *Concrete wall*
2. *Glass Cover*
3. *Black paint*
4, 11. *Air stream*
5, 6. *Vents*
7. *Window*
8. *Louvres for ventilation (summer)*
9. *Hot air intake*
10. *Living area*
12. *Basement*
13. *Recessed supply channel to prevent night-time backdraft*
14, 15. *Filter and cool air intake (summer)*

33

As mentioned before, heat distribution from the radiant masonry wall is difficult to control and can result in overheating the interior. One solution to avoid this is to add a layer of insulation, either fixed or movable, to the inner surface of the masonry wall.

If the insulation is fixed, the heat is drawn from the top of the air space between the outer glass and the masonry wall, and is easily ducted into a space that is **above** the collector wall—for example, in multiple-storied construction. To recover the heat within the collector/storage wall, one might thus rely upon the natural upward flow of heat, or "thermosyphoning." (This term is used to describe solar heating systems that use the natural upward flow of heated liquid or air to remove heat from the collector and that therefore require no pumps or fans.)

A small fan is much more effective, however. By using fans, the heat can be ducted to colder parts of the building or to a thermal storage unit.

If the insulation is movable, such as by a panel or shutter, then the radiant effect of the collector/storage can be used as needed by opening the insulating panel to expose the masonry to the room. If any overheating is felt, the direct radiant heating effect to the interior can be stopped by replacing the insulating panel over the collector/storage wall and the interior space.

Insulating layers also can be added to the **outer side** of the collector/storage wall. In this location, the insulating panel could control overheating somewhat by being closed on warm days, but this has the disadvantage that the sun's heat is wasted, and the heat effect from storage will last several hours after the insulating panel is closed. This outside location of an insulating panel does have advantages, however, in insulating the wall at night.

An installation of the masonry collector/storage wall has been completed in New Hampshire using the Beadwall insulating system between two exterior cover sheets of translucent fiberglass (Figure 3.7). The value of an insulating layer on the outside is particularly apparent in such cold regions to prevent undue heat loss from the collector/storage wall on sunless days and at night.

The advantages of the masonry collector/storage wall are its low construction cost (since its uses stan-

Figure 3.7. *Tyrrell Residence, Bedford, NH (1975). Beadwall insulating system between fiberglass covers in front of a concrete wall. Total Environmental Action, designers.*

dard building elements) and the ease with which it can be included into conventional building construction. Colors other than black can be used if within the absorbent color spectrum (such as dark reds and blues).

One disadvantage of wall collector/storage elements, in addition to those of limited thermal control discussed above, is that wall space is taken up by the storage elements on the sunny side of the building, where windows, patio doors, balconies or other architectural features might also be desired.

Architect Dave Kelbaugh has completed his own house in Princeton, New Jersey using the glass-covered masonry wall system, and overcomes these disadvantages by placing a greenhouse and windows within the south facing collector/storage wall (Figure 3.8, next page).

3.2.2 DRUMWALL

The collector/storage wall described above relies upon the mass of masonry as the heat storage element, but water containers also can be used. This has been demonstrated in the solar home of Steve and Holly Baer near Albuquerque, New Mexico (Figure 3.9). In their system, called Drumwall, steel oil drums are filled with water and stacked in vertical racks on the inside of a glass window wall. The drums, painted black on the end that faces the sun, absorb solar heat and then release it slowly into the interior after the sun is down (Figure 3.10).

Because there are spaces between the drums in the racks, natural light and the sun's heat are also directly admitted to the interior, and one can see between the drums to the outside. The direct sunlight into the interior space also provides a faster warm-up time in the morning than with the solid masonry collector/storage wall. And the water potentially stores more heat than would an equivalent volume of masonry.

The system thus combines the advantages of solar windows and collector/storage walls. By admitting light and some visibility through the storage drums, it also may overcome the architectural

Figure 3.9. *Drumwall System in Steve and Holly Baer's Residence (1972). (Courtesy Zomeworks Corporation)*

Figure 3.10. *Drumwall System, interior.*

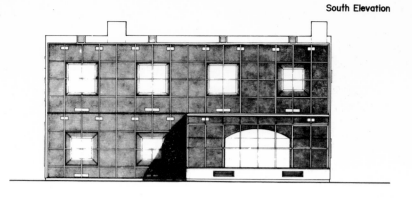

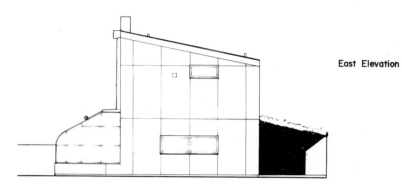

Below: View between cover glass and concrete.

Figure 3.8. *Kelbaugh Residence, Princeton, New Jersey (1976).*

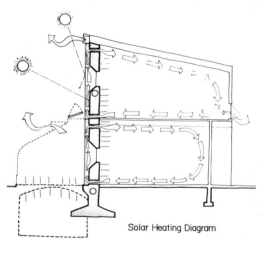

Solar Heating Diagram

1. living room
2. dining
3. kitchen
4. greenhouse
5. w.c.
6. entrance
7. coat closet
8. garden storage
9. circulating fireplace
10. trap door to cellar
11. utility closet
12. candle niche
13. arbor

14. master bedroom
15. study
16. child's bedroom
17. sleeping loft
18. sink, bidet, laundry
19. bath
20. w.c.
21. linen closet
22. storage left
23. movable closet

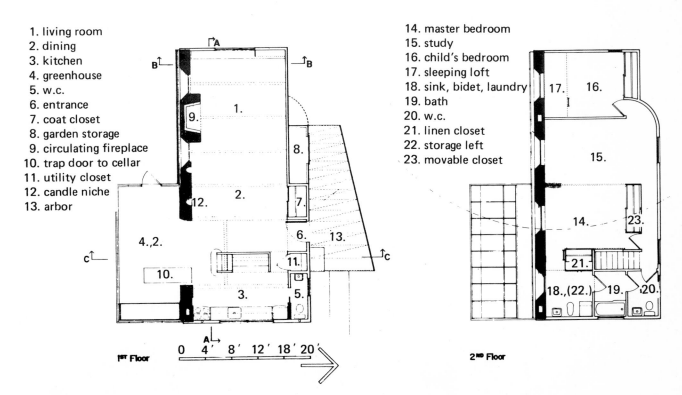

1st Floor

0   4'   8' 12' 18' 20'

2ND Floor

limitations presented by solid masonry collector/storage walls.

The Baers control overheating in summer and heat loss on winter nights by the operation of an outside insulating panel which also serves as a reflector when in the open position. The advantage of reflectors, which can increase the heat gain when used in conjunction with solar collectors, is discussed in a separate section later.

An alternative to a wall of steel water drums has been proposed by the Kalwall Corporation: vertical columns of translucent water containers that absorb some of the sun's heat and provide some time lag and heat-storage effect while admitting natural light to the interior. The house designs of Bill Mingenbach have also featured such water storage columns, as shown in Figure 3.11.

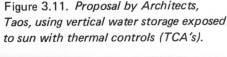

Figure 3.11. *Proposal by Architects, Taos, using vertical water storage exposed to sun with thermal controls (TCA's).*

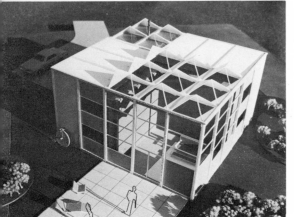

Figure 3.12A. *The Skytherm System House, Atascadero, CA (1973).*

Solar HWH

Evaporation Cooling Ponds

TCA's on all exterior glass

Thermal Storage Tanks

Ventilator for room temperature control

Full height rotating TCA on all tanks for radiation control

Underslab ducts for supplemental heating system

Building Section

0   10

These collector/storage walls, either with masonry or with liquid containers, can thus be used to advantage when incorporated into a house design with large window exposures. The problem of slow warm-up can be helped by east windows and by an effective fireplace or stove back-up system. The problem of overheating can be taken care of by insulating panels or a low-speed fan distribution system.

3.2.3 ROOF POND SYSTEMS

A roof pond—water contained in a clear plastic bag placed on a black metal roof of a home—has been developed into a combined system for winter solar

38

heating and summer night radiant cooling. Designed and patented as the Skytherm System by Harold Hay, it has been demonstrated by experimental installations in Arizona (1967) and in California (1973). Its use of natural heating and cooling effects to create house comfort is ingeniously simple and elegant. It is ideally suited to the unique conditions of hot-dry climates as found in the United States southwest. Here the need for summer cooling is the principal design requirement, and nighttime temperatures fall considerably below daytime temperatures both in winter and summer. Adaptions to other climates are being developed by its inventor.

In the Skytherm design (Figure 3.12) the solar collector/storage element—a water-filled clear plastic water bag about 8 inches deep—is placed on a flat roof of the dwelling. Movable insulating panels are positioned on tracks above the water bags for insulation during winter nights (Figure 3.13). During sunny winter days, the panels are opened to expose the water bags to the sun's heat. Warmed during the day, the heat then radiates downward through the metal deck ceiling to warm the building interior below. Masonry walls exposed to the interior help to balance the temperature swings and control overheating.

In the summer, the positioning of the insulating panels is reversed—closed during the day to prevent their being heated by the sun and then opened at night. Exposed to the cool night sky, the "thermoponds" lose heat by radiant cooling. When the temperature of the water cools below the house temperature, they absorb the heat from the building and thus offer in summer, with the same elements used for solar heating in winter, a method of natural cooling. The only moving parts of the system are the insulating panels, which can be operated manually or automatically with a small electric motor.

In the Skytherm test house in Atascadero, California, occupied year round, comfort was maintained for the entire heating and cooling season without any additional fuel requirements. Currently, five Skytherm houses are under construction by Self-Help Enterprises of Visalia, California. This project

3.12B. *Water-filled plastic bags on roof.*

3.12C. *Electrically operated insulating panels on roof over water bags.*

3.12D. *Interior of Skytherm house.*

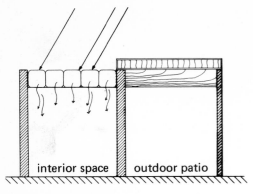

Figure 3.13A. *Winter Day.*

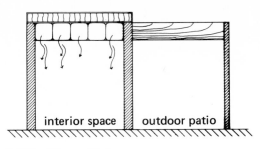

3.13B. *Winter Night.*

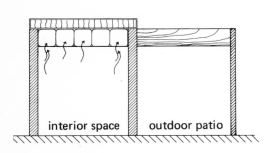

3.13C. *Summer Day.*

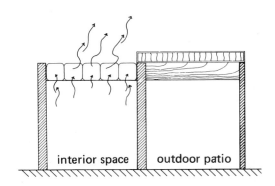

3.13D. *Summer Night. When additional cooling is needed, the thermopond bag is covered with water to cool by evaporation.*

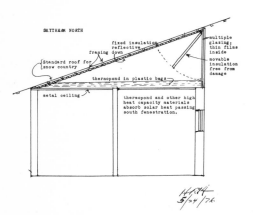

Figure 3.14. *Skytherm North. Harold Hay's sketch of the adaption of Skytherm principles to northern climates.*

thus will combine natural energy systems in house designs which can be built by the owners themselves in a "sweat equity" construction program.

The use of the roof ponds for radiant cooling is effective in areas where the night sky is clear, in which case temperatures do fall well below the daytime range.

In hot-humid climates, however, overcast skies and the moisture in the air may hold the air temperatures only a few degrees lower than daytime. In such cases, light building structures (with low "thermal mass") will cool more rapidly than buildings that have high heat-storage capacity and a resulting slow response-time in cooling. House designs based on such climate variations are discussed further in Chapter 6.

In a development of the Skytherm system for heating in cold climates, Harold Hay proposes to locate the thermopond with a movable insulating panel and reflective surfaces within a protected roof structure (Figure 3.14).

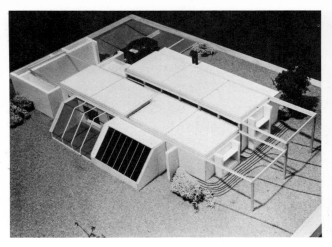

3.2.4 THERMIC DIODE SOLAR BUILDING PANELS

A proposed collector/storage design, now under development by Professor Shawn Buckley at the Massachusetts Institute of Technology, combines passive solar heating with a modular building panel (Figure 3.15). Its operation is based on two liquid chambers, one on the exterior face of a building wall (or roof) panel exposed to the sun and the other on the interior face exposed to the inside rooms.

The liquid chambers on both sides of the wall, separated by a layer of insulation, are filled with water. When the water in the outer face is heated by the sun, it flows naturally upward and passes through a control valve into the inner chamber, at the same time drawing the cooler water from the room side through an open gate at the bottom of the panel. The control valve permits the flow of heat in one direction only from the outer to inner faces when the outer chamber has gained usable heat.

The temperature in the inner chamber would never fall much below room temperature, even under cloudy day and night conditions, because then it would pick up heat from the interior room air that is supplied by the back-up or auxiliary heating system. Although the panels are intended mainly for warm climates, where freezing is not a problem, the present design of the panel allows for freezing expansion in the construction of the outer chamber.

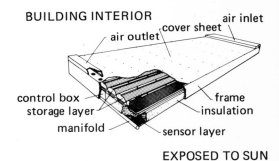

Figure 3.15. *Thermic Diode Collector/ Storage Panel. Construction detail.*

41

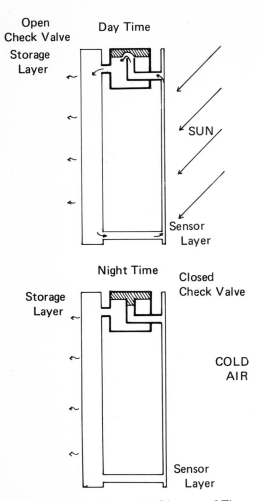

Open Check Valve
Storage Layer

Day Time

SUN

Sensor Layer

Night Time

Storage Layer

Closed Check Valve

COLD AIR

Sensor Layer

Figure 3.16. *Schematic Diagram of Thermic Diode Collector Operation.*

After experimenting with flaps—to permit the liquid to flow from outer to inner face and to prevent "backflow"—Professor Buckley has devised a means of using oil as the valving control (Figure 3.16).

The oil is heavy enough to block the flow of water at room temperature from the inner to outer chamber, but it is sensitive enough to slight differences in pressure to permit water that is 5° F. warmer to lift the head of oil and then spill into the inner chamber. Because of this one-directional flow feature, the system is referred to as a "thermic diode solar panel."

In the basic panel design described above, the inner water chamber can either be installed to radiate heat directly to the interior or can heat air spaces between the liquid chambers from which the heated air can be ducted to other parts of the building.

In summer the control valve is reversed, allowing the flow of warm water from the inner chamber to the outer face of the building at night to be cooled by the night air. Further modifications of the system include the addition of glazing to the outer face so that the system might also be used in temperate and cool climates as well.

3.3 Reflectors

The ground, the roofs of buildings, and surrounding surfaces—such as the sides of buildings and even nearby mountains—reflect the sun rays on a building. Thus, solar heat reflected from snow, water, or ground and roof surfaces can be used to advantage on solar-oriented windows, collector/storage elements or solar collectors. The typical reflectivity values of common ground surfaces are listed in Figure 3.17.

Highly reflective surfaces have been used to increase heat gains on passive collector devices, as illustrated earlier with the Drum Wall. Reflectors also can be used with the solar collectors described in the following chapters on active systems.

Reflectors are, of themselves, a passive means of increasing solar heat gain. Because of their wide use

Figure 3.17. *Reflectivity of Surfaces*

Perfect Mirror (theoretical)	1.00
Polished Aluminum (Alzak)	0.75-0.85
Polished Stainless Steel	0.60-0.80
Aluminized Mylar (clean)	0.60-0.80
Fresh Snow	0.60-0.80
Dirty Snow	0.40-0.70
Sand	0.10-0.25
Water	0.08-0.10

for improving the performance of solar collection (whether through windows or solar collector panels), reflectors deserve mention here to explain how they can work with any solar heating system.

Panels with a reflecting surface—positioned at an advantageous angle with respect to the sun and the collector—increase the amount of solar radiation received by reflecting the sun's rays from an area larger than the collector itself. Reflecting panels are easy to construct and thus may be more economical or practical than building a larger collector area to capture the same amount of solar heat.

The projects of architect James Lambeth illustrate the inventiveness with which reflectors can be used—one for melting snow at an entryway of a ski lodge (Figure 3.18), a second to help heat an outdoor courtyard and swimming pool (Figure 3.19).

Flat reflecting panels are easily fabricated and installed to augment the heat gain of passive or active solar collectors. The sun's direct radiation arrives in rays that are parallel to one another, and their effect therefore is predictable. They are reflected from a smooth surface at an angle equal to their incoming angle (or "angle of incidence"). Thus, for different times of the year, the direct radiation received by a

Figure 3.18. *Solar lens, Ski Lodge, Snowmass, CO. Fabricated of gold mirrored glass and positioned to concentrate solar rays on entry from September to March for snow evaporation and melting. (Courtesy James Lambeth)*

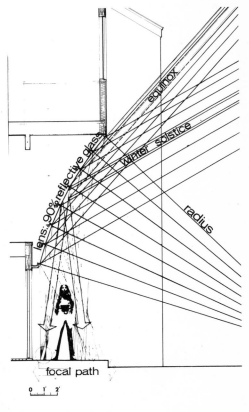

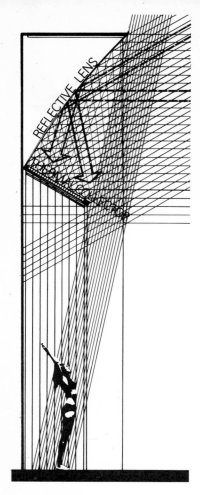

Figure 3.19. *Solar lens, swimming pool, Springfield, MO. Fabricated of stainless steel to concentrate solar rays on solar collectors and pool area. (Courtesy James Lambeth)*

Figure 3.20. *Reflected Heat Gain on a Collector Window. The angle of reflection is the same as the angle of incidence. The effectiveness of a reflector can be established by tracing the sun's rays from given solar altitudes to a given collector window area.*

reflector (which then in turn is reflected on a collecting surface) can be determined by a simple exercise of geometry called "ray tracing," which then gives the best position of a reflector (see Figure 3.20).

The surfaces of a window or a collector also reflect the incoming solar rays—with the result that when the angle of solar rays is less than 30° with respect to the glass, more heat is lost by reflection to the outside of the window or collector than is transmitted through the glass.

In subsequent chapters, it will be seen that the orientation angle of a solar collector with respect to the sun's altitude in winter is important in order to minimize "reflection losses"—the loss of potential heat that is reflected away from the collector by its

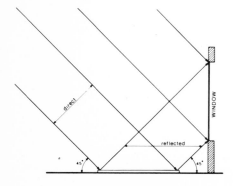
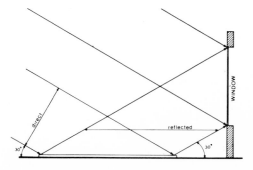

glass cover. Changing the position of a reflector once a month can improve the incident angle of reflected radiation as the sun changes in altitude throughout the year, a simpler adjustment than changing the position of a large collector area.

Reflectors are useful for the passive systems that were detailed in this chapter, especially in southern locations where the sun's altitude in winter averages about 45° — a less-than-ideal angle of incidence either to vertical solar walls or horizontal roof ponds (Figure 3.21).

3.3.1 REFLECTIVE/INSULATING PANELS

In Steve Baer's Drumwall design, a panel is dropped to the ground during sunlight hours to expose a reflecting (aluminum) surface to the sun at the base of the collector wall. Ideally, one could fix the panel at calculated angles during the heating season to accommodate the variable solar altitude. At night and during the summer, the panel is raised to insulate the collector wall. The use of operable reflective/insulating panels is well suited to solar window and collector/storage concepts—offering a simple method to increase the heat gain as well as providing an insulating layer at night.

The least expensive reflecting surface is aluminized Mylar bonded to a rigid backing, such as plywood. Rigid foam board insulation, normally used in standard wall construction, is available with a reflecting surface of Mylar already bonded to it. A permanent but more expensive reflector can be built of stainless steel.

Because reflecting surfaces are susceptible to damage from air pollutants, dust and rain-splashed dirt, with a resulting loss of reflectivity, the cost of maintenance, replacement and operation has to be considered.

3.3.2 PYRAMIDAL OPTIC REFLECTORS

The name **Pyramidal Optics** has been given by its inventor to describe a solar collector system that uses reflecting panels to concentrate solar radiation

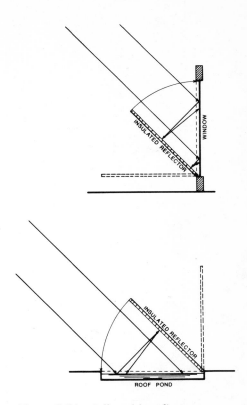

Figure 3.21. *Adjustable reflectors positioned to increase the area exposed to the sun (as shown in dotted lines) or to re-reflect back to the collector surface the solar rays that are reflected off the cover sheet when the angle of solar rays is less than 45 degrees to the collector surface (as shown in solid lines).*

45

Ryan Studio

Figure 3.22. *Prototype, Pyramidal Optic installation in Stamford, CT. Outside panel is closed at night and during inclement weather.*

from a large area to a small solar collector. The system, developed by Eric Wormser, is demonstrated in an experimental installation in Stamford, Connecticut (Figure 3.22).

A reflecting panel is opened automatically during sunlight hours and closed during inclement weather and at night. The inside surfaces of the roof shed also are covered with reflecting surfaces (Mylar glued to plywood). The result of careful positioning of the reflectors is that all of the solar radiation that falls on the roof opening is reflected upon a small solar collector, in effect receiving the same heat gain of a collector many times its size. The system promises potential economies because the solar collectors themselves are costly, while reflecting panels can be installed economically.

Although the solar collector itself may not be exposed directly to day-long sun due to shading by the roof shed, the temperature of the air in the roof shed area is raised because it is, in effect, an air pocket, protected from the wind. As will be shown in the next chapter, higher temperatures of the air outside a collector directly improve its performance.

In recent modifications, Wormser has installed the reflecting panels within a plastic-covered roof

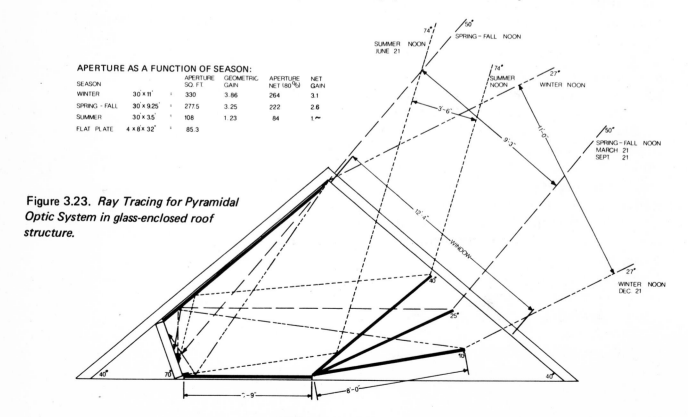

APERTURE AS A FUNCTION OF SEASON:

SEASON		APERTURE SQ. FT.	GEOMETRIC GAIN	APERTURE NET (80%)	NET GAIN
WINTER	30' x 11'	330	3.86	264	3.1
SPRING - FALL	30' x 9.25'	277.5	3.25	222	2.6
SUMMER	30' x 3.5'	108	1.23	84	1.~
FLAT PLATE	4 x 8 x 32"	85.3			

Figure 3.23. *Ray Tracing for Pyramidal Optic System in glass-enclosed roof structure.*

Figure 3.24. *Pyramidal Optic installation in Columbia, South Carolina. (Courtesy Wormser Scientific Corporation)*

shed (Figures 3.23 and 3.24). This protects the reflecting surfaces from dirt and pollution and permits a more carefree operation of the moving reflector panel, which would otherwise have to be designed to withstand wind and snow loads.

Solar heating with the passive means described in this chapter is often ignored by advocates of more technically complex solar heating systems. Passive solar heating methods put emphasis on the design of a building itself, its basic planning, orientation and construction materials, rather than on the solar mechanical equipment which will be discussed in the next chapter.

The major disadvantages presented by reliance on passive systems have been mentioned throughout this chapter: a wide variation in indoor temperature due to slow warm-up time on cold mornings and overheating on extremely sunny days.

These disadvantages can be overcome by using insulating devices and by using fan-controlled heat distribution systems. In a recent report from the Los Alamos Scientific Laboratory, various passive devices were compared by computer simulation, which confirm that, in the southwest, passive systems can be used with operating controls to supply the entire house heating requirements (Figure 3.25). Some systems, such as Skytherm, also provide a passive means of house cooling. With reflecting and insulating devices, passive collector and storage systems can be applied in cooler climates as well.

3.4
Collecting, Storing and Distributing Heat through Passive Means

Advantages and Disadvantages

Figure 3.25. *Comparison of Four Passive Systems.*

Case 1: *Interior storage (such as masonry fireplace) is heated by room air only (out of direct sunlight).*

Case 2: *Storage is placed in direct sun (as in glass-covered masonry design) with no insulating controls between storage and room.*

Case 3: *Storage is out of direct sun but is part of building structure (as in masonry wall and roof) insulated on outside.*

Case 4: *Storage is in direct sun but with insulating control against heat loss outside (as in Drumwall system).*

A computer simulation study by J. D. Balcomb and J. C. Hedstrom compared the performance of these four alternatives under yearly weather conditions of New Mexico. Case 3 was better than Case 1, due mainly to the increased surface area of the masonry storage exposed to the room air. Cases 2 and 4 were superior to either of these, due to the direct heating of the storage by its exposure to the sun. The insulating controls used in Case 4 made it the best of all the cases, due to reduced nighttime heat loss. Water storage was judged to be superior to the masonry wall due to its more even temperature difference between the outer (sun exposed) and inner surface (room exposed). The high temperature between the two faces of the masonry wall (as shown in Figure 3.5) results in a greater heat loss back to the outside than to the interior. Such passive systems with proper insulating controls were shown to be practical for house heating in the United States Southwest. (Source: Simulation Analysis of Passive Solar Heated Buildings, Los Alamos Scientific Laboratory)

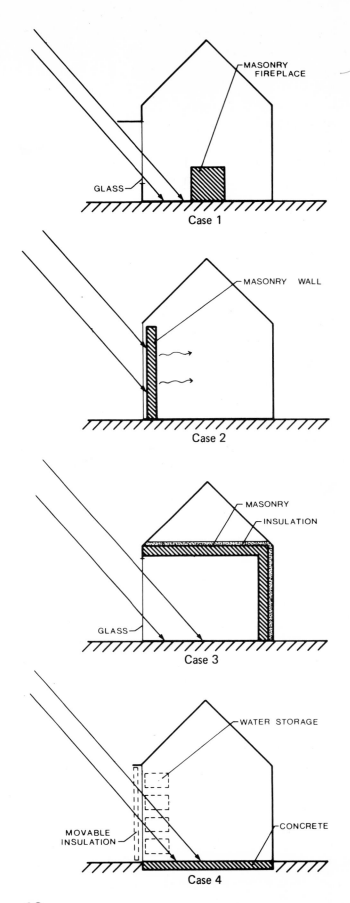

48

The advantage of passive systems is one of construction economics. The passive systems are built of materials that can be easily obtained. They can be installed in a house by local contractors as well as by relatively unskilled owner-builders.

Many of the passive devices strike the average homebuyer as unconventional. Also, due to the slow response times of high thermal-capacity construction, passive systems impose their own regime on the home owner, who may be used to the more easily controlled, conventional heating systems. Thus, despite their simplicity, passive systems have been slow to attract the wide acceptance in home building that they deserve.

In the chapters that follow, more technically advanced solar heating systems are discussed, which have the advantage over the passive systems of higher and more easily controlled heat and which can be applied to conventional house design and construction—particularly to existing houses.

But installing mechanical heating equipment in a building, whether it is new or an existing structure, always proves to be expensive. As a result, a basic principle of practical solar house design emerges: to first use passive means of solar heating to best possible advantage, as appropriate for each climate, and thus lighten the load on the mechanical heating equipment, whether it is an active solar heating system or not.

CHAPTER 4

ACTIVE SYSTEMS: THE THREE BASIC PARTS

In contrast to the passive approach, which relies on elements of building design and construction for natural control of climate, "active" systems use mechanical means (pumps, fans, automatic controls) to collect, store, and distribute the sun's heat to a building.

Equipment has been developed and can be commercially supplied or custom-fabricated to perform the separate steps of solar heating—heat collection, storage and distribution.

A solar heating system must perform adequately with heat supplied from solar collectors, which is generally lower in temperature than what is normally produced by a conventional furnace or boiler. Local climate factors determine the amount of sunshine available, which in turn determines the appropriate collector and heat storage type. The mode of heat distribution from heat storage to the house must then be designed to supply heat from storage to the house in a manner that is comfortable for the house occupants.

In this chapter the individual steps involved in collecting, storing and distributing solar heat are taken up separately. Solar heating with collectors and storage units which utilize temperatures in the "low" temperature range (90° to 140° F. in northern climates) will occupy most of the discussion in this chapter because it represents the most common system and, to be efficient, requires careful planning of the house itself.

Whether a solar collector is a simple device made at the building site or a factory-made product, the design considerations are similar: to use solar radiation to heat an absorber through which a transport medium (air or liquid) is circulated to heat a building, either directly or via a heat storage unit.

In the solar collectors, air or liquid is heated as it passes through an absorber material exposed to the sun. The most common collectors used for heating buildings are in the shape of flat panels and, when made part of a building, have the appearance of a dark window or a skylight. Other collectors under development use curved shapes, with reflectors to focus or concentrate the sun's rays on a small absorber.

Flat-plate solar collectors are composed of an **absorber** (usually sheet metal with air or liquid passages attached, a translucent **cover sheet** of glass or plastic, and **insulating material** behind the absorber. Such collectors usually can be placed directly on a roof or wall of a building.

The absorber and the cover sheet both play a role in efficient heat collection, with the same general principles that apply to passive collector/storage walls as well as to more advanced collector types.

In an air-type collector, air is heated as it passes across the absorber (usually in an air space behind the absorber), and then is ducted to the building space or to the heat storage unit. In a liquid-type collector, water or a similar liquid (oil or antifreeze mixtures) is heated as it passes through channels or tubes in the absorber plate, and then is piped to storage.

The collector is controlled automatically to operate when the temperature in the collector is usable (that is, when it is warmer than either the heat storage or the interior of the building). Heat is drawn from the collector until the temperature in the storage unit or the house exceeds that which is available from the collector.

4.1
Solar Collectors

The First Step in Using
the Sun's Heat
in Active Systems

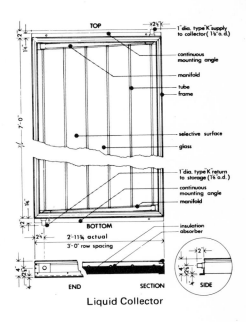

Liquid Collector

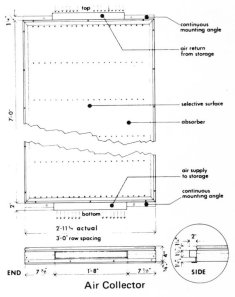

Air Collector

*Typical collector construction.
(Courtesy Sunworks, Inc.)*

THE ABSORBER

An **absorber** could be any material that can be exposed to the sun's radiation for its heat absorption and transfer capacity. In one of the collector/storage wall systems described in the previous chapter, masonry is used. In flat-plate solar collectors, sheet metal—such as copper, aluminum or steel—commonly is used. Figure 4.1 shows the typical heat-energy flow in a flat-plate collector.

Only part of the heat that is received by a collector eventually reaches the transfer medium—liquid or air—as it passes through the collector. Some solar radiation is reflected away from the absorber by the cover sheet or is absorbed within the cover itself. The remainder strikes the absorber plate which, like the cover sheet, may reflect some radiation back to the sky, depending upon the angle at which the incoming rays strike it. The rest, however, heats the absorber material.

Absorbers vary in their capacity to absorb and hold heat, depending upon the material used and the coating or finish on the outer surface that faces the sun.

Black paint on masonry or metal will increase the

Figure 4.1. *Heat Energy Flow. Single glazed collector with selective coating. (Source: Sunworks, Inc.)*

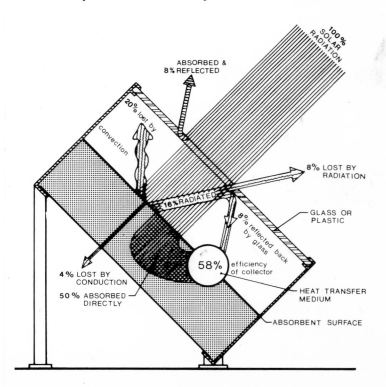

heat-absorption capacity of the material many times above a light color. However, while a heated black material absorbs radiation well, it also re-radiates heat back to the outside, and the rate that it does so is called its "emissivity."

The amount of emissivity (and resulting heat loss) depends largely upon the type of coating used on the metal absorber. Thus, while it is intended that the heat in an absorber plate be picked up by the air or liquid heat-transfer medium, heat is lost back to the air between the cover sheet and the absorber. As the temperature in the air space between absorber and cover sheet rises, there is an increased heat loss to the outside through the driving force of convection within the air space, and through conduction back out through the cover sheet.

In 1955, Israeli engineer Harry Tabor developed a "selective surface" coating for metal absorber plates which has a high absorptivity, but also has a low emissivity due to particular properties of the surface coating. So, unlike black-painted absorbers, one with the selective surface does not re-radiate and thus lose much of the heat it absorbs. The "Tabor Surface" was the first of what is now a number of coatings that can be applied to solar collector absorber plates by a chemical or electrolitic process or by vacuum deposition. Absorbers with a selective surface often appear bluish-grey or violet rather than black (similar to the coating on a gun barrel, where a selective coating is applied to reduce reflection and glare).

At present, selective coatings require a shop or factory application. On-site or job-built solar collectors, which can only be blackened by paints, do not provide low emissivity. Paints that have selective properties that can be painted to metals at the construction site are being developed but are not yet available.

THE COVER SHEET

An efficient collector requires one or more translucent glass or plastic **cover sheets** to reduce the heat loss from the absorber by wind cooling. The cover sheets create an insulating air space between

Table 4.1. *Absorptivities and Emissivities of Various Surfaces.*

Material or color	Shortwave absorptivity	Longwave emissivity
Aluminum foil, bright	0.05	0.05
Whitewash, new	0.12	0.90
Grey color, dark	0.70	0.90
Black paint	0.85	0.90
Selective Coating	0.90	0.10

A factory application of selective surface being applied to steel Miromit collector. (Courtesy American Heliothermal Corporation)

the outside air and the absorber. (Collectors used in southern climates for swimming pool heating may not require any cover sheet.)

A cover sheet also increases the efficiency of heat collection due to the "greenhouse effect." Glass is "transparent" to solar radiation which is in the short wave length—and thus admits the sun's heating rays. However, the heat that is re-radiated back towards the sky from the absorber is in a longer wave length spectrum, to which glass is "opaque."

Thus the heat re-radiated back to the sky from an absorber is trapped by the glass cover sheet, part of which is then given back to the air space between cover sheet and absorber.

Some plastic materials used as collector cover sheets do not have the same property as glass in acting as a greenhouse trap, but Teflon and Lexan do have similar properties and often are used for cover sheets. Lexan also is highly resistant to breakage and thus, despite a higher cost than glass, may be used in areas where a solar collector might be exposed to vandalism. Many plastics are deformed by high temperatures, but fiberglass and thermosetting plastics are not affected by heat, and are commonly used for collector covers.

A single sheet of glass alone does not provide the best insulation against heat losses from the absorber to the outside, and in some climates two or even three cover sheets are required, depending upon the particular application for which the heat is used.

However, each layer of glass that is used also reduces the solar heat gain to the collector—for three reasons. First, each layer **absorbs** some heat, part of which is lost again to the outside through conduction and convection. Second, each layer **shades** solar radiation, depending on its material composition. (Cover sheets are thus selected which have a high solar transmittance.) Finally, each layer of glass **reflects** some heat back to the outside, rather than transmitting it to the absorber.

Thus, a compromise must be made. For good insulation against heat loss to the outside air, the more cover sheets the better. But to block the sun least, the fewer the better. Because selectively coated collectors hold heat better within the absorber plate, one glass cover sheet is often sufficient for such collectors in climates that would otherwise require two.

Because of reflection losses off the cover sheets, the direction that a collector faces is critical in any solar installation. If it faces too far away from the sun's rays, both cover sheet and absorber will reflect more heat than is usefully trapped. Anti-reflective films can be used on the cover sheets to reduce reflection losses, but these do not preclude the need to face collectors so as to gain the most winter sun.

As mentioned previously, when the angle of the incoming solar rays is less than 30° with respect to the collector cover, most of the heat is reflected away from the collector and thus is comparatively useless.

Ideally, a collector would be oriented to face directly (or "normal") to the sun at all times. To do so all day would require that the collector be moved to follow the hourly and seasonal angle of the sun. Such sun-tracking collector mountings have been devised and are used for advanced collector designs. For practical reasons, however, one fixed position is chosen in most cases based on the average position of the sun during the months when the solar collectors need to operate most efficiently.

The long-term durability and performance of many collector designs is difficult to predict at this early stage of what is becoming a growing solar equipment industry. However, solar collectors have been in continuous use for water heating in Florida, Arizona, and California as well as in other countries —notably Australia and Israel—for more than 50 years.

The description of collectors given here is intended to introduce the items that are more completely described in manufacturers' literature. A summary review of points to look for in selecting a solar collector is given in Chapter 8.

FLAT-PLATE COLLECTORS

Until more advanced collectors are developed to become more economically attractive, the flat-plate types are the most economic and practical solution for a number of problems that are related to active solar heating systems. These problems are worth reviewing here to outline the advantages of flat-plate collectors, as well as to indicate their disadvantages—which have led to the search for more efficient collector devices.

Flat-plate collectors can be made part of a roof or wall, either placed on the outside surface or actually built in as part of the structure itself. To avoid problems of weathertight connections, the weatherproof building enclosure can be completed and the collector fixed to the outside roof or wall or to a specially built support.

The advantage of placing the collectors on the building is that the distances between collector, heat storage and the space to be heated are as short as possible. There also may be an additional advantage if, in placing collectors high on a building roof, shading from surrounding buildings or trees is avoided.

Collectors normally are installed in one fixed position due to the additional cost and maintenance required with movable elements. Thus the flat plate solar collectors that are discussed below usually are fixed at a tilt angle and an orientation which is calculated for maximum winter heat gain at the particular latitude where the building is located. The recommended tilt and orientation of solar collectors are detailed in later chapters.

There are limits to the number of collectors that can be placed on a building in a practical and aesthetically pleasing manner. The problem is not made much easier by placing collectors on the ground, for here they may meet with additional shading or vandalism problems.

The collector area needed for each installation of course varies according to the heating requirements of the building and the amount of solar radiation available. Also, solar collectors now available from different manufacturers vary widely in their efficiency. These factors and their effect on the real cost of heat gained are discussed throughout this book.

4.1.1 AIR-TYPE COLLECTOR

Flat-plate collectors that use air as the heat transfer medium were first developed many years ago,

Site-fabricated air-type collector installation. (Courtesy Crowther Solar Group)

notably by Maria Telkes (1948), R. Bliss and M. Donovan (1954), and George Löf (1957).

An air-type solar heating system in the Denver, Colorado residence of George Löf—described in detail in the next chapter—has been in continuous operation since it was installed in 1957, and this fact alone may indicate the chief advantage of air-type solar collectors—they are free of freezing and corrosion problems that have complicated the use of liquid-type collectors. In addition, the air that is heated can be ducted either directly into the interior space of a building or into a rock storage unit (and then into the building interior), thus avoiding the heat transfer inefficiencies that are incurred in liquid systems.

The disadvantages of air-type collector systems are these: air collectors are not as efficient for domestic water heating as are liquid collectors (and domestic water heating is a logical part of most solar installations). Large air ducts are needed, also, to move air from the collectors to heat storage, and fans are required to move the air, so that more electrical power is required than for a comparable liquid system.

Manufacturers who now supply air-type solar collectors use one of two approaches for ducting the air to and from the collectors. One is with outside manifolds—whereby a main air duct runs along the top or bottom of the collectors (air can be supplied from top or from bottom). The other is by "self-manifolding," whereby the air is delivered through the back of one of the collectors and then allowed to flow horizontally or vertically between adjacent collectors. Common designs for air-type collectors are shown in Figure 4.2.

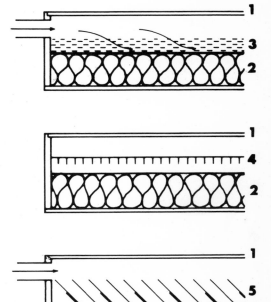

Figure 4.2. *Typical Air Collector Designs.*

1. *Glass or plastic cover sheet*
2. *Insulation.*
3. *Layers of black cloth or wire mesh (after R. Bliss and M. Donovan)*
4. *Metal Absorber sheet designed for heat transfer.*
5. *Glass or metal louvers (after G. Löf)*

(Source: J. I. Yellott and G. Rand)

4.1.2 WATER-TRICKLING COLLECTOR

At present the least expensive solar collectors to construct are those built from commonly available materials and assembled at the site, often by the building owners themselves. Higher efficiency, factory-assembled solar collector units eventually may become just as economical if larger markets justify their mass production. But many solar house builders have had to rely upon designs that could be built on the construction site. The water-trickling collector is one of the most common of these solar heating systems built from standard building materials.

The first design for a water-trickling collector, developed and patented by Harry Thomason, is shown in Figure 4.3. Its absorber is a standard corrugated aluminum roofing panel painted black and covered with one sheet of glass.

Water is pumped to a horizontal feeder pipe or "manifold" which runs along the top ridge of the collectors. The manifold is pitched slightly to allow the water to flow down its entire length and then exit through holes located at a spacing which coincides with the corrugations or channels in the absorber sheets. To pick up the heat from the metal absorber effectively, the water should flow in a thin film over the entire surface of the corrugated sheets, rather than in the valleys or corrugations alone. Imprinted patterns available in some metal sheets help to create such a flow through surface tension.

The water, heated in its passage down the absorber, is collected in a gutter at the bottom and piped to a thermal storage unit. In the Thomason "Solaris" system, illustrated in the next chapter, the heat storage consists of a metal water tank embedded in a rock storage bin.

Compared to collectors in which the liquid passages are enclosed (see 4.1.3 below), the Thomason design and other open water collectors lose heat efficiency through evaporation of water from the absorber channels and condensation on the cover sheet, which further reduces the radiation received by the absorber, since the water drops on the underside of the cover sheet reflect some of the sun's rays back to the sky. This heat loss is the more critical in cold climates as the temperature difference increases between outside air and the collector.

In one attempt to control condensation in a water-trickling design, a variation of the open collector uses two corrugated metal sheets nested close enough together to force the water that flows between them to remain in contact with the upper absorber sheet, in effect creating a closed water-trickling collector.

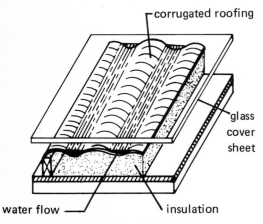

Detail, Thomason collector installation.

Figure 4.3. *Water-trickling collector.*

corrugated roofing

glass cover sheet

water flow

insulation

58

Harry Teague

The Thomason Solaris system has been in use for more than a dozen years in the Washington, D. C. area. Other houses with water-trickling collectors have been constructed in colder climates, assembled and installed by their owner-builders, such as the Snowmass, Colorado house built by owner Ron Shore, using a nesting water-trickling collector, (Figure 4.4).

4.1.3 LIQUID-TYPE COLLECTOR

Liquid-type solar collectors have been developed and improved continuously since the early experimental houses built at the Massachusetts Institute of Technology. (The system operation of the MIT Solar House IV is explained in the next chapter.)

Liquid collectors, currently available in various designs from a growing number of nationally recognized manufacturers, are the most common

Figure 4.4. Shore House, Snowmass, CO (1974). Designer/owner/builder: Ron Shore. Nesting-type water-trickling collector consists of two glass covers and two sheets of corrugated roofing approximately 1/32 inch apart so that water flow remains in contact with both sheets. To prevent freezing, water is drained into storage tank at end of day. Collector vented in summer. Reflector/insulating panels located over skylights. Beadwall insulation system on south windows. No auxiliary heating used.

59

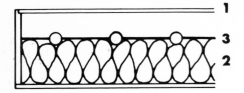

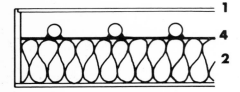

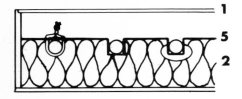

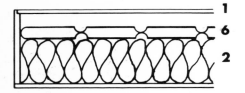

Figure 4.5. *Typical Liquid Collector Designs:*

1. *Glass or plastic cover sheet.*
2. *Insulation.*
3. *Liquid passages integrated with absorber sheet by Rollbond process (similar to refrigerator backs).*
4. *Tubes attached to absorber (typically by soldering).*
5. *Tubes nested in fold within absorber and attached by various methods.*
6. *Liquid flow passages between two metal sheets joined only at points.*
(Source: J. I. Yellott and G. Rand)

type in use today. Water or a water/antifreeze solution is used in the collectors, piped under pressure through tubing that is attached to or integral with the metal absorber plate. There are numerous methods for passing the liquid through the absorber plate, some of which are shown in Figure 4.5.

Some liquid systems are designed to be drained-down at night to avoid freezing, rather than to depend upon antifreeze, which is costly and which is corrosive to some metals.

Copper is the most durable fluid conduit commonly used in absorber plates, attached to a copper or aluminum absorber sheet. Corrosion is a constant concern when aluminum is used for the fluid conduits. Galvanized steel, a third metal commonly used, is least expensive but has the lowest heat-conduction properties.

The liquid is piped to the collectors through a manifold which may be built into the collector or through piping that is connected at the time of installation to the top and bottom of the row of collectors. The liquid in the collector-to-storage loop can be pumped from top to bottom of a collector, or from bottom to top.

A principal advantage of all liquid collectors is that they can supply domestic hot water, which makes use of the collectors year-round. Fuel for domestic hot water requirements of a family of four can represent from 10 to 20 percent of the annual heating bill. When compared to electric rates for heating hot water, the fuel savings that are possible with a solar domestic water heater can pay back the initial installation cost within a very few years.

A second advantage of liquid systems is that heat can be pumped easily in small pipes from collector to storage, with less electric power than is needed for fans to move heat in air systems. For this reason, if the collectors must be located a considerable distance from the heat storage, liquid collector systems may be the only practical choice—especially for large buildings or for existing homes.

A third advantage is that liquid system's water storage takes up much less space than the rock storage that is used with air systems.

Liquid collectors do have two disadvantages, however, when compared to air systems—those of

60

freezing and of corrosion—but careful installation and maintenance can overcome them.

The possibility of water freezing requires that anti-freeze be used in the collector-to-storage loop or that the collectors be drained down automatically when the outside temperature approaches the freezing point. (In northern climates, this generally requires that antifreeze systems be used.) Anti-freeze-filled collector-to-storage loops must be completely closed, of course, and full precautions taken against the possibility of the antifreeze entering the domestic water supply loop. Some anti-freeze liquids are toxic. Propylene glycol, a non-toxic antifreeze, is therefore recommended where compatible with the metal used in the collector.

Liquid-type collectors also are more subject to corrosion than air collectors, particularly if a neutral water or antifreeze solution used in them is not properly maintained. Aluminum collectors, while less expensive than copper, are particularly suscep-tible. Although less efficient in heat transfer than water, oil admixtures are also used in aluminum sys-tems to minimize the risk of corrosion. Electrolysis between the dissimilar metals will cause corrosion, too, so that one metal is generally used for the entire collector and piping loop. Where dissimilar metals must be used in contact with liquid, they must be separated by non-metallic or "dielectric" unions.

Most factory-made liquid collectors are pressure-tested for leaks before leaving the factory, and the system is normally tested again under pressure after installation (in the same way that any house plumb-ing system is tested).

Liquid-type collector with external manifold connection at bottom. (Courtesy Sunworks, Inc.)

When installing collectors of any type, however, provision must be made for future access and ser-vicing, including replacement of parts, and such provisions are especially important with liquid systems.

Often air may become trapped in the passages within a liquid collector, causing blockage of the liquid flow through that part of the collector array. Provided the assembly is installed for easy access, this can be checked by placing one's hand on the collectors. If one is hotter than the others, this would indicate that heat is not being removed from that collector area at the proper rate due to blockage of some sort.

61

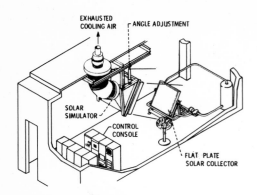

Solar simulator used for testing solar collectors.

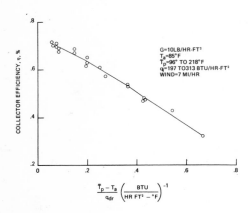

G=10LB/HR-FT²
Ta=85°F
Tp=96° TO 218°F
q=197 TO313 BTU/HR-FT²
WIND=7 MI/HR

COLLECTOR EFFICIENCY, η, %

$$\frac{T_p - T_a}{q_{dr}} \left(\frac{BTU}{HR\ FT^2 - °F}\right)^{-1}$$

Figure 4.6. *Typical Instantaneous Efficiency Curve. Results of an experimental collector tested on a solar simulator. Actual performance efficiency is established at various points as a function of the temperature difference between the collector (Tp) and outside air (Ta) divided by the available solar radiation (Qdr). The line (or "curve") is drawn as the average of the test result points to represent performance under other conditions. This format has been recommended by the National Bureau of Standards as the industry standard in representing instantaneous collector performance. (F. Lewis Technical Memorandum NASA TM X-71793). Table II.9 (Appendix II) shows typical curves for commonly used collector types.*

Both liquid and air collectors each have advantages in meeting specific needs of solar installations in different climates. Therefore the choice between collectors—and particularly between air-type and liquid-type systems—is often made on the basis of individual preferences and circumstances.

PERFORMANCE OF FLAT-PLATE COLLECTORS

The performance efficiency of a solar collector is determined by the amount of heat that it produces compared to the amount of solar radiation available. Climatic factors, of course, affect this performance: the varying amount of solar radiation available, the type of the incoming radiation (diffuse vs. direct), outside air temperature, and the outside wind speed.

Use conditions also can affect the performance: the rate of flow of heat removal from the collector, and the temperature range that is necessary for the effective use of the solar heat in a particular system.

Swimming pool heating, for example, requires only a 30° to 50° F. difference in temperature above that of the outside air. On the other hand, solar-powered air conditioning requires temperatures from the collector well above 190° F. to operate well with absorption chillers. Space heating, to be effective, generally requires temperatures from the collectors in the range of 130° F.—or 80° to 100° F. above the outside air temperature in winter.

Most established solar collector manufacturers supply test data on performance of their collectors. In comparing the performances, of course, the specific conditions of climate mentioned above and the test procedures must be the same.

The graph most commonly used by solar collector manufacturers indicates the **instantaneous efficiency** of performance of the collector, with the solar radiation assumed to be directly facing, or "normal" to, the collector—which only occurs with a fixed south-facing collector when the sun is at solar noon (Figure 4.6). The actual day-long efficiency may be 10 to 20 percent less than what is shown by the instantaneous efficiency, due to the reflection losses off the cover sheet when the sun is at different angles to the collector, or because of insufficient solar radiation available to operate the heat collection cycle (Figure 4.7).

Day-long performance data may not be available from all manufacturers, but one can expect that industry standards soon will be adopted that recommend or require publication of all such performance test data in the same form, to permit easy consumer evaluation.

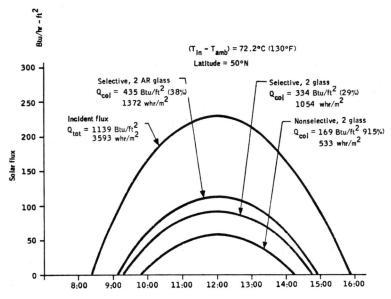

Figure 4.7. *Day-long Collector Perform-ance. Clear day performance of various collector types (in a fixed position) as a function of time. (Source:* Development of Flat-Plate Collectors, *NASA Report CR-134804)*

Winter performance (December 21).

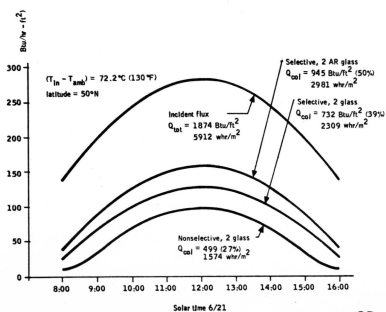

Summer performance (June 21).

Figure 4.8. *A Comparison of Five Collector Types. Each of the four performance efficiency charts compares a different solar collector type to a "baseline" collector, a selectively surfaced double-glass collector (dotted line). (Source: Development of Flat-Plate Solar Collectors, NASA Report CR-134804)*

A guide to what one can expect from liquid-type collectors, based on construction and materials, can be seen in Figure 4.8, taken from a report published in 1975 for the National Aeronautics and Space Administration, entitled "Development of Flat-Plate Solar Collectors." The report shows results of performance tests run on many different collectors under identical test conditions, and thus it offers objective guidelines by which to compare them.

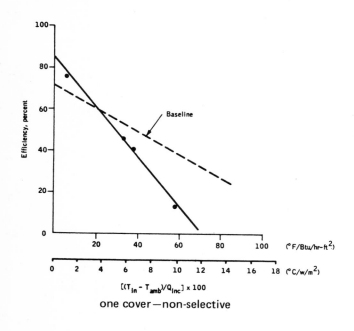

one cover—non-selective

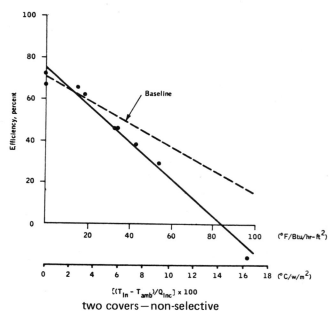

two covers—non-selective

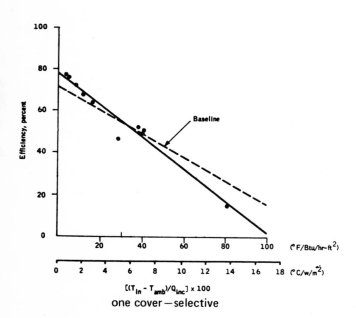

one cover—selective

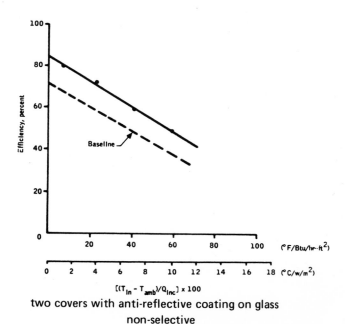

two covers with anti-reflective coating on glass
non-selective

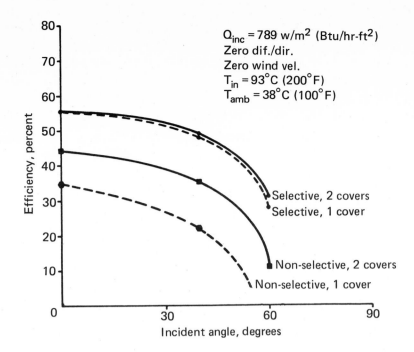

Q_inc = 789 w/m² (Btu/hr-ft²)
Zero dif./dir.
Zero wind vel.
T_in = 93°C (200°F)
T_amb = 38°C (100°F)

$Q_{inc} = 789$ w/m² (Btu/hr-ft²)
Zero dif./dir.
Zero wind vel.
$T_{in} = 93°C$ (200°F)
$T_{amb} = 38°C$ (100°F)

Selective, 2 covers
Selective, 1 cover

Non-selective, 2 covers
Non-selective, 1 cover

Efficiency, percent

Incident angle, degrees

Effect of Off-Normal Solar Incidence. *The performance efficiency of various collector types as a function of the angle of solar incidence. When the angle of solar incidence is more than 60 degrees (that is, 30 degrees in relation to the collector surface), collection efficiency decreases rapidly. (Source:* Development of Flat-Plate Collectors, *NASA Report CR 134804)*

The performance curves show, for example, that collectors with a selective coating and only one glass cover perform better than painted black collectors with two glass covers. In having only one cover sheet, the single-glazed collector has less reflection losses. The best performer of the collectors tested had an anti-reflective coating on all the surfaces of the glass cover sheets. Other experimental collector designs that perform even better are described later in this chapter.

Details of a collector's construction also can affect its performance. Absorber designs vary, for instance, in their effective heat-conductance and transfer capability. If the air space between cover sheet and absorber is too wide, air currents within the air space (due to the rise of heated air) result in "convection losses."

Heat loss from the collector can occur, also, due to insufficient back and side insulation or air leakage through holes that are used to control condensation. Raised edge detailing can cause shading and reduce the effective absorber area exposed to the sun. (The effects of shading and reflection losses from the cover sheet on a particular collector design would only show up on a day-long performance curve.)

The amount of heat that a collector can produce at a given location can be estimated by determining the average amount of available winter sun and the collector's heat-collection efficiency factor. These calculation methods are detailed in Appendix II.

FLAT-PLATE COLLECTORS
ON ADJUSTABLE MOUNTINGS

Flat-plate collectors, as we have seen, are used because they are relatively simple and inexpensive to produce, install and maintain. But when these collectors are fixed—even at an optimal angle for winter sun—the day-long heat yield is limited to the hours when the sun is within a given range.

However, to improve the potential heat collection efficiency for a given collector, mounting devices that move the collector to follow the sun have been used, despite the added cost and operational energy.

The supports for adjustable mountings are complicated by the need to resist wind forces at all positions. Furthermore, to allow room for collector adjustment and to avoid shading of one collector by another, more area is needed for an adjustable mounting system than with fixed collectors. The inlet and outlet connections to the collector, too, whether liquid or air-type, must be flexible to accommodate the change in collector position while maintaining a continuous and well-sealed fitting.

From a practical standpoint, when collectors are used for space heating alone, the potential increase in efficiency that is attained by tilting a flat-plate collector probably does not justify the cost of an adjustable mounting.

On the other hand, when a collector panel is used for domestic water heating, a monthly adjustment in the tilt angle makes good sense, because the panels are used year-round. The annual variation in the sun's altitude between June and December is about 47°.

Usually only two or three panels are required for domestic hot water heating, so that the adjustable frame need not be complicated. The adjustment can be made manually if the collectors are mounted on the ground or on an accessible roof deck.

It is possible, also, to rotate a collector automatically on a sun-tracking or "heliostatic"

Collectors on an adjustable Mount.
(Courtesy: American Heliothermal Corporation)

66

mount, so that the collector faces the sun directly at all times during the day. The controls and the frame for such a system are complex and costly, as one would expect. However the theoretical increase in collector efficiency—due to reduced reflection losses and the larger absorber area that is exposed directly to the sun on a day-long basis—can approach 200 percent more annually than that of the same flat-plate collector mounted at one fixed, though optimal, position.

ADVANCED COLLECTOR DESIGNS

The collector devices discussed up to this point often are referred to as "medium-grade heat" collectors, capable of collecting heat efficiently in a range of 80° to 100° F. above the outside air temperature, but not often above 200° F.

These temperatures are sufficient to meet the space heating requirements for dwellings that are properly designed and that are constructed with every effort made to reduce heat losses. There are, however, several reasons why more efficient solar collectors are needed.

First, it is not always possible to fix a large collector area on or near a building at the optimal solar orientation. Applying collectors to existing dwellings and to multi-storied buildings in northern climates also is severely restricted by collector coverage and orientation requirements. Solar collectors of higher efficiency therefore could reduce the large area required with current collectors.

Second, higher average temperature yields from solar collectors would allow a reduced size for heat storage and heat distribution.

Third, if the cost of the solar equipment is to be reduced by mass production, a wider range of applications must be developed for solar collectors, including air conditioning through "solar-powered" cooling. Such a use for cooling, now in a more developmental stage than is solar heating, promises an appropriate use of solar energy for both heating and cooling in southern climates.

All of these considerations provide incentives for developing solar collectors that are more efficient and that produce higher temperatures than are now typical of flat-plate collectors. With technical breakthroughs, some of them may come within range of economic and practical application to homes.

No matter what a collector's design, the amount of radiation that it can receive is determined by climatic conditions. However, of the amount of solar radiation that is received, the heat that a collector can effectively recover will vary greatly, depending upon the design. The designs that will be described shortly attempt to increase the efficiency of heat collection by reducing or eliminating one or more of the sources of heat loss inherent in typical flat-plate collector construction.

One source of such loss is the convection through air movement in the space between the cover sheet and the absorber. As the air is heated, it tends to flow upward and outward from the collector.

Two alterations in flat-plate collector design attempt to reduce convection losses. One is to use louvers in the space between the cover plate and the absorber to reduce air movement. The second method is to create a vacuum in the space between cover sheet and absorber, which effectively eliminates convection losses and increases the insulation value of the space (Figure 4.9).

Another source of heat loss in collectors lies in the design of the absorber plate itself and its heat-transfer capability to the pipes or conduits, where heat is picked up by the liquid or air heat-transport medium.

In most of the new collector designs described below, the flat absorber plate is abandoned in favor of directing the sun's rays onto the absorber conduit itself, thus attempting a greater efficiency in heat transfer and removal.

In some of these designs, reflectors focus the sun's rays onto an absorber pipe. Such collectors receive no more solar radiation than a flat-plate collector with equal exposed surface. But by focusing the rays on a smaller absorber, high temperatures are built up more quickly at the point of heat transfer. The reflectors thus make up for the smaller absorber area by obtaining an improved heat transfer efficiency.

Figure 4.9. *Experimental Evacuated Flat Plate Collector. Wood pegs support plastic cover sheet that encloses an aluminum Rollbond absorber plate. A vacuum is created in the space between absorber and cover sheet. (Courtesy of Solar Systems, Inc.)*

Some of the focusing collectors are effective only with direct radiation and do not perform as well in climates where there is a large percentage of diffuse sky radiation. However, due to the concentration of energy on a small target in focusing collectors, the temperature that can be recovered from the absorber is high. Some (but not all) reliably produce temperatures 160° F. above the outside air temperature, and therefore are most applicable where high temperatures are required, such as solar heating for cooling and for industrial uses.

4.1.4 FLAT-PLATE COLLECTOR WITH INTERNAL HEAT TRAP

Flat-plate collectors are improved in their performance by the addition of an internal heat trap made up of slat or grid louvers between the glass cover and the absorber plate to reduce convection losses (Figure 4.10). Such spacers also may cause shading of the absorber and reduce the direct radiation gain to it, but transparent or reflective spacers help compensate for the shading losses.

As noted earlier, all collectors should be designed to withstand temperatures of at least 400° F., or even higher temperatures in warm climates. This is of particular concern if plastic spacers are used inside the collector (many of which deform with temperatures in the range of 300° F.) so that provisions against overheating are essential with such collectors.

EVACUATED TUBE AND FOCUSING COLLECTORS

A number of collector designs apply the technology of glass lighting fixture manufacture, eliminate the flat cover sheet and absorber plate, and instead intercept or focus the sun's rays directly on an absorber tube. Such collectors now are expensive due to custom fabrication. They are adaptable to mass production, however, and could thus become competitive in cost with flat-plate collectors.

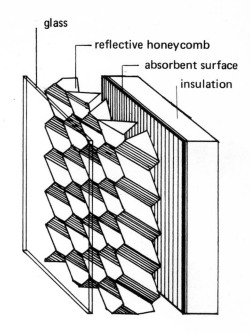

glass
reflective honeycomb
absorbent surface
insulation

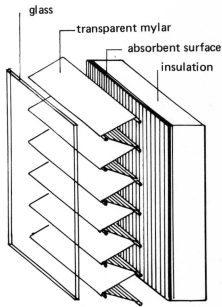

glass
transparent mylar
absorbent surface
insulation

Figure 4.10. *Flat Plate Collector with Internal Heat Trap. Various designs to reduce convection losses between absorber and cover sheet with reflective honeycomb grid (A) and with transparent mylar (B). (K. T. G. Hollands. "Honeycomb Devices in Flat-plate Solar Collectors" Solar Energy, July-Sept. 1965.)*

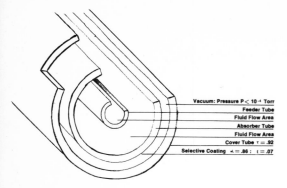

Figure 4.11A. *Sunpak*^{TM} *Solar Collector. Feeder tube provides the return flow passage for liquid that is supplied to the absorber tube.*

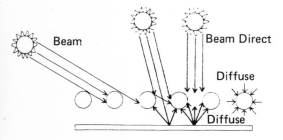

4.11B. *The tubes collect the diffuse component of insolation efficiently due to their curved surfaces, which intercept more diffuse light from the sky dome than a flat surface with the same projected area. The overall performance of the collector array would be enhanced by incorporating shaped reflector surfaces behind the collector tubes.*

4.1.5 OWENS-ILLINOIS'S TUBULAR COLLECTOR

Owens-Illinois's "Sunpak™" design, currently under experimental development, is composed of three glass pipes or tubes inserted one inside another (Figure 4.11). The name "evacuated tube," often given to such collectors, describes only one characteristic—its vacuum between the absorber and cover tubes.

The collector's innermost pipe serves as the "supply" to the outer end of the collector tube, the liquid picking up solar heat on its return flow through the second pipe, which is coated with a selective surface to increase heat retention. The outer tube serves as the cover enclosure.

The space between the absorber tube and the outer tube is under vacuum pressure, which eliminates condensation and convection losses. Since the supply and the return flow are within each tube, they are simply connected at one end to a trunk line or manifold (Figure 4.12).

This tubular collector design has advantages over flat-plate collectors because the round tubes receive radiation from all angles with less reflection losses and also utilize a wider range of diffuse radiation than a flat-plate. For the same reason, early morning and late afternoon sun is more usable, and they therefore perform better than flat-plate designs on a day-long basis, especially under diffuse and cloudy sky conditions.

Figure 4.12. *The Sunpak Collector Array with the main trunk supply and return. (Courtesy: Owens-Illinois)*

4.1.6 OTHER TUBULAR COLLECTORS

Variations of the tube design principles are being developed, notably by Corning Glass Works and by Philips Research of Holland, both of which use an absorber pipe placed within a glass tube under vacuum pressure. Unlike the Sunpak design, however, which relies upon the flat surface behind the tubes to reflect some radiation back to the absorber pipe, these tubular collectors use a reflective surface on the lower half of the inner glass cover tube itself (Figure 4.13).

The heat-collection efficiency of these designs is higher than for flat-plate collectors or the Owens-Illinois tubular design for several reasons. Like the Sunpak, day-long reflection losses are less, and the vacuum provides perfect insulation.

Moreover, the inner surfaces of the glass tubes used in the Corning and Philips designs are mirror-coated to focus the reflected radiation onto the absorber pipe. This eliminates the back losses incurred with flat-plate designs and produces much higher temperatures at the absorber tube.

4.1.7 NORTHROP CONCENTRATING COLLECTOR

In any focusing arrangement that relies upon direct solar radiation, the focal point changes with the sun's movement through the day (as shown in Figure 4.14). One way to accommodate this daily movement is to dimension the reflectors to create a wider focal area or image.

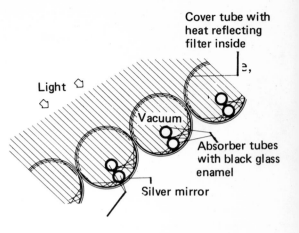

Figure 4.13. *Evacuated Tubular Collector Design, developed by Philips Research Laboratory, Aachen, Germany.*

Figure 4.14. *Fixed Cylindrical Reflector with a fixed tube absorber. The sun's rays focus on the absorber only when the reflector is directly facing the sun.*

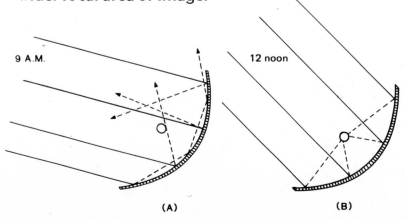

(A)   (B)

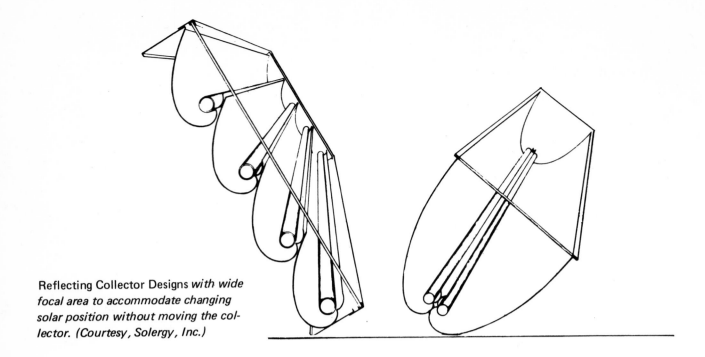

Reflecting Collector Designs *with wide focal area to accommodate changing solar position without moving the collector. (Courtesy, Solergy, Inc.)*

A second strategy, the one adopted in the Northrop design, is to rotate a refracting lens so that it tracks the sun in its daily path across the sky (Figure 4.15).

The Northrop collector uses a pipe absorber on which direct solar radiation is focused by a linear Fresnel lens in which miniature prisms focus the sun's rays on the absorber tube. Each unit is rotated on a polar mount to follow the sun.

Figure 4.15. *Northrop Tracking Collector.*

J. Busse

4.1.8 COMPOUND PARABOLIC CONCENTRATOR (CPC) COLLECTOR

Another collector design, developed by Dr. Roland Winston at the University of Chicago and Argonne National Laboratories, uses compound parabolic or related-shaped troughs with reflecting sides to concentrate the sun's rays on an absorber tube (Figure 4.16). Similar collectors have been developed in the Soviet Union by Dr. V. K. Varanov.

The troughs can be grouped to make up a large collector array which then is covered with a glass or plastic cover sheet, just as is a flat-plate collector.

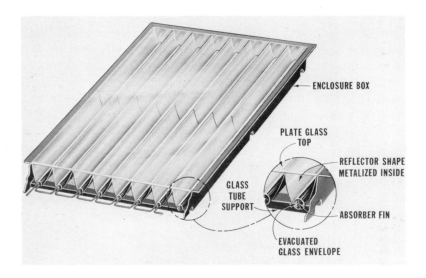

Figure 4.16. *Compound Parabolic Concentrator (CPC) Collector. (Courtesy Dr. Roland Winston)*

This collector thus has the same reflection losses as a flat-plate collector and does not "receive" more radiation than a flat-plate collector of the same size. Instead, the trough design serves both as reflectors and also as heat trap louvers, in the same way as the modified flat collectors described earlier—which reduce convection heat losses in the space between absorber and cover sheet.

The CPC collector, however, concentrates solar radiation from a large area on a small tube. In addition to increased collection temperatures, this promises economy in manufacture by reducing the net absorber area required.

Because of the mathematically derived shape of the reflector, solar rays from a wide arc of the sky can be directed to the absorber. For this reason, the CPC does not require a daily tracking device.

Figure 4.17. *High Temperature Linear Focusing Collector, with movable reflector, University of Arizona.*

Figure 4.18. *Circular Focusing Collector with tracking mount. (Patent Pending). (Suntrak Division of Wyatt-Townsend Corporation)*

Portable Solar Cooker. *Collapsible umbrella opens to focusing collector shape for water boiling. (Courtesy Department of Mechanical Engineering, University of Florida)*

4.1.9 OTHER FOCUSING COLLECTORS

Focusing collectors—both linear reflector (Figure 4.17), and circular reflector types (Figure 4.18)—have been proposed, in some cases as part of the building shape itself. These solar heaters are effective in producing extremely high temperatures—200° to 1000°F.

The requirement to follow the sun's changing position can be met either by moving the reflector or by moving the absorber to follow the changing position of the focal point (Figure 4.19).

The drawbacks of all the focusing collectors for space heating are that they are not as effective as flat-plate collectors for utilizing diffuse radiation, and the focal point moves with the daily arc of the

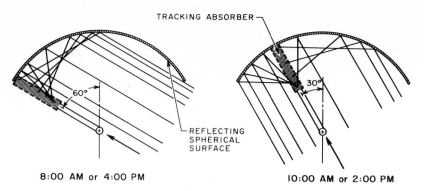

TRACKING ABSORBER

60°

REFLECTING
SPHERICAL
SURFACE

8:00 AM or 4:00 PM

30°

10:00 AM or 2:00 PM

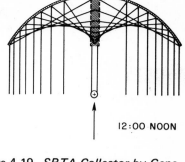

12:00 NOON

Figure 4.19. *SRTA Collector by Gene Stewart proposes a fixed reflector and a movable absorber tube to follow the changing focal point during the day. Drawings show solar reflection from a spherical mirror and the resulting position for the absorber.*

Stewart House, *Boulder, CO. Proposal to incorporate SRTA collector in roof shape. Charles A. Haertling, Architect.*

sun. Nonetheless they may prove of practical value in warm, dry climates which experience relatively clear sky conditions in winter. The higher temperature heat can be used here also for solar-powered summer cooling (Figure 4.20), as well as for commercial applications. The progress that is made in developing solar-power cooling may determine whether the advanced collector concepts that have been described here are developed from the experimental stage to the point of widespread application for home energy needs.

Figure 4.20. *Solar Village Proposal by James Lambeth for focusing collectors on row housing. Moving absorber tube to follow changing focal point. Winner: Misawa Homes Competition, Japan.*

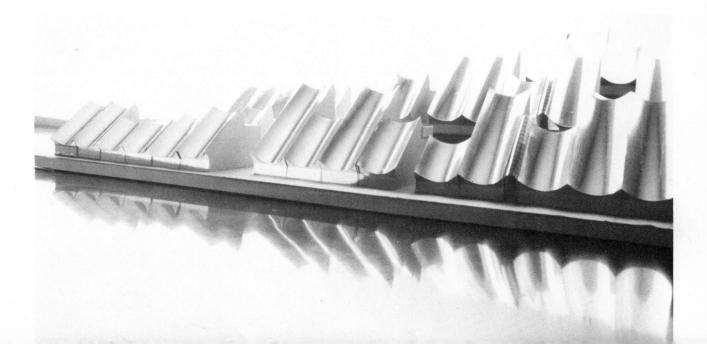

4.2
Heat Storage

**The Second Step in
Using the Sun's Heat**

Since northern climates typically experience many consecutive days without sunshine, a solar-heated house requires some form of storage to hold excess heat from sunny days in a recoverable form, usually above 90° F.

Depending on the heat distribution system used, heat from storage as low as 80° F. can provide comfort conditions, but below this temperature, auxiliary or back-up heating must be called upon.

In theory, usable heat could be stored for periods long enough to minimize back-up needs, to the point that only a fireplace/stove or a small amount of electric heat would be all the auxiliary heat required—but only if one disregarded installation cost and solar equipment size considerations.

Most solar installations today use either water or rock to store heat in a large, well-insulated container. As described previously, solar collectors are connected to the storage by a heat-transport loop (pipes or ducts) which is operated when the temperature in the collector is higher than that in storage. The collector-to-storage-loop is turned off automatically when the stored heat exceeds the temperature available from the collector. For this reason, the size of storage must be calculated according to the specific conditions of climate and collector size used in the installation.

Water and rock both hold heat due to their **sensible heat capacity** (the ability of a material to hold heat without a change in its physical state, due to its composition and density). Water storage normally is used with liquid-type collectors and rock storage with air-type collectors, although there are systems which combine both types.

Storage materials are under development that use the **latent heat capacity** of a chemical compound as it undergoes a change in state or "phase" from solid to liquid at its melting point.

Salt hydrates, which have melting points between 75° and 120° F., are the most commonly used chemical for "phase change" solar heat storage, because they are readily available materials and have melting points in the temperature ranges that can be obtained from solar collectors (see Figure 4.21).

	Chemical Compound	Melting Point (°F)	Heat of Fusion (Btu/lb)	Density (lb/ft^3)
Calcium chloride Hexahydrate	$CaCl_2.6H_2O$	84-102	75	102
Sodium carbonate decahydrate	$Na_2CO_3 \cdot 10H_2O$	90-97	106	90
Disodium phosphate dodecahydrate	$Na_2HPO_4 \cdot 12H_2O$	97	114	95
Sodium sulfate decahydrate	$Na_2SO_4 \cdot 10H_2O$	88-90	108	91
Sodium thiosulfate pentahydrate	$Na_2S_2O_3 \cdot 5H_2O$	118-120	90	104

Figure 4.21. *Properties of Salt Hydrate Compounds Used in Latent Heat Storage. (Source: Maria Telkes)*

The chemical compounds are placed in sealed plastic containers and are stacked in trays that allow air to pass by them, within an insulated storage container. If, for example, a chemical compound used has a freeze-thaw temperature of 85° F., the chemical storage unit (in a solid state below 85° F.) absorbs heat supplied by the solar collectors until it reaches a liquid state. The additional heat that is absorbed from the surrounding air to raise the chemical storage above its freeze-thaw temperature, even by one degree, is much more heat than is represented by the small rise in temperature and thus is called "latent," (or hidden) heat.

When heat is taken out of storage to the house distribution system, the storage is "cooled" to the point of freezing again, at which time it releases its latent heat for house heating. In addition, the chemical compounds hold heat due to the sensible heat capacity of the materials.

Chemical "phase-change" heat storage systems are still under development and have been installed in only a few experimental homes, one of which is detailed in the next chapter. The advantage, if salt systems do become available, is that a much smaller area will be needed for heat storage than is required presently using water or rock storage methods.

The large size required for the thermal storage unit, whether liquid or rock, can be seen in Figure 4.22. If one wishes the stored solar heat to carry over for a two- to three-day period (which is certainly desirable in northern climates) a water container approximately 6 feet in diameter and 12 feet long is

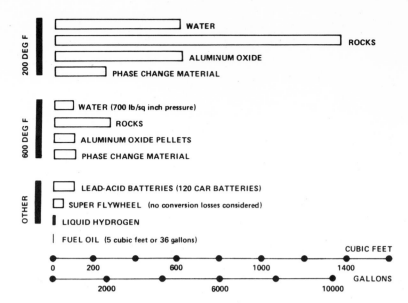

Figure 4.22. *Comparative Storage Volume Energy Storage Requirements for Three Days. (Source: Solar Dwelling Concepts, U. S. Dept. H. U. D.)*

needed. The equivalent heat storage capacity in rock requires a volume more than three times this size.

Large storage volumes, therefore, are practical only under particular conditions of climate, house design and cost. In most instances, the size of the storage unit is limited by the building design and cost, rather than by what would be its ideal size to maintain the house's heat during extended periods without sunshine.

In most of today's solar houses, the heat storage is custom-built for the particular installation. However, as solar heating becomes more established, equipment manufacturers may develop standard storage elements for use in conjunction with a particular collector design.

The two types of heat storage used today in solar houses—water and rock—are briefly introduced below, and are further detailed in subsequent chapters. Appendix II includes methods for calculating the heat capacity and volume of the heat storage systems.

4.2.1 WATER STORAGE

Water is excellent for heat storage in conjunction with liquid-type solar collectors, because it is inexpensive, readily available and remains relatively stable under the temperature range typical of solar systems. It has a high specific heat, which means that it can hold a large amount of heat relative to its volume. A stored volume of water can be heated efficiently, piped entirely through solar collectors themselves (open loop systems) or, more commonly, by heat exchangers placed in the storage tank (closed loop systems). When raised to sufficiently high temperatures, it can transport the heat efficiently throughout a building to the interior spaces.

The drawbacks to the use of water in collectors mentioned in the previous section, freezing and corrosion, must both be considered in the design and construction of the storage container as well.

Durable containers made especially for solar heat storage can be supplied by manufacturers or can be built as part of the house construction. If planned for solar heating from the start, part of the basement or foundation wall can be built to contain the heat storage, with an applied waterproofing or a replaceable lining to contain the water. In the ideal situation the storage should be located within the house to help insulate it—so that heat that is lost from the storage would be gained by the house anyway.

4.2.2 ROCK STORAGE

In an air-type collector and storage system, air that is heated in the collector is ducted through an insulated storage container filled with rock. It is cooled in its passage through the rock as it gives up heat, and is cycled again through the collectors.

This continues until the temperature in the rocks is the same as that recovered from the collector. The drop in temperature as the air passes through the rock storage causes a temperature difference within the storage, often referred to as temperature "stratification," typical to that shown in Figure 4.23.

The size of rocks that is appropriate to use for heat storage varies from 1 to 5 inches, depending upon the volume of storage and the distance that the air must travel to get through the storage from inlet to outlet. The smaller the rock, the more efficient the heat transfer, but more fan power is

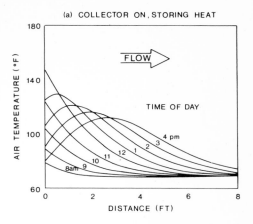

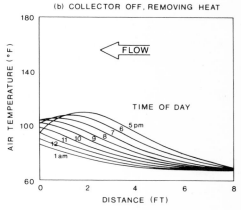

Figure 4.23. *Rock Bed Temperature Distribution as a Function of Time and Distance from Heat Inlet. Assume the bed is cold in the morning. As the day progresses, air temperature from the collector rises, peaking at noon, and decreasing in the afternoon. The resulting air temperature distributions in the rock bed are shown at different times during the day. Note that the exit air from the bed is always cold and therefore the collector operates at peak efficiency all day. In the evening, when the collector is off and the building needs heat, air flow direction through the bed is reversed so that the air exits from the hottest part of the bed. (If flow were not reversed, one would have to wait hours to wash the heat through the bed and even then would get only moderately warm air.) As evening progresses, temperature out of the bed rises until 8 o'clock and then falls, resembling the time profile of the inlet temperature during the day, but in reverse. (Source: Los Alamos Scientific Laboratory Report LA-5967)*

79

required, due to the increased resistance or "pressure drop" offered by the rock.

The best size for a rock storage unit thus depends upon specific conditions, such as the local climate, the house size, and the desired rate of air flow through the heating system. Several ways of arranging the air flow between air collectors, rock storage and warm air distribution systems are examined in the discussion of total systems in the next chapter.

4.3
Heat Distribution

**The Last Step in
Using the Sun's Heat**

The temperatures that are obtainable through solar collector and heat storage systems vary considerably, depending on the climate and the collection and storage efficiencies.

In collectors used for house heating, the temperature yields should average 100° F. above the outside air temperature on days with good sunshine. (Thus, if it is 20° F. outside, the heat from the collectors should rise to about 120° F.)

If the collectors are located relatively close to the storage unit, most of the heat gathered by the collectors is transferred to storage without significant losses, since heat lost from pipes or ducts would be gained by the house interior. In northern climates, however, the average winter temperatures that can be maintained in solar heat storage typically range between 85° to 120° F.

It is necessary, therefore, to design a means of distributing heat to the building rooms at low temperatures—around 85° to 90° F.—and still achieve a high level of comfort for the building occupants.

The temperatures delivered to a building by conventional furnaces and boilers range from 140° F. from warm air furnaces to 180° F. from boilers. In comparison, the 85° to 120° F. temperatures typical of solar heating impose special requirements for heat distribution methods—which are directly related to the house plan. Thus the distribution plan becomes as important a factor in solar house design as collector and storage.

In the United States, there are two common methods of heat distribution in homes: **hydronic systems** (in which hot water is circulated from a boiler to baseboard hot water radiators—and **forced-air systems** (in which warm air is ducted from a furnace to separate outlets or registers in each room).

The efficiency of these two methods using currently available equipment is based on operating temperatures higher than 120° F., so they must be adapted carefully to accommodate the lower temperatures of solar heating.

4.3.1 WARM-AIR DISTRIBUTION

Of the two distribution systems, the most commonly chosen for solar heating is forced-air, but with duct sizes that are larger than used with conventional fuel heating in order to carry low-temperature air efficiently.

The lower the temperature of the air delivered to a room, the larger the distribution duct should be. (Air systems sized for air-conditioning usually are close to the proper size for distributing low-temperature heat. Thus if an existing home has a warm-air system already sized for air-conditioning loads, it may be easily adapted to solar heating.)

Warm-air distribution is the most practical system with air-type collectors and storage. Liquid collectors and storage systems also are commonly used with warm-air distribution systems. Heated water from storage is piped through a "fan coil" unit, in which air is blown across an extended section of pipe or coil, so that it transfers its heat into the warm-air distribution ducts.

When air is delivered to the interior rooms in the lower temperature ranges, the flow must be slow and even. We often sense that air coming from the registers, even when in the 90° F. range, feels cold, because we expect to feel much warmer air from heating registers. Because of this, supply registers for solar-heated air distribution should be located where the movement of air will not be felt by the occupants, especially when seated.

In most homes, the heat **supply** registers are located at the outside walls, most often under windows (Figure 4.24). This is done to counteract the cold air that falls down along window surfaces on winter days and nights.

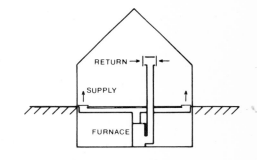

low supply—high return

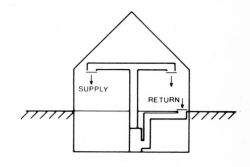

high supply—low return

Figure 4.24. *Heat Distribution Modes. Two methods of warm air flow can be used depending on house design and construction and operating temperatures.*

81

Because such heat distribution locations must fight that cold draft, the lowest temperature that should be used when the heat is supplied "low," is in the range of 95° F. or above.

A second method to distribute space heat with a forced-air system is to supply it "high," the reverse of the air flow described above. One anticipates that cold air will drop down outside walls, and instead of allowing it to then cross along the floor, **return** air registers are located under windows. The heat supply outlets then are located high on an inside wall of each space, to create an even air flow through the room.

This method is recommendable only if such a heat flow pattern—along the ceiling of a room and down the outside wall—can be evenly maintained and does not counteract any natural upward flow of heat such as occurs in double-height spaces and up stairwells. The house must be well insulated, too, and thus free of cold drafts that are common above uninsulated basements and near entryways. If a "high supply-low return" heat duct layout can be installed, then the supply air from storage can be as low as 85° F., thus utilizing an additional 10° F. of heat from the solar storage system.

4.3.2 BASEBOARD RADIATOR DISTRIBUTION

The baseboard-type "hydronic" hot water system that is commonly installed in homes is not effective with temperatures below 130° F., simply because the baseboard "fin-tubes" are designed to operate only with higher temperatures.

Because the average temperature range from solar heat storage is lower, this method of heat distribution is not generally recommendable in solar heating systems. (It can be used in warm and temperate climates with high performance collectors or with a heat pump system.)

But because so many homes have baseboard heating systems in them, the high-performance collectors (which reliably maintain temperatures in storage above 130° F.) would have to be used in order to "retrofit" such houses to solar heating without changing the heat distribution system.

As an alternative, more efficient radiators with a larger radiating surface could be developed as a distribution method with the typical liquid collector and storage systems.

4.3.3 RADIANT FLOOR AND CEILING DISTRIBUTION

Another method of heat distribution that performs well with low-temperature heat can be matched with solar heating: **radiant floor or ceiling systems.**

A liquid-type radiant floor system consists of a grid of small water pipes imbedded in a concrete floor. Water in the range of 100° to 120° F. is pumped through the pipes so that the entire floor is heated to a warm, comfortable temperature.

Instead of water, warm air also can be ducted through concrete ducts under a floor or through a rock bed covered with a concrete slab to create an air-type radiant floor system. In such a case, even air at 80° F. can give a comfortable heating effect to a masonry floor. Heat recovered from a greenhouse or a house with south-facing glass wall areas often rises above 80° F., so that it, too, can be used to supply warm air to a radiant slab system. Water pipes imbedded in a plaster ceiling are used for radiant ceiling heating (Figure 4.25).

The one drawback of radiant heating systems is

Figure 4.25. *Radiant Ceiling Heating. Piping in room ceiling before plaster is applied for use with low water temperature from solar heat storage.*

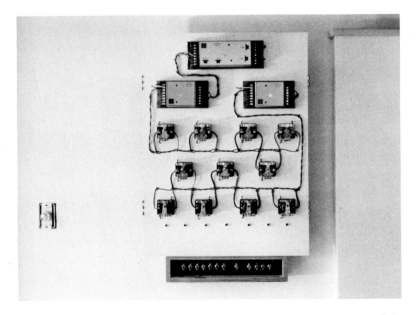

Controls for a solar installation in a residence for numerous temperature settings and distribution zones.

COLLECTOR   STORAGE   DISTRIBUTION

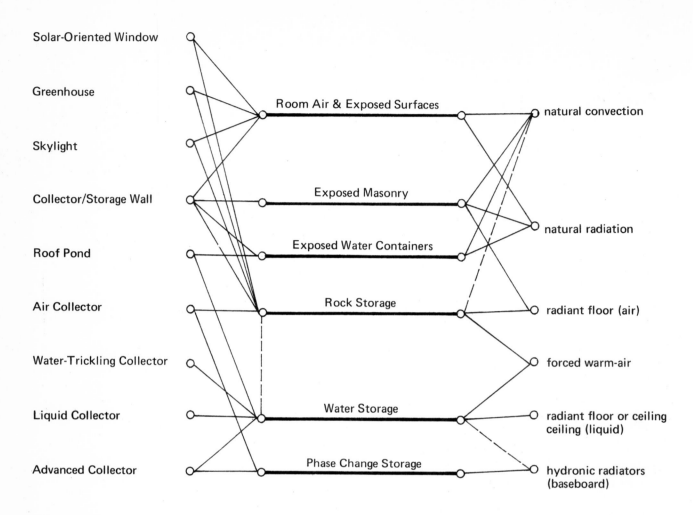

Figure 4.26. *Various Collector Storage and Distribution Systems in Combination.*

that the time needed to heat the entire floor or ceiling mass is slower than with other systems, and once heated, it is slow to cool. However, this aspect can be somewhat improved by proper sizing and controls.

The collector, storage and distribution systems described in this chapter can be used with one another to fit individual circumstances. Figure 4.26 depicts some of these combinations, including passive methods. The most common of these solar systems are detailed in the following chapter.

CHAPTER 5

ACTIVE SYSTEMS: HOW THE PARTS WORK TOGETHER

In the last chapter, the different methods of solar heat collection, storage and distribution were discussed individually. As mentioned, different combinations of collector, storage and distribution methods can be used with equal effectiveness. In this chapter, the basic types of active systems are described to illustrate how solar equipment is combined into effective home-energy systems.

As introduced in Chapter 2, there are three general types of active solar heating systems:

1. Active Collector, Storage, Distribution Systems

2. Active Systems with Special Heating (or Cooling) Equipment

3. Solar Photovoltaic Cells for Electric Conversion

The first two of these, the most common systems in use today, are properly called "solar thermal" heating because they operate by using the sun's heat radiation. In the first type, discussed in Section 5.1 below, the solar heating systems operate with comparatively low temperatures, relying upon the sun to heat a storage unit to the point that it can be used to comfortably heat a house.

The second active system type uses solar thermal energy as a heat supply to special mechanical heating equipment. This system type, discussed in Section 5.2 below, includes heat pump systems which raise the temperature from solar thermal storage to a much higher level, so that it can then be distributed by conventional heat distribution methods. Solar energy systems which use solar heat to drive mechanical refrigeration machines for air conditioning also fit this system type.

The last active system type, to be described in Section 5.3, differs fundamentally from solar "thermal" applications. It uses solar cells that convert the sun's rays to electricity—often referred to as "photovoltaic conversion." The electric energy is converted from DC to AC current or is stored in batteries for lighting and electric heating—either baseboard heaters in each room or electric coils inserted in a warm-air duct distribution system. Or, as will be shown by description of an experimental house installation using solar cells, the solar photoelectric panels can be combined with solar thermal heating methods.

5.1
Active Solar Heating Systems

Active systems that utilize the sun's thermal energy to supply low-temperature heat are the most common type of solar heating used for houses. In this section both air and liquid systems are reviewed by reference to some original or "prototype" houses that first demonstrated unique approaches to active solar heating system design.

5.1.1 HOUSE-HEAT RECOVERY SYSTEMS

A House-Heat Recovery System stores for re-use the heat generated from use of the house—from cooking, from solar-oriented windows, and from fireplace and furnace flues. Depending on the system, temperatures from 80° F. to 100° F. can be obtained from such sources and used to maintain a rock storage unit at temperatures that are usable (depending upon the distribution method), between 70° to 85° F.

Such low-temperature storage does not have the large carryover capacity of storage heated with solar collectors. The moderating effect of low-temperature heat storage can be used to great advantage, however, in houses with a lot of south-facing glass. In such cases, much of the excess heat available during sunny hours is wasted unless the inside air is circulated to all parts of the house. This super-heated air, from a greenhouse or the house proper, can be ducted through a rock storage unit.

Two ways of distributing the heat thus stored are shown in the examples below.

The residence of Everett and Virginia Barber in Guilford, Conn., demonstrates a wide range of energy-saving features, including provision for future liquid-type solar collectors. The house itself has been occupied since 1975 without the solar collector system, which is not yet installed. It has been possible, therefore, to test in practice a unique method of house-heat recovery, developed by Everett Barber, which can operate with a conventionally fueled heating system.

In the Barber residence, the normal house heat—generated during the day by window heat, use of the kitchen and the fireplace, and by the activity of occupancy itself—rises through an open, double-height living room to the top of the house. Here a return air duct draws the heat out of the space and channels it past what will be the future solar heat storage tank, into a rock storage area built under the concrete floor of the first level of the house (Figure 5.1).

The duct layout in the rock storage area allows the house heat that is thus recovered to pass through the rocks and return to living space through warm-air supply outlets at the outside walls. The rock storage in the Barber design is not insulated

Robert Perron

View of Barber residence living room showing the fireplace and its exposed flue. The large tank behind fireplace will be used for future solar-heated water storage.

Figure 5.1. *Schematic of Heating System, Barber Residence, Guilford, CT (1975).*

Winter. *Night-time heating: D1, D2, D3, closed; D4 open, fan on. Daytime storage of occupancy and solar heat through windows into stone under floor: D2, D3, D4 closed; D1 open, fan on.*

Summer. *Night-time cooling from outside air into stone: Windows open, D1, D3, D4 closed; D2 open, fan on. Daytime cooling of house from coolness stored in stone: stone: D1, D2, D4 closed; D3 open, fan on.*

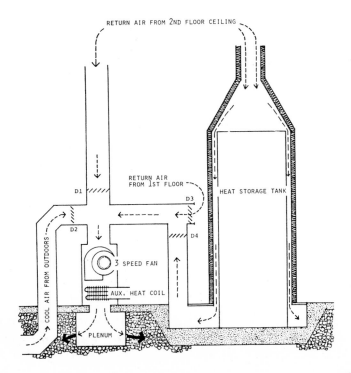

RETURN AIR FROM 2ND FLOOR CEILING

RETURN AIR FROM 1ST FLOOR

HEAT STORAGE TANK

D1
D2
D3
D4

COOL AIR FROM OUTDOORS

3 SPEED FAN

AUX. HEAT COIL

PLENUM

87

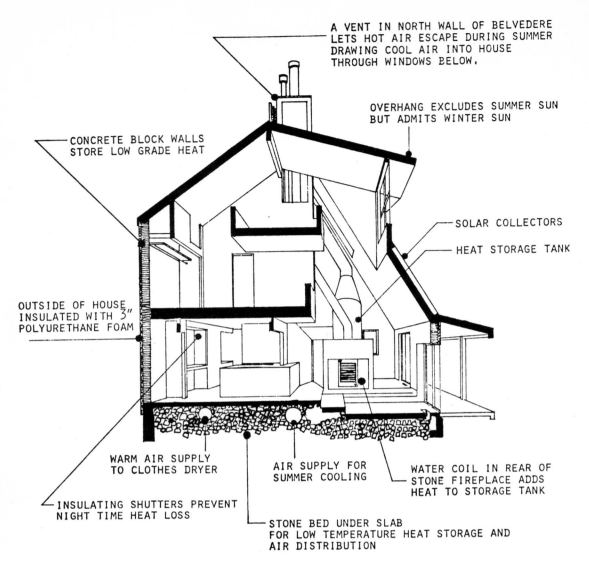

A VENT IN NORTH WALL OF BELVEDERE LETS HOT AIR ESCAPE DURING SUMMER DRAWING COOL AIR INTO HOUSE THROUGH WINDOWS BELOW.

OVERHANG EXCLUDES SUMMER SUN BUT ADMITS WINTER SUN

CONCRETE BLOCK WALLS STORE LOW GRADE HEAT

SOLAR COLLECTORS

HEAT STORAGE TANK

OUTSIDE OF HOUSE INSULATED WITH 3" POLYURETHANE FOAM

WARM AIR SUPPLY TO CLOTHES DRYER

AIR SUPPLY FOR SUMMER COOLING

WATER COIL IN REAR OF STONE FIREPLACE ADDS HEAT TO STORAGE TANK

INSULATING SHUTTERS PREVENT NIGHT TIME HEAT LOSS

STONE BED UNDER SLAB FOR LOW TEMPERATURE HEAT STORAGE AND AIR DISTRIBUTION

5.1A. *Cutaway view of Barber house. (Drawings courtesy of Charles Moore & Associates)*

from the concrete floor above, so that it too is heated and serves as a low-temperature radiant slab (see Section 4.3.3).

In the Barber residence, the heat accumulated in the rock storage passes through the air registers at the outside walls and radiates through the concrete slab that covers the rock storage, which becomes, in effect, a combined duct and radiant slab. This is an effective means by which to store and distribute heat in the range of 70° to 85° F. which is easily recoverable in most houses.

Under-floor rock storage can be incorporated into conventional "slab-on grade" house construction. Typically, foundations are placed three feet or more in the ground (below the frost line) and the area inside then is filled with compacted earth and gravel to prepare the base for a concrete slab floor.

5.1B. *Barber house, showing urethane foam exterior, solar collectors not yet installed.*

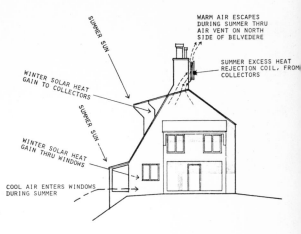

WARM AIR ESCAPES DURING SUMMER THRU AIR VENT ON NORTH SIDE OF BELVEDERE

SUMMER SUN

SUMMER EXCESS HEAT REJECTION COIL, FROM COLLECTORS

WINTER SOLAR HEAT GAIN TO COLLECTORS

SUMMER SUN

WINTER SOLAR HEAT GAIN THRU WINDOWS

COOL AIR ENTERS WINDOWS DURING SUMMER

5.1E. *East elevation.*

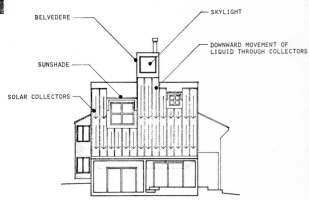

BELVEDERE

SKYLIGHT

SUNSHADE

DOWNWARD MOVEMENT OF LIQUID THROUGH COLLECTORS

SOLAR COLLECTORS

5.1F. *South elevation.*

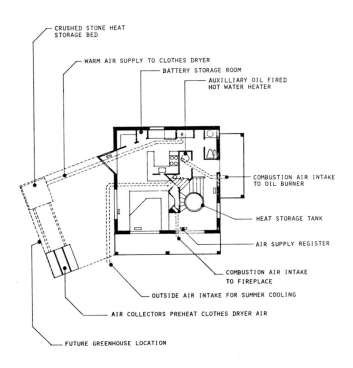

CRUSHED STONE HEAT STORAGE BED

WARM AIR SUPPLY TO CLOTHES DRYER

BATTERY STORAGE ROOM

AUXILLIARY OIL FIRED HOT WATER HEATER

COMBUSTION AIR INTAKE TO OIL BURNER

HEAT STORAGE TANK

AIR SUPPLY REGISTER

COMBUSTION AIR INTAKE TO FIREPLACE

OUTSIDE AIR INTAKE FOR SUMMER COOLING

AIR COLLECTORS PREHEAT CLOTHES DRYER AIR

FUTURE GREENHOUSE LOCATION

5.1C. *First floor plan.*

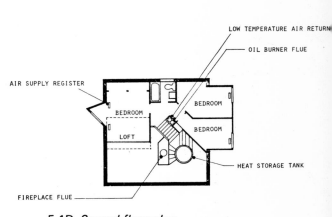

LOW TEMPERATURE AIR RETURN

OIL BURNER FLUE

AIR SUPPLY REGISTER

BEDROOM

BEDROOM

LOFT

BEDROOM

HEAT STORAGE TANK

FIREPLACE FLUE

5.1D. *Second floor plan.*

To incorporate a rock heat storage into such an underfloor area, insulation is added on all sides and the foundation area is filled with rock. A normal concrete slab then is installed over the rock, with heat supply ducts located at the center of the storage. Depending on the house plan, a combination of ducts and loose rock fill is placed in the under-floor area so that heat can easily reach the outside walls of the house. Thus, where "slab-on-grade" construction normally is used in construction, an underfloor heat storage and radiant slab system is quite practical to build.

There are disadvantages to this method: radiant floor heating has been used for over a decade in heating systems which pass heated water through piping imbedded in the concrete floor. The problem always has been the slow response time required—first to bring the concrete up to temperature when the building first calls for heat (say, early morning), and then to cool the building in times of overheating (say, during variable sunny weather).

A further disadvantage is that, to be effective, a masonry floor must be used. There are rugs and linoleum floor coverings designed for radiant floor heating, but these tend to reduce the heating effect when the rock storage temperature drops below 75° F.

To overcome disadvantages of slow thermal control and response time, the same rock storage approach can be used, but completely insulated and without the radiant slab, so that the standard wood floor could be constructed.

In this case the top of the rock storage is insulated to prevent any heat loss through the floor. The accumulated heat from the recovery system can then be supplied to augment the conventional forced warm air system. However, heat recovered from storage can be used effectively in forced air distribution systems only when temperatures of 80° F. or higher can be attained—higher than that which is effectively utilized with the radiant slab.

Houses in temperate and warm climates, which obtain a good deal of direct solar heat gain from south-facing windows or greenhouses, may supply such storage temperatures. In northern climates,

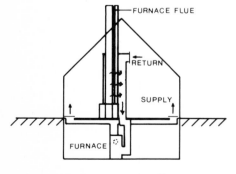

Figure 5.2. *Chimney Heat Recovery. Air duct passes by outside of fireplace and furnace flues and picks up heat radiated through flue masonry for return to house heating system.*

90

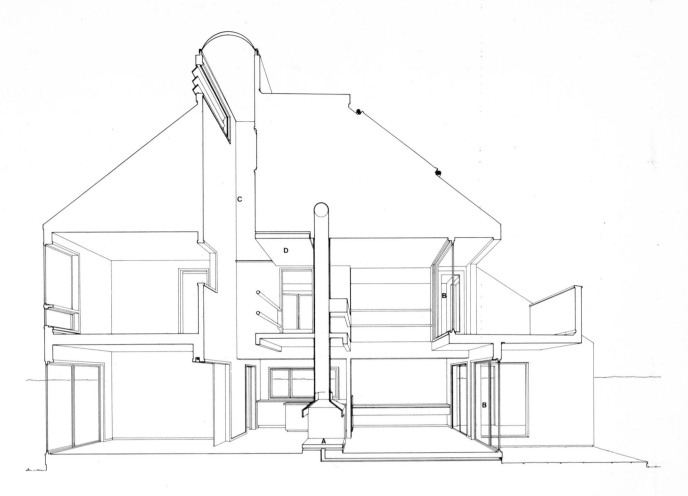

chimney- and flue-heat recovery systems can supply additional heat to rock storage (Figure 5.2).

House-heat recovery systems work best with open house plans, with ample south windows and with centrally located fireplace/stoves, in which case the free air movement helps to control the overheating and utilize the heat throughout the entire house (Figure 5.3).

Figure 5.3. *Stoker Residence, Groton,CT (1976). Open house plan for balanced heat effect from central fireplace (A) and from large south-facing glass area (B). High return air register in ventilating air shaft (C), controlled by insulating translucent panel (D). Donald Watson, AIA, Architect: Ahmed Dadi, P. E., Engineer.*

5.1.2 AIR-TYPE SOLAR COLLECTOR AND STORAGE SYSTEMS

In the house-heat recovery systems described above, heat from windows and from the house use itself is supplied to thermal storage in the range of 80° to 100° F. In the systems described in the remainder of this section, solar heat collectors are used to heat storage to 90° to 130° F.—high enough to be effective in a forced warm-air distribution system.

91

Figure 5.4A. *Löf Residence, Denver, Colorado (1957). Air is used as the heat transport medium and crushed rock as the solar energy storage medium. The system consists of two solar collector banks, two vertical heat storage cylinders, hot water preheater, blower and conventional natural gas furnace, control equipment and a warm-air distribution system.*

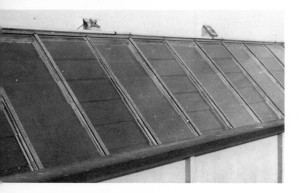

5.4B. *Air collectors on Löf residence composed of glass louvers, with bottom half of every other glass louver painted black. (See bottom drawing, Figure 4.2.)*

5.4C. *Heat storage columns in Löf residence as seen from entry hall.*

Löf residence: One of the original air-type solar installations still in operation today, the Löf residence in Denver, Colorado, pioneered many concepts of air-type collector and storage solar heating (Figure 5.4).

Schematic drawings of the Löf system are shown in Figure 5.5. These and the following commentary are based on published drawings and descriptions of the house (principally an article by George Löf in the United National Conference Proceedings **New Sources of Energy** Volume 5, 1961).

In the Löf design, the thermal rock storage is contained in two vertical cylinders (fiberboard tubes used normally for concrete formwork), each three feet in diameter by 18 feet high. The house air-return duct is located in the center of one cylinder, shown on the right in the illustrations. Crushed rock, approximately one inch in diameter, fills the cylinders except for the lower two feet, which contain wire mesh to allow air to pass between the cylinders.

The operation of the various modes in the Löf system is detailed in Figures 5.5A through 5.5D. The last mode (shown in Figure 5.5E) is not used in the Löf house but is included to illustrate a means of cooling the rock storage on summer nights, an option that is easily added to air-type systems.

In evaluating the performance of the system, Löf concluded that electric power requirements could be greatly reduced by other duct layouts that would permit a short-cutting of the rock storage when the house is heated by the back-up furnace. The small rock size chosen, while efficient in picking up heat from the air, requires a large amount of electric power consumption. Based on the documentation of the Löf installation, the collectors operated at an average of 35 percent annual efficiency, while the system itself utilized 24.5 percent of the total solar radiation available to the collectors. Air leaks in the system (particularly in the collectors which were made on the job), are reported by Löf as a source of considerable heat loss and inefficiency, leading to his conclusion that higher quality factory-made collectors would greatly improve the system efficiency.

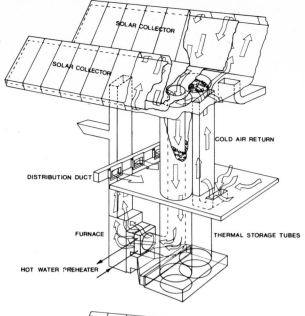

Figure 5.5A. *House Heating from Collectors. Hot air is supplied directly from the collectors to the rooms of the house when heat is demanded and when adequate solar energy is being received. Cold air from the house enters the cold air return duct and is distributed to the solar collectors. The air is heated and delivered to the rooms via the hot air manifold and distribution ducts. When required, gas heat may be supplied to the warm solar air to boost it to useful temperatures.*

SOLAR COLLECTOR

SOLAR COLLECTOR

COLD AIR RETURN

DISTRIBUTION DUCT

FURNACE

THERMAL STORAGE TUBES

HOT WATER PREHEATER

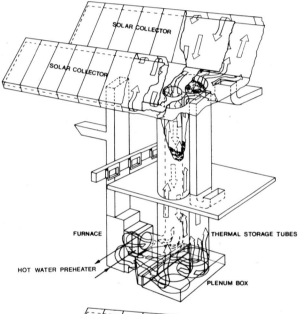

5.5B. *Storing Heat from Collectors. This cycle operates when the house does not need heat and the intensity of solar radiation is great enough to justify collection. Cold air from the storage tubes enters the cold air manifold and is distributed to the solar collectors. The heated air moves down the vertical duct, through the hot water preheater and into the rock storage bins. The air loses its heat to the rocks as it is passed through the storage tubes, and thus cooled, returns to the collectors.*

SOLAR COLLECTOR

SOLAR COLLECTOR

FURNACE

THERMAL STORAGE TUBES

HOT WATER PREHEATER

PLENUM BOX

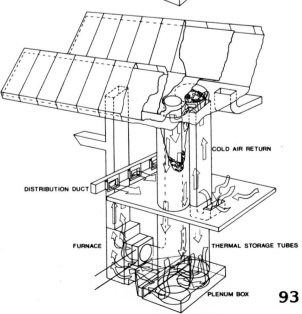

5.5C. *House Heating from Storage. This cycle operates intermittently, usually during evening or night hours. Cold air enters the cold air return duct. The air passes through the storage bins absorbing heat. If temperatures are too low, gas heat is added to the air before distribution in the house. Air is circulated through the storage unit even if it contains little or no heat, thereby ensuring its full utilization but at greater pumping costs.*

COLD AIR RETURN

DISTRIBUTION DUCT

FURNACE

THERMAL STORAGE TUBES

PLENUM BOX

5.5D. *Summer Water Heating. An air to water heat exchanger in the hot air duct is used as a preheater for the house hot water supply. After being preheated, the water passes to an automatic gas-fired heater. Ambient air enters the solar collectors, is heated and passes down the vertical air duct that forms the center of one of the storage containers, and enters the hot water preheater. A portion of heat is transferred to the water, after which the warm air is recirculated through the collector via the summer by-pass duct.*

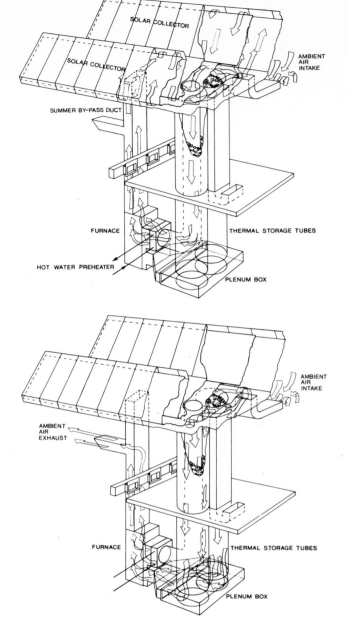

5.5E. *Summer Night Cooling of Storage. (A possible mode, but not used in the Löf Residence due to negligible cooling requirement.) Cool night air is circulated through the rock storage bins, extracting the "coolness" from the air (actually by removing heat from the rock). The then-warm air is exhausted to the outside. During the day hours, house air is circulated through the storage bins, extracting the "coolness" for use in the rooms (by absorbing heat from the air).*

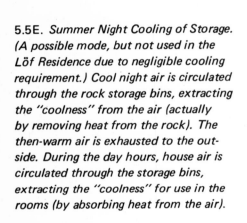

Solaron system. Since the original Löf installation, operating efficiencies of air systems have been improved with factory-produced collectors and with rock storage and air distribution layouts that do not require as much fan power.

The Solaron Company of Denver, founded by George Löf, now supplies complete air systems as shown in Figure 5.6. The installation of such a system is relatively straightforward for several reasons:

1. The collectors can be connected to one another side by side and top to bottom. Thus air can be

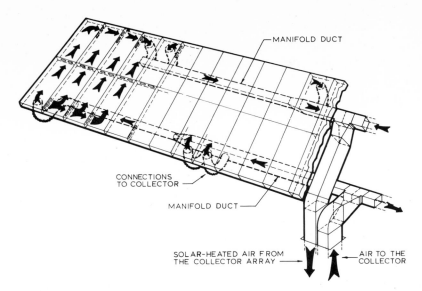

Figure 5.6A. *Solaron Collector Array.*
Drawings courtesy of Solaron Corp.

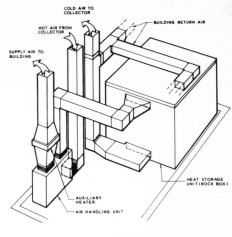

5.6B. *Typical Mechanical Room Layout.*

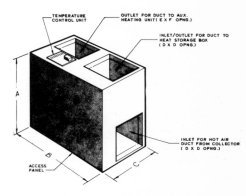

5.6C. *Solaron Air Handling Unit.*

circulated through them without additional "manifolds."

2. The heating systems including collectors and an air-handling unit, which combines a fan and temperature controls in one piece of equipment, is supplied by one manufacturer.

3. The thermal storage compartment recommended for use with the Solaron system is compact and can be included in any house plan without sacrificing floor area (½ cubic foot of rock for each square foot of a collector). Larger heat storage may be recommended according to the house design and the climate characteristics at the location.

Other air systems. Other air collector and storage systems have been developed with differences from the Solaron System in one or more of the following areas:

Large storage volume: Small storage volumes are sufficient in climates where there is a fairly constant and frequent amount of sunshine throughout the winter—such as in the southwest. In cloudier climates, a larger volume of storage may be economically justified to increase the carryover capacity of a solar heating system.

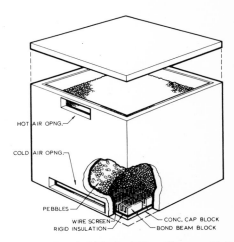

5.6D. *The Pebble-Bed Heat Storage Unit recommended by Solaron, with pebbles between ¾ inch and 1½ inches, and a volume sized for only one day's carryover of heat during the winter season.*

Ducting the collectors: In extended paths through many collectors, the resistance to air flow is increased and, as a result, requires more fan power to move the air. External supply and return manifolds to each collector are recommended by several air-type collector manufacturers, as shown in Figure 5.7, to balance the heat collection more evenly across the entire absorber area. While the heat-collection efficiency thus is improved, there may be greater cost in installing the additional connections.

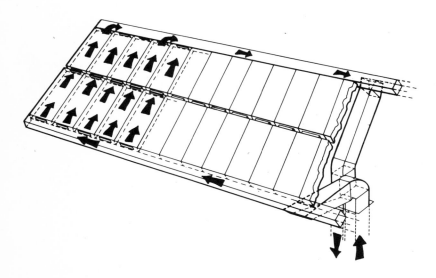

Figure 5.7. *External Manifold for supply and return to air collectors. Direction of flow can also be designed from the top to the bottom of the collectors— in reverse of that shown—so that the cool air from storage meets the warmest part of the collector first for more even utilization of the absorber heat.*

System layout: The way in which the air is ducted through the collectors, the storage and the house greatly affects the cost and the effectiveness of an air-type solar heating system. Duct lengths should be as short as possible, with a minimum number of bends to reduce the fan power requirements. A system devised by Fred Broberg, P.E., shown in Figure 5.8, attempts to reduce installation costs by using one fan and relying upon gravity dampers to control air flow in the system.

Many such individual variations can be developed for specific house plans. In the Paul Davis house at Corrales, New Mexico, the collector, storage and distribution are closely located one above the other so that the system works without fans by the thermosyphoning action of heated air. If fans were used, the electrical power requirements in such a design would be minimized because the direction of heat flow follows the natural upward movement of heated air (Figure 5.9).

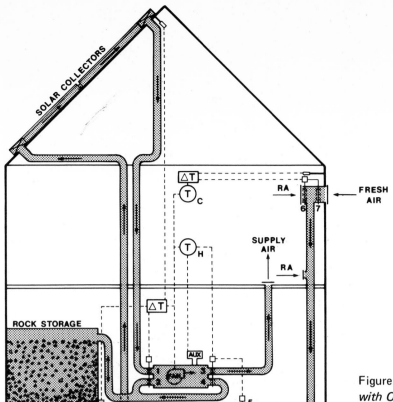

Figure 5.8. *Schematic of Air System with One Fan.*

Damper Number (o = open, s = shut)	1	2	3	4	5	6	7	Fan	Back up
Normal position	s	o	s	o	s	o	s	off	off
Solar heating storage	o	s	s	o	s	o	s	on	off
Solar heating house	o	s	o	s	o	o	s	on	off
Storage heating house	s	o	o	s	o	o	s	on	off
Back up heating house	s	o	o	s	o	o	s	on	on
Fresh air cooling storage	s	o	o	s	o	s	o	on	off
Storage cooling house	s	o	o	s	o	s	o	on	off

Figure 5.9. Air System with No Fans. *Davis House, Corrales NM (1972). In the system used in the Davis residence the collector is composed of 6 layers of black-painted expanded metal lath. The heated air then rises and flows to the top of a rock bed storage bin which is located beneath the south facing porch of the house. The rocks are cooler than the air, and so, as the air gives up its heat to the rocks, it begins to move slowly downward to the bottom of the rock bed and then back to the bottom of the collector. Heat can be drawn directly into the house, which is located higher than the collector/storage area. (Baer residence in background).*

97

Figure 5.10. *Residence, Cork County, Ireland (1976). (Courtesy W. A. McDonough).*

In a solar house in Ireland (the first to be constructed there), Bill McDonough has placed a large rock storage area into the chimney and fireplace mass, thereby establishing a built-in heat recovery arrangement (Figure 5.10).

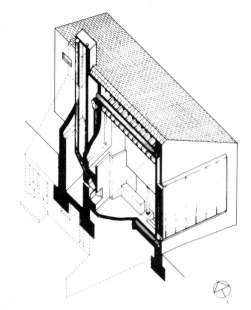

5.10A. *Cutaway view through the collector and storage units.*

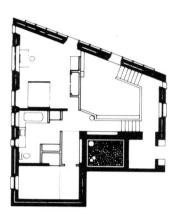

5.10B. *Plans.*

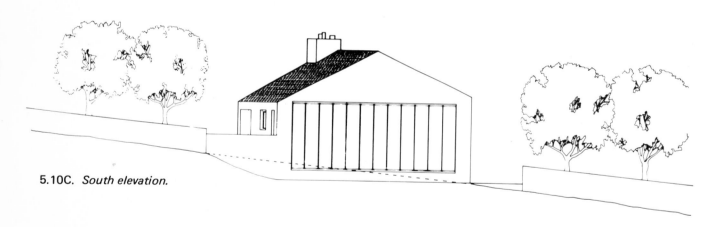

5.10C. *South elevation.*

5.10D. *View from south before collector installation.*

5.1.3 LIQUID-TYPE SOLAR COLLECTOR AND STORAGE SYSTEMS

Two types of liquid systems were demonstrated in occupied houses in the mid-1950's and are detailed below in order to show how the original installations have led to more recent developments.

The Thomason solar system. As described earlier (in Section 4.1.1), the open-water collector was developed by Harry Thomason and installed in his own home in Washington, D. C. in 1959. (His experience with the original design and subsequent installations is reported in the United Nations Proceedings **New Sources of Energy,** Volume 5, 1961.)

The operation of the Thomason Solar House No. 1 is shown in Figures 5.11A through C. The roof-top evaporative cooling system shown in Figure 5.11C was operated for two summers and has since been replaced in favor of simply cooling the storage with

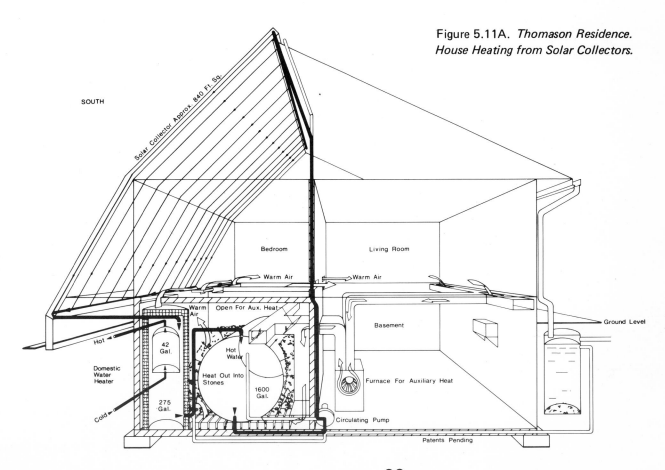

Figure 5.11A. *Thomason Residence. House Heating from Solar Collectors.*

SOUTH

Solar Collector Approx. 840 Ft. Sq.

Bedroom

Living Room

Warm Air

Warm Air

Warm Air

Open For Aux. Heat

Ground Level

Hot

42 Gal.

Hot Water

Basement

Domestic Water Heater

Heat Out Into Stones

1600 Gal.

Furnace For Auxiliary Heat

275 Gal.

Cold

Circulating Pump

Patents Pending

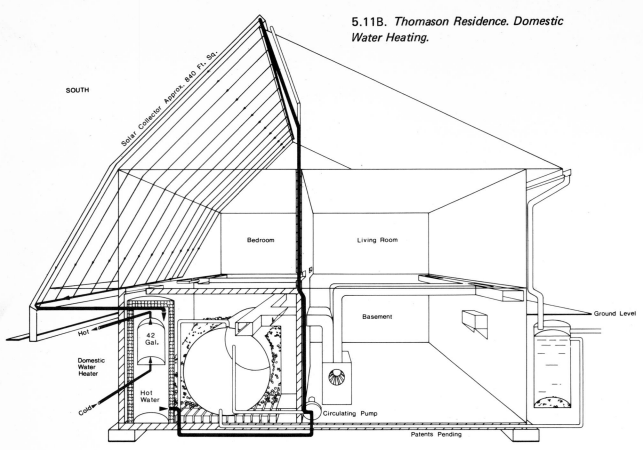

5.11B. *Thomason Residence. Domestic Water Heating.*

SOUTH

Solar Collector Approx. 840 Ft. Sq.

Bedroom

Living Room

Basement

Ground Level

Hot

42 Gal.

Domestic Water Heater

Cold

Hot Water

Circulating Pump

Patents Pending

5.11C. *Thomason Residence. Original Installation of natural evaporative cooling (removed after two years of operation).*

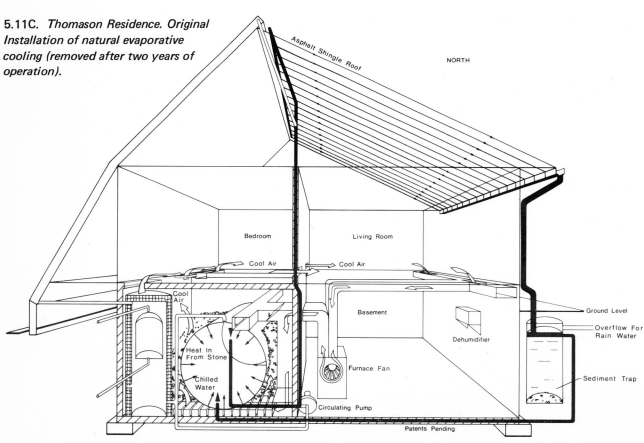

Asphalt Shingle Roof

NORTH

Bedroom

Living Room

Cool Air

Cool Air

Cool Air

Basement

Ground Level

Overflow For Rain Water

Dehumidifier

Heat In From Stone

Sediment Trap

Chilled Water

Furnace Fan

Circulating Pump

Patents Pending

100

a conventional refrigeration compressor at night, which operates more efficiently when outside air temperatures are lower. (This would also be advantageous where off-peak electric rates are available.)

While the initial installation has experienced normal problems of maintenance and repair, the Thomason design—now patented and marketed as the Solaris System—is economical to construct with standard building materials and is efficient in its use of low-temperature heat. The water tank and the rocks serve as the heat exchanger. The placement of the supply outlet in the heat distribution arrangement, shown in Figure 5.11A, has been changed in subsequent installations to a high location near the ceiling, to offer the "high supply-low return" advantages described in Section 4.3.1.

Figure 5.12. *Thomason Solaris Home No. 6, Calvert County, MD (1976). Design patents applied for. (Courtesy Harry Thomason)*

MIT Solar House IV. The Massachusetts Institute of Technology experiments from 1939 to 1960, which used liquid collector and storage systems, and which culminated with the construction and instrumentation of an occupied solar house in Lexington, Mass., are the basis of the most common type of solar heating today (Figure 5.13). The MIT Solar House IV in Lexington was fully documented for two years which provided very thorough data on the operation of liquid-type solar systems. (The descriptive information and illustrations presented here are based on a report by C. D. Engebretson from the United Nations Conference Proceedings **New Sources of Energy, Volume 5, 1961.**)

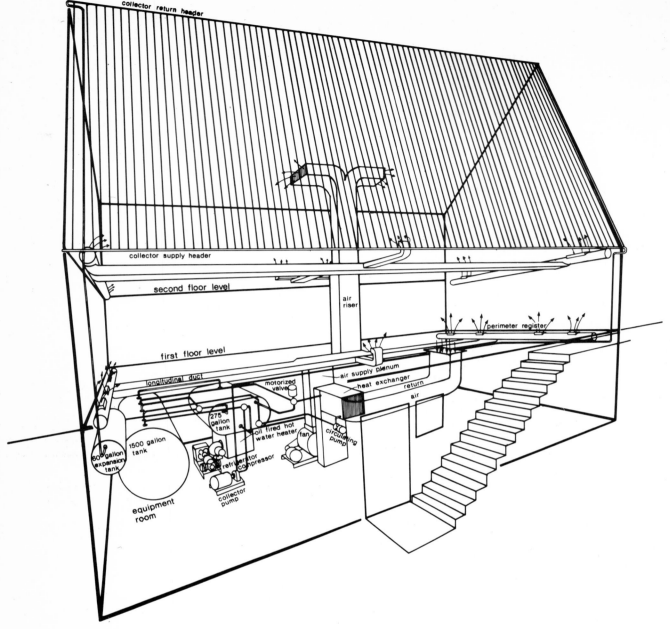

labels in figure:
collector return header
collector supply header
second floor level
first floor level
air riser
perimeter register
longitudinal duct
motorized valve
air supply plenum
heat exchanger
return air
275 gallon tank
oil fired hot water heater
fan
circulating pump
60 gallon expansion tank
1500 gallon tank
refrigerator compressor
collector pump
equipment room

Figure 5.13. *Perspective Diagram of MIT Solar House IV solar heating system.*

Figures 5.14A through C show in diagram form the use of the system for space heating, for domestic hot water heating and for air conditioning. The cooling operation does not use the solar collectors, but like the Thomason system described above, chills the water storage tank for summer cooling. Because of the size of storage, only a small refrigerator compressor is needed to maintain a large cooling capacity and to avoid peak hour overloads.

A summary of the performance of the solar collector used on the Solar House IV over two years shows the monthly and yearly variations (Figure

102

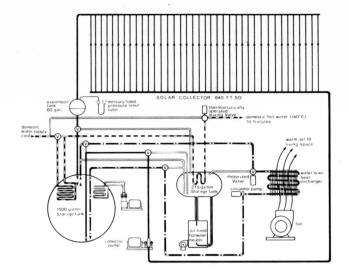

Figure 5.14A. *MIT Solar House IV: Winter Cycle with Solar Heat.*

———— *Collector to Storage Loop. The Solar hot water circulates from collectors to the top of the 1,500 gallon storage tank, drawing the colder water from the bottom of the storage tank back to the collectors.*

—·—·—· *Storage to Space Distribution Loop. Solar heated water from storage circulates through the water-to-air heat exchanger, heating the living space.*

·—·—·—· *Solar Domestic Hot Water Loop. Cold water is heated in the heat storage tank. The water is further heated to 140 degrees F. in the 275-gallon oil-fired hot water storage tank before use at the fixtures.*

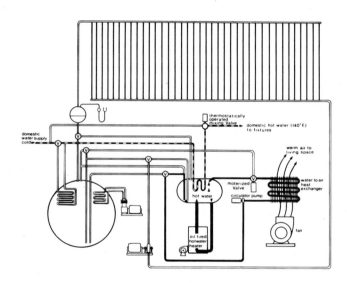

5.14B. *MIT Solar House IV: Winter Cycle with Back-up Heating System.*

———— *Space Heating Circulation Path. Heated water from hot water storage circulates through the water-to-air heat exchanger, heating the living space.*

----------- *Cold water is heated to 140 degrees F. in the hot water storage tank prior to use at plumbing fixtures.*

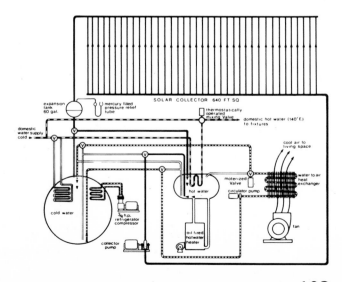

5.14C. *MIT Solar House IV: Summer Cycle (originally proposed but not installed).*

———— *Solar Hot Water Circulation Path. The Solar heated water circulates from the collectors through the 275-gallon storage tank.*

·········· *Cooling Cycle. The ¾ h.p. refrigerant compressor is operated at night to cool the storage water. The compressor is operated at times of off-peak (reduced) electrical rates. Cold water is pumped from storage through the water-to-air heat exchanger when house cooling is desired.*

———— *Domestic Hot Water Heated by Solar. Cold water is heated in the hot water storage tank by a combination of solar and the oil fired hot water heater.*

		Oct.	Nov.	Dec.	Jan.	Feb.	Mar.	April	Total	Ave.
Solar incidence on 60° plane (Btu/ft.²)	1959-1960	33,720	19,330	26,160	34,140	33,890	44,000	32,530	233,780	31,961
	1960-1961	39,360	33,090	40,730	43,125	36,750	44,208		237,263	39,544
Solar incidence on 60° plane while collector operating (Btu/ft.²)	1959-1960	22,890	12,920	18,360	25,730	27,020	34,690	24,790	166,400	23,771
	1960-1961	26,380	27,860	33,480	36,984	29,734	35,322		189,760	31,627
Collection (Btu/ft.²)	1959-1960	9,890	5,390	8,520	11,590	12,630	15,770	11,040	74,830	10,690
	1960-1961	9,910	11,640	13,810	15,375	12,656	13,944		77,335	12,889
Average hourly collection, q_u/A (Btu/hr ft.²)	1959-1960	96.1	88.3	103.3	103.1	102.3	106.6	80.9		99.3
	1960-1961	80.8	86.0	92.9	92.8	102.2	89.3			90.9
Average collector efficiency (percent)	1959-1960	43.2	41.8	46.4	45.1	46.7	45.4	44.5		45.0
	1960-1961	37.6	41.8	41.3	41.5	42.6	39.5			40.8
Utilization factor (percent)	1959-1960	67.9	66.8	71.6	75.4	79.7	78.8	76.2		74.4
	1960-1961	67.0	84.3	82.2	85.4	80.9	79.9			80.0
Over-all efficiency (percent)	1959-1960	29.3	27.9	33.2	34.0	37.3	35.8	33.9		33.4
	1960-1961	25.2	35.2	33.9	34.0	34.4	31.5			32.6

Figure 5.15. *MIT Solar House IV: Solar Collector Performance during the heating seasons of 1959-60 and 1960-61. The average collector efficiency over the two years = 42.9% during the times that the collector was operating. The actual utilization of the available solar heat equalled 77.2%, for an overall average collection efficiency of 33%. (Source: (C. D. Engebretson 1961)*

5.15). Of particular interest, because of the thoroughness of the test procedures used, is the annual efficiency of collection and overall system performance, which averaged over two years 42.9 and 33 percent respectively. These results indicate what percentage of the total solar radiation available during the heating season was effectively recovered by the collector and then utilized by the heating system, and remain an important reference for current predictions of collector efficiency and overall system performance.

The research team responsible for the solar houses at MIT, under the direction of Professor H. C. Hottel, reported that inefficiencies resulted from aspects of the collector design and in the control settings chosen for system operation. Their work has provided the basis for the many improvements that will continue to be made in collector and system design.

Other liquid systems. The vast majority of solar collectors now being marketed are of the liquid type, installed with water heat-storage units that are sized for each particular installation. The following are important areas where efficiency can be improved over that achieved in the MIT installations.

Collector design: The collector used in the MIT Solar House IV was custom-fabricated, with black-painted aluminum and two glass cover sheets. Because of the connection and edge detail, which were made part of the roof, there were efficiency losses due to shading from vertical edges, snow collection at the horizontal edges, and "back losses" through the frame. As described in the previous chapter, collector efficiency has been improved in designs with selective coatings on the absorber, with better insulation and edge detailing, and with anti-reflective coatings on the glass cover sheets.

Collector piping: The manner in which the piping is arranged in the collector greatly affects heat-removal efficiency. Improved combinations of collector material, thickness, coating, pipe size and spacing are being developed, based on extensive performance testing.

One way of piping the liquid in the collector-to-storage loop supplies the water from storage to the bottom of the collector for return to storage from the top. Or the direction of flow can be in the opposite direction—from top to bottom.

The argument for the latter arrangement is that the absorber plate is hottest at the top, and by exposing the "cooler" water from storage to the hottest part of the collector, the overall absorber is used more efficiently. Air pockets are likely to occur within the piping, particularly if the system is "drained down" as a precaution against freezing. In such cases, provision for venting the collectors must be made by sloping the supply and return manifold pipes and by providing pressure release vents.

Heat exchange in storage: In several early solar installations, heat losses have resulted due to inadequate insulation of the storage tank. Particularly when the thermal storage is underground, heat losses from storage can seriously reduce the system's efficiency.

Stratification of water at different temperatures within the storage is considered desirable by most solar engineers. Stratification occurs naturally, as the warmest water rises to the top of storage. In closed loop systems, the collector-to-storage loop heat exchanger usually is placed at the bottom of the storage unit, leaving the top of storage available for the storage-to-house loop heat exchanger.

In liquid systems that drain down when collector temperatures approach freezing, the water from storage itself is circulated through the collectors, thus eliminating one heat exchanger. Baffles often are placed in the storage unit to prevent too much mixing of the water between inlet and outlet.

Heat exchanger in the distribution system: The temperature at which the distribution system can provide comfortable heating is the key to effective use of the temperatures that are characteristic of solar heating—higher than those needed in building interiors, but not as high as those supplied by conventionally fueled furnaces or boilers.

Thus, as discussed in the previous chapter, the proper sizing and layout of heat distribution can greatly improve the efficiency of solar heating systems.

In the typical liquid-type system, the water from storage is passed through a heat coil in front of a fan, so that the heat is transferred into the air-duct distribution network. Other distribution systems use low-temperature water directly from storage without heat exchangers (as has been mentioned previously), where heated water is passed through pipes imbedded in masonry floors or plaster ceilings.

In the Barber residence, described earlier to illustrate the under-floor storage and radiant slab system, the liquid storage tank itself will serve as the heat exchanger. Air will be circulated around the outside of the metal tank before it is passed into the distribution network.

5.1.4 DOMESTIC WATER HEATING

The use of liquid solar collectors to provide domestic hot water is perhaps the most economic and widespread application of solar energy. It requires only a small collector area, it is used year-round, and all other parts of the installation are standard plumbing items. Because they are used year-round, solar collectors used only for domestic water can be installed at a lower angle than that used for space heating—equal to the local latitude.

Solar domestic water packages are available throughout the U.S. from many manufacturers, some of whom have been in production for several decades in Florida and in the southwest. Figure 5.16 illustrates common systems of such solar domestic hot water heating.

Figure 5.16. *Solar Domestic Water System Types.*

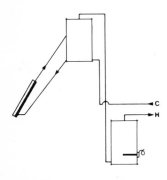

5.16A. *Gravity Hot Water System. Based on the thermosyphon principle, water heated in the collector becomes lighter and rises while colder (heavier) water will flow from the bottom of the storage tank to the bottom of the collector. The system is shown in series with a conventional hot water tank.*

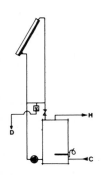

5.16B. *Forced Drain-Down Hot Water System. A pump circulates water from the bottom of the storage tank through the collector back to storage.*

When a freeze condition occurs, an automatic sensing device activates a solenoid valve (v), draining the water from the collector. A non-freezing automatic vent at the top of the collector is required.

106

The SAV Domestic Water Heater. *A unique combination of collector/storage tank exposed to direct solar heating. (Courtesy Fred Rice Productions)*

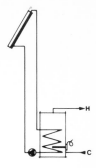

516C. *Closed Loop Hot Water System. Heat from the collector is transferred to storage water through a water to water heat exchanger, placed within the storage tank. A freeze inhibitor is circulated through the closed loop, eliminating the need to drain the solar panels when a freeze condition occurs. (Nontoxic antifreeze, such as propylene glycol, recommended.)*

5.1.5 AUXILIARY SOLAR SPACE HEATING

An alternative to the large collector and storage systems used for space heating described up to this point is to use solar collectors to supply heat directly to the space distribution system—without heat storage and the controls required to regulate different collector, storage and space heating modes.

One such auxiliary solar space heating system, developed by Everett Barber, can be used with a domestic hot water installation, by adding a few more collectors than required for domestic water heating alone and a heat exchanger, connected either to baseboard radiator or warm-air distribution systems (Figure 5.17). The controls can be set to first supply the domestic hot water requirement (where electric rates are high), with the excess then piped directly into the space-heating distribution system. Or, depending on decisions of system operation, it can be set to first supply space heating requirements.

Air collectors also can be used to supply heated air directly to a building interior, but without the domestic hot water heating system described

107

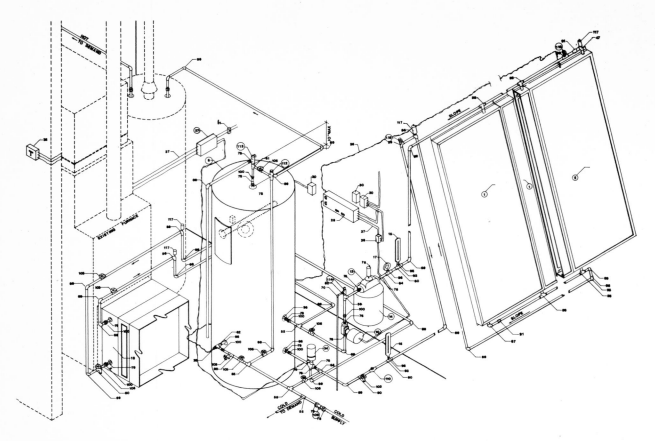

Figure 5.17. *Auxiliary Space Heating System. Currently under development, proposed for combined domestic-water heating and small percentage of space heating. (Courtesy Sunworks, Inc.)*

above. A backyard air-type collector and storage unit is shown in Figure 5.18.

Auxiliary solar heating provides heat only during sunny winter days. It can be installed on almost any house, new or existing. The heat obtained directly from the collector can range up to 130° F. or more, at which point it can add an effective supplement to conventional heat distribution systems. It is a fairly simple matter to find space on most building roofs or in the backyard for 100 square feet of collector.

FES Delta Collector. *A backyard collector with adjustable reflector for domestic water, pool, or auxiliary space heating. (Courtesy Falbel Energy Systems, Inc.)*

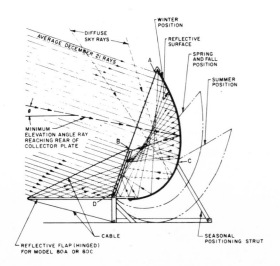

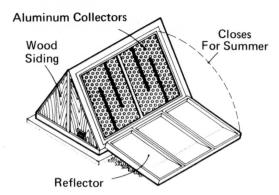

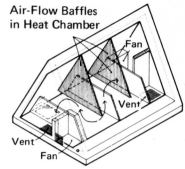

Figure 5.18. *Sungazer* ™ *Solar Furnace, an air type collector/storage unit for auxiliary solar heating. (Courtesy International Solarthermics, Inc.)*

Because the design of the house is a less critical matter with solar domestic water heating and auxiliary space heating, such installations should see widespread use, as more companies bring such equipment packages on the market. Their relative economic merit compared to large capacity solar heating is detailed in the next chapter.

5.2 Active Systems with Special Mechanical Equipment

Instead of designing the entire house-heating distribution system to be effective with the relatively low temperatures produced by solar collectors, many systems use solar heat to supply special mechanical heating or cooling equipment.

The most common of these is the heat-pump system in which the solar panels are used to pre-heat water or air for a heat pump, which then brings it to higher temperature for use in conventional heat-distribution systems.

Similarly, solar collectors can be used to provide heat to drive an absorption chiller or mechanical refrigeration devices that provide air conditioning.

5.2.1 SOLAR HEAT-PUMP SYSTEMS

The heat pump is a device that, by compression or by absorption, raises low-temperature air or water to a higher temperature (Figure 5.19). Heat pumps

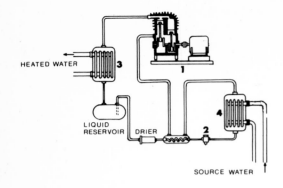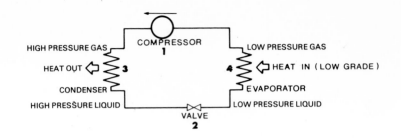

5.19. *Heat Pump Operation. The heat pump is a refrigeration machine used in reverse. A refrigerant such as Freon 11 is circulated in a closed loop by the compressor (1). A pressure release valve (2) keeps it under pressure at the hot end in the condenser (3) and under a reduced pressure at the cold end in the evaporator (4). When compressed, the temperature of the refrigerant is increased and it will liquify, giving off heat at the condenser (heat out). Passing through the pressure release valve, it rapidly evaporates and drops in temperature taking up heat from its environment (heat in). (After S. Szokolay,* Solar Energy in Building)

have been used for many years, particularly in the United States south, for air conditioning (by removing heat from a house interior). By reversing the cycle, solar collectors can be used to preheat water, which the heat pump then raises to the temperature needed in conventional space-heating distribution systems.

A heat pump uses electric energy more efficiently than other heating and cooling equipment when the temperature difference between the air (or liquid) supplied and that delivered is less than 40° F. In northern climates, the heat pump operation can be inefficient in winter due to undesired ice buildup on the evaporator coil. However, solar collectors can be used to supply low temperature air or liquid which can be boosted with a heat pump for use in conventional forced warm-air distribution systems or hot-water baseboard radiators.

Two systems of solar heating with heat pumps have been analyzed by Jesse Denton at the University of Pennsylvania (Figure 5.20). In a conventional Solar-Heat Pump System, the heat pump is the sole source of high temperatures for heating, making up with electric energy for heat not available from the solar heat storage. In an alternate Solar-Heat Pump System analyzed by Denton, heat can be taken directly from the solar collectors to a fan-coil unit in the distribution system, thus "shortcutting" the storage and heat pump units. When the temperature available from the collectors is high enough to supply the distribution directly, the storage and heat pump elements therefore can be by-passed.

In comparing the two solar-heat pump systems, the alternate (with the by-pass) was found to consume 15 percent less auxiliary electrical energy than the conventional arrangement, which itself was

110

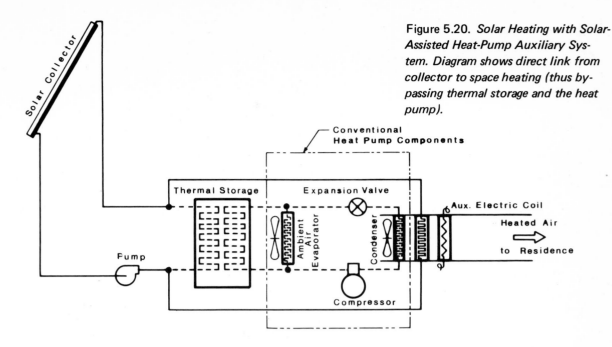

Figure 5.20. *Solar Heating with Solar-Assisted Heat-Pump Auxiliary System. Diagram shows direct link from collector to space heating (thus bypassing thermal storage and the heat pump).*

found to be less energy-efficient than solar heating without a heat pump (Figure 5.21), because the pump consumes the heat from the thermal storage so quickly as to eliminate any carryover capacity.

Many heat-pump systems are being developed to be combined with solar collectors for space heating. While a reliable comparison of energy efficiency—with and without heat pumps—awaits actual performance testing, the promise is that heat pumps can reduce the requirement for consistently high temperatures from the solar collectors themselves and instead can usefully recover heat from storage as low as 45° F.

Figure 5.21. *Conventional Energy Requirement of Heat Pump System with By-Pass[1] compared to five other systems. (Source: Jesse C. Denton, "Integrated Solar-Powered Climate Conditioning Systems," 1974, Univ. of Pennsylvania, Center of Energy Management)*

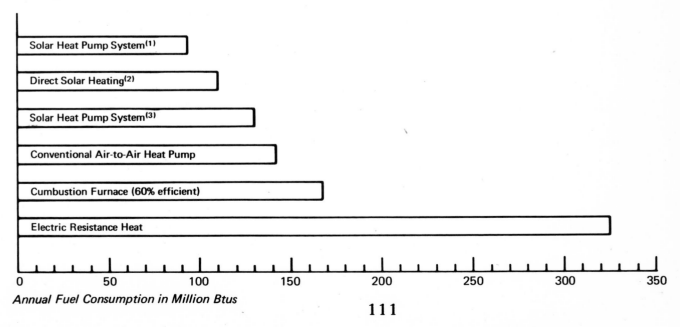

Annual Fuel Consumption in Million Btus

111

5.2.2 SOLAR-POWERED AIR CONDITIONING

Methods for cooling a house have been illustrated throughout this book. Roof monitors and well-placed window openings provide a means of cooling by **natural convection.** The Thomason House (Figure 5.11C) demonstrated one method of **evaporative cooling,** which has also been attempted in hot-dry regions by roof spraying. The Skytherm system provides a means of **natural radiant cooling.**

The storage mass can also be cooled at night either by mechanical convection—simply circulating cooler night air through rock storage (Figure 5.5E)—or by refrigeration (Figure 5.14C).

A new system of long-run energy storage for heating and cooling has been proposed, based on a liquid storage component (Figure 5.22). Here the storage unit that is built into a solar house can also be used in summer as a source of cooling.

Figure 5.22. *Proposed Annual Cycle Energy System (ACES), based on equalizing year-round energy requirements for heating and cooling by long-term energy storage. In winter, heat is obtained from a water storage bin by a heat pump which draws the heat from the water in much the same manner that the conventional home heat pump draws heat from air. Heat drawn from the water is used to warm the building and to provide domestic hot water. This removal of the heat from the water gradually turns the water into ice over a period of months. In the summer months, the chilled water from the bin is used to provide air conditioning for the building without the operation of the heat pump compressor. This action causes a gradual melting of the ice over a period of months and thus stores heat for use in the winter. Prototype installation to be constructed at the University of Tennessee.*

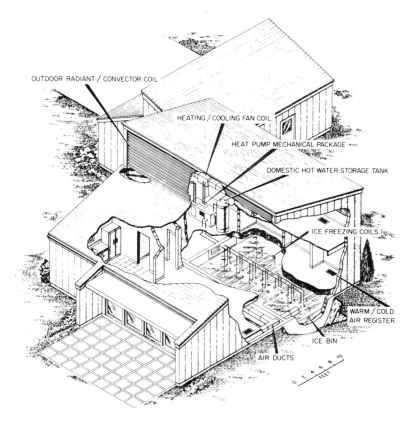

OUTDOOR RADIANT / CONVECTOR COIL

HEATING / COOLING FAN COIL

HEAT PUMP MECHANICAL PACKAGE

DOMESTIC HOT WATER STORAGE TANK

ICE FREEZING COILS

WARM / COLD AIR REGISTER

ICE BIN

AIR DUCTS

0 2 4 6 8 10 FEET

Solar collectors themselves can be used to supply heat to machines which utilize the heat to drive a refrigeration process, and several of these machine processes can use solar heated water as low as 190° F.—including Rankine cycle engines and absorption chillers. All of these machines convert heat energy into mechanical energy by means of changing the state of a circulating fluid from liquid to gas (Figure 5.23, next page).

Because the need for cooling occurs at the same time of the day that solar energy is most available, and because electric air conditioning's energy costs are high, this use of solar collectors may be developed to the point that is proves practical for house cooling. In many parts of the United States the cost of cooling is a large part of the annual fuel bill. Here combined solar heating and cooling could utilize the same equipment effectively year 'round (Figures 5.24 and 5.25).

Figure 5.25. Sugarmill Woods Solar Home. *Homosassa Springs, Florida (1976). Combined solar space heating, pool heating and cooling. (Courtesy: Burt, Hill and Associates)*

Figure 5.24. *Geographic comparison of percent of total energy requirement supplied to 1,500 SF house by 750 SF collector: (Source:* Development of Flat-Plate Collectors, *NASA Report CR-134804)*

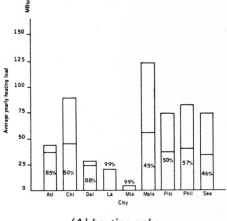

(A) heating only

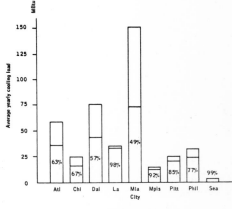

(B) cooling only

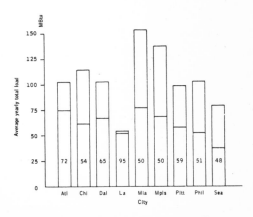

(C) combined heating and cooling

113

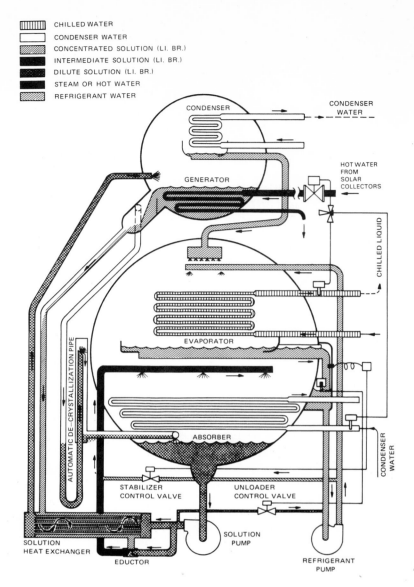

Figure 5.23. *Absorption Chiller.*
The principle of refrigeration is the exchange of heat, and in absorption liquid chilling, there are four basic heat exchange surfaces: the evaporator, the absorber, the generator and the condenser.

In absorption chilling, the refrigerant is water. But like any refrigeration system, absorption chilling uses evaporation and condensation to remove heat. To maintain effective evaporation and condensation, absorption chilling employs two shells which operate at different controlled vacuums.

The lower shell (Evaporator and Absorber) has an internal pressure of about one-hundredth that of the outside atmosphere—or six millimeters of mercury, a relatively high vacuum. The vacuum allows water (the refrigerant) to boil at a temperature below that of the liquid being chilled. This chilled liquid entering the evaporator can be cooled for air conditioning purposes in four steps, as shown on the opposite page.

CHILLED WATER
CONDENSER WATER
CONCENTRATED SOLUTION (LI. BR.)
INTERMEDIATE SOLUTION (LI. BR.)
DILUTE SOLUTION (LI. BR.)
STEAM OR HOT WATER
REFRIGERANT WATER

CONDENSER
CONDENSER WATER
GENERATOR
HOT WATER FROM SOLAR COLLECTORS
CHILLED LIQUID
EVAPORATOR
AUTOMATIC DE-CRYSTALLIZATION PIPE
ABSORBER
CONDENSER WATER
STABILIZER CONTROL VALVE
UNLOADER CONTROL VALVE
SOLUTION HEAT EXCHANGER
EDUCTOR
SOLUTION PUMP
REFRIGERANT PUMP

Absorption Liquid Chiller
(Courtesy YORK BORG-WARNER)

However, a flat-plate collector—efficient and cost-effective for space heating—may not necessarily meet the higher temperature requirements of refrigeration. A larger collector area is required to provide the heat necessary for cooling than is needed for heat only—and installation costs are proportionately higher.

To gain maximum heat for cooling the optimal collector tilt is more towards the horizontal (to face the higher summer sun), so that, depending on the angle of tilt, flat-plate collectors that are oriented for both heating and cooling may not operate at good efficiency for one or the other mode.

114

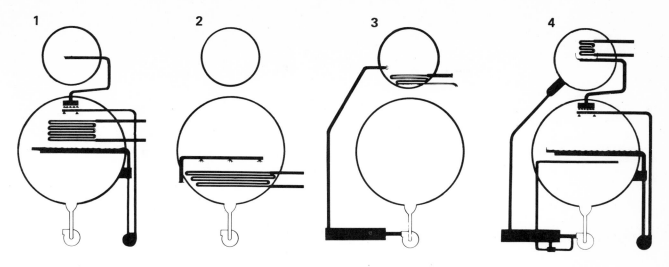

1. Evaporator. *Refrigerant enters the top of the lower shell and is sprayed over the evaporator tube bundle. Heat from the liquid being chilled evaporates the refrigerant.*

2. Absorber. *The refrigerant vapor then migrates to the bottom half of the lower shell. Here the vapor is absorbed by a lithium bromide solution. Lithium bromide is, basically, nothing more than salt water. But lithium bromide is a salt with an especially strong attraction for water. With the lithium bromide spray, it is as if hundreds of little sponges are sucking up the refrigerant vapor. The mixture of lithium bromide and the refrigerant vapor—called the "dilute solution"—now collects in the bottom of the lower shell.*

3. Generator. *The dilute solution is then pumped through the heat exchanger where it is preheated by hot concentrated solution from the generator. The heat exchanger improves the efficiency of*

the cycle by reducing the amount of steam or hot water required to heat the dilute solution in the generator.

The dilute solution then continues to the upper shell containing the Generator and Condenser, where the pressure is approximately one-tenth that of the outside atmosphere, or seventy millimeters of mercury. The dilute solution flows over the generator tubes and is heated by solar-heated water. The amount of heat input from the solar hot water is controlled by a valve and is in response to the required cooling load. The hot generator tubes boil the dilute solution releasing refrigerant vapor.

4. Condenser. *The refrigerant vapor rises to the condenser and is condensed. The liquid refrigerant flows back to the lower shell, and is once again sprayed over the evaporator. The refrigerant cycle has been completed. Now the concentrated lithium bromide solution flows from the generator back to the absorber in the lower shell ready to absorb more refrigerant. Its cycle has also been completed.*

Thus the new high-performance collectors may find a market in supplying combined heating and cooling. At present the increased use of solar cooling awaits further developments in research and in marketing. These might be in the form of combined solar heating/cooling equipment —often referred to as solar climate control packages.

115

5.3
Solar Photovoltaic Cells for Electric Conversion

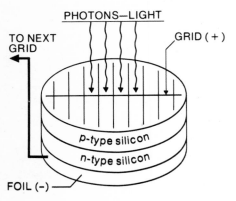

Figure 5.26. *Solar Cell. A schematic diagram of a single silicon solar cell shows wafer between upper and lower contact. The composition causes electron flow when light strikes the surface. Bottom of the cell is coated with foil to collect current for next cell. (Solar Power Corporation)*

Solar Cell—Actual Size, *showing pattern of metal contact on outer surface. (Courtesy McGraw-Edison Company)*

Instead of converting solar radiation to heat energy as in all of the solar collectors described up to this point, photovoltaic cells convert solar radiation directly into electricity. The present cost of producing photovoltaic cells is prohibitive, and converters and storage batteries also are required to provide electricity for home use. However, these solar cells, used as the primary source of energy for space satellites since the 1950's, are now subject to intensive research, with the goal of reducing production costs for energy applications to buildings.

5.3.1 SOLAR PHOTOVOLTAIC CELLS

A solar cell is fabricated in the form of a thin wafer or chip from a semi-conductor material, such as silicon or cadmium-copper sulfide, that sustains an electric field when exposed to sunlight. When photons from sunlight are absorbed by the outer surface of the solar cell, free electrons are created, which then cross to the bottom surface (Figure 5.26). The cells are attached in series or parallel in a grid to create an electric current.

The common method used to fabricate individual solar cells is to form silicon crystals—with an impurity added to increase its semi-conductor properties—into cylindrical ingots approximately three inches in diameter. The hardened ingot is then sawn into thin wafers and polished to a thickness of about 0.012 inches. Depending upon the specific fabrication method, the surfaces of the silicon wafer are treated, first to add another impurity on the outer surface (so that upper and lower sides will have dissimilar electrical properties) and then to apply a metal contact grid and protective coating on the outer surface and a metal conductor on the bottom.

This process of fabrication has been slow and expensive, with waste and damage inherent in the silicon cutting process. In 1975, a new method of producing thin ribbons of silicon was developed at Tyco Labs in Massachusetts, eliminating waste and facilitating the continuous automated assembly of individual cells cut from the ribbon (Figure 5.27).

Cadmium-copper sulfide solar cells are based on a similar photovoltaic process but are fabricated by electroplating a thin layer of cadmium sulfide to one of copper sulfide to create the electric field. Cadmium-copper sulfide cells tend to degrade under high temperatures, so that they must be cooled by removing heat from behind the collectors.

Thus, as will be seen in the house to be described below, the solar heating design approach that has been described in this book also applies to the use of photovoltaic collectors.

Solar cells typically operate at efficiencies between 5 and 16 percent, a relatively low figure for the production cost involved. Increased efficiency can be achieved by using reflectors to concentrate a wider area of sunlight on the small collector target. Designs such as the Winston CPC Collector and other focusing collectors have been proposed for photovoltaic applications.

5.3.2 UNIVERSITY OF DELAWARE "SOLAR ONE HOUSE"

An experimental house has been built in 1971 at the University of Delaware Institute of Energy Conversion to test several approaches to solar energy use, including solar photovoltaic cells.

Cadmium-copper sulfide cells are used to supply the electric utility needs—lighting, kitchen appliances and fans. Unused electric energy is stored in batteries.

Heat is removed from the back of the solar cell array to keep the cells from overheating, which thus acts as an air-type collector to supply space heating requirements.

In addition to the use of solar cells, the Solar One House uses a heat pump and salt storage units to meet heating and cooling energy requirements. These various modes are described in Figures 5.28A through 5.28F. on pages 118-119.

The Solar One House is designed to obtain up to 80 percent of its heat and electric needs from solar energy. The storage components permit the additional electric energy requirements to be supplied at off-peak rates.

117

Figure 5.27. *Extrusion of Continuous Silicon Ribbon by EFG Process. Ribbon is then cut into individual wafers and fabricated into solar cells. (Courtesy Mobil-Tyco Corporation)*

Figure 5.28. *University of Delaware Solar One House. An experimental house which combines solar photovoltaic cells and solar thermal collectors for electric power and heating. (Courtesy Institute of Energy Conversion, University of Delaware)*

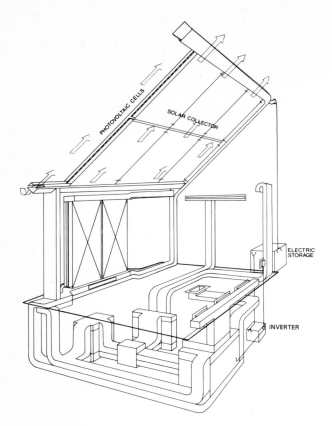

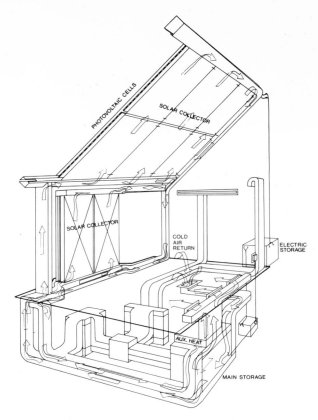

5.28A. *Solar One: D. C. Current Generated by Photovoltaic Cells. When sunlight strikes the solar cells on the roof, D. C. electricity is generated by the CdS Solar Cells. A D. C. to A. C. invertor is used to provide energy to residential appliances (refrigerator, motors, TV, etc). When there is little or no demand for electrical current, the energy is directed to storage batteries for later use. The arrows indicate convective air flow through the collector panels. Outside air enters at the bottom of the collectors and is vented from the top to prevent overheating of the photovoltaic cells.*

5.28B. *Solar One: House Heating from Collectors. Sunlight striking the solar panels heats the photovoltaic cell collector array. Cool air is forced through the solar collectors, heated by contact to the back of the solar cells. Additional black surface louvers placed vertically improve heat transfer. The warm air is supplied directly to the living space through the supply registers. Cool room air is returned to the solar panels.*

5.28C. *Solar One: Storing Heat from Collectors. Ductwork conducts the hot air from the solar panels through a storage system containing eutectic salts. As the air passes over the eutectic salt containers, heat is transferred to the salt and causes it to melt at 120 degrees F. (main storage) and 75 degrees F. (auxiliary storage). In the process of melting, the salts absorb a large amount of heat, known as Heat of Fusion. In this way heat can be stored in a much smaller volume (6 ft. x 6 ft. x 6 ft.) main storage and (2 ft. x 2 ft. x 6 ft.) auxiliary storage than would be required by rock or water storage.*

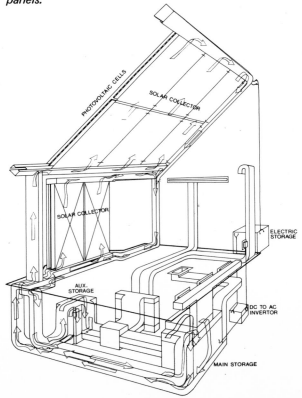

118

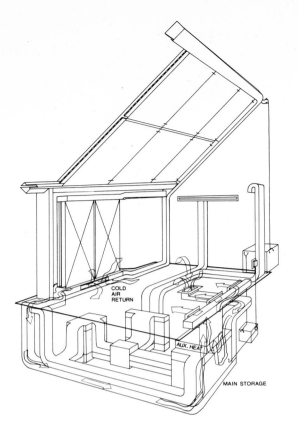

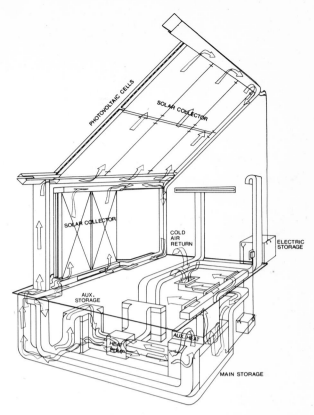

5.28D. *Solar One: House Heating from Storage.
During the evening and night hours when the house
cools down, its air is circulated through the storage
containers, cooling the salt compounds and thus
"extracting" their latent heat of fusion.*

5.28E. *Solar One: House Heating with Low Temperature Solar Heat. Incident solar levels may be
insufficient at times to heat the house. The heat
pump is then used to boost the temperature of
heat from the collector which passes through auxiliary storage to the heat pump where it is raised to
the required temperature. The hot air then passes
through the main storage bin for distribution to
the house.*

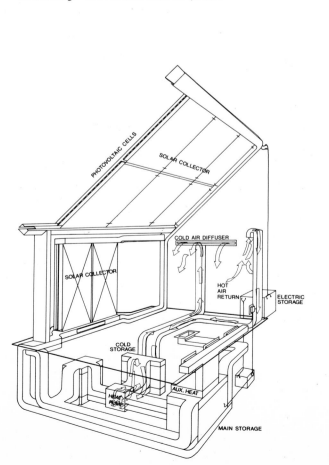

5.28F. *Solar One: House Cooling from Cold Storage. During the summer, the heat pump is used as an
air conditioner and will operate predominantly
during night hours to take advantage of reduced
electrical rates and lower outside air temperature. The
heat pump freezes the eutectic salts in the cold
storage bin at 55° F. During the day hours, house
air is circulated through these salt containers to
extract the "coolness" from the salt (by giving up
its heat to storage), thus cooling the house.*

119

CHAPTER 6

ECODESIGN: DESIGNING A BUILDING FOR ENERGY CONSERVATION

One of the first purposes of a building is to protect the occupants from the extremes of the outside weather, for compared to varying weather conditions, we are comfortable only within extremely narrow limits of temperature and humidity (Figure 6.1).

Part of the task of creating comfort can be achieved without energy-consuming mechanical heating or cooling equipment, by responding to given climatic conditions in the design of the building shape, its orientation and its materials.

Figure 6.1. *Bioclimatic Chart. Relative zones of comfort as a function of temperature and humidity. Building design can create natural means of comfort by shade, ventilation, wind protection and solar heating, both direct and time delayed. (After V. Olgyay,* Design with Climate, *1964)*

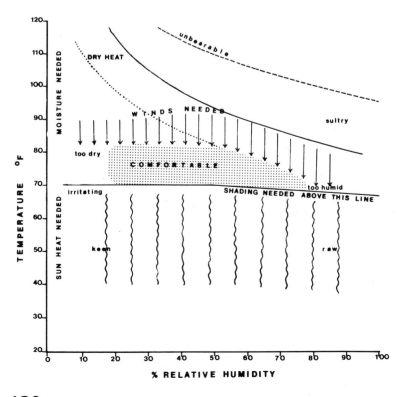

If a building is properly designed, mechanical methods of heating or cooling should be required only to take over during those periods when passive means are inadequate. Furthermore, if passive means are first made part of the building construction, then solar collectors and any other mechanical heating or cooling equipment can be held to a size that is economically practical and does not "take over" the design of the house.

This chapter reviews principles by which to design a building to fit its particular climate and to thus reduce the energy requirement on its heating and cooling equipment. The principles combine to offer an energy-efficient approach to building which can best be called "ecodesign."

A building structure, its roof and walls, delays the effect of heat or cold to which it is exposed from sun and wind. Depending upon daily and seasonal temperature variations, heat lag through the building surfaces can be used to store daytime heat and help reduce the effect of cool night temperatures. If the building is poorly designed, however, it can create conditions inside the building more uncomfortable than outdoors.

There is a variety of house design solutions that are appropriate to the different climates in North America. In southern areas, where the predominant need is for summer cooling, the building should provide sun protection, natural ventilation and

Climate Variable	Range of Variation
Solar Radiation absorbed in walls	15 to 90% of incident radiation
Solar Radiation penetrating through windows	10 to 90% of incident radiation
Indoor Air Temperature Amplitude	10 to 150% of outdoor amplitude
Indoor Maximum Air Temperature	−18° to +18°F from outdoor maximum
Indoor Minimum Air Temperature	0° to 54°F from outdoor minimum
Indoor Surface Temperature	14° to 54°F from outdoor maximum and minimum
Average Internal Air Speed, windows open	15 to 60% of outdoor wind speed
Actual air speeds at any point in room	10 to 120% of outdoor wind speed

Interior Climate in Buildings Compared to Outside Climate Conditions as affected by building design and construction variables. (Source: B. Givoni, Man, Climate and Architecture.)

121

methods of radiant or evaporative cooling. In northern areas, where the main need is for heating, the building design should provide solar heat and protection from wind.

Buildings in any climate, however, experience periods both of overheating and underheating, so that combined methods of heating and cooling should be selected as needed in each climate—to the extent that is practical—by economic building design. Inevitably, a design that attempts to fit different extremes of climate involves compromises. A building design feature that works well under summer conditions may work against effective winter solutions. For example, high interior spaces, ideal for natural ventilation in summer, are difficult to heat in winter; windows or skylights that obtain beneficial solar heat in winter can be a source of overheating in summer.

In the end, such factors as the appearance of a house or the building costs limit the number of solutions that can be used. However, in view of escalating fuel costs over the life of a building, the ecodesign approach to energy conservation through building design has become both worthwhile and necessary. Fuel-consuming heating and cooling equipment no longer can be expected to make up by brute force what has been ignored in the basic building design.

The United States is generally designated by four basic climatic types: **cool** (Minneapolis), **temperate** (New York City), **hot-dry** (Phoenix), and **hot-wet** (Miami). Every part of the United States, however, experiences most of these weather extremes at some time of the year. Conditions vary locally, also, due to the effect of nearby land features, large bodies of water or vegetation.

Comparison of Climates: *Average annual requirements for comfort. Zones shown in map are approximate only, with wide variation possible within each zone.*
(Source: V. Olgyay, Design with Climate*)*

	comfort by shading only	shading needed	heat needed	cool breeze needed	wind protection needed
COOL	15%	24%	76%	4%	76%
TEMPERATE	31%	28%	72%	7%	72%
HOT-DRY	16%	63%	37%	19%	37%
HOT-WET	26%	88%	12%	62%	2%

122

Buildings that are in the same region therefore may actually experience wide differences in actual weather conditions.

In **cool** climates, the main ecodesign objectives are to maximize winter solar heat gain and to minimize heat losses caused by cold winter winds.

In **temperate** climates, while some of the same "cool climate" objectives apply for winter heating, the need to control humidity both in and around the building leads to distinct design solutions that do not necessarily apply to cooler or to drier zones. In temperate-to-cool climate areas, natural ventilation often can be used to eliminate the need for mechanical air conditioning.

In **hot** climates, the main ecodesign objectives are to minimize heat gain to the structure and to maximize natural cooling, but in other respects design solutions appropriate to hot-dry areas are quite distinct from those of hot-wet areas.

In **hot-dry** zones, natural cooling can be accomplished by radiant cooling (such as the Skytherm system) and by evaporative cooling.

Houses in **hot-wet** climates cannot rely on radiant cooling devices because night skies are not clear and the temperature drop between day and night is slight. Similarly, the air is generally too humid for effective evaporative cooling. The main technique for natural cooling in hot-wet zones is to increase comfort by maximum air flow and ventilation.

The design solutions appropriate to temperate and cool climate areas are similar to one another, varying only in the amount of heating required. The colder the climate, the larger the solar collector and storage system must be to provide a major portion of the annual heating. The designs discussed in this book, therefore, are based principally on solar heating requirements for temperate to cool climates, where the heating requirement is the major energy demand. In southern climates, a solar heating system can be smaller and is easier to incorporate into the house design. Advanced collector designs for heating and cooling are still experimental but even if they become economically feasible, the same ecodesign objectives set forth in this chapter will still apply.

6.1
Ecodesign
Techniques

The solar heating methods described in previous chapters are part of a number of design features that can be used to meet ecodesign objectives (Figure 6.2). These techniques can be combined in many ways, based on personal preferences and on local design and construction practices.

Interestingly enough, many of the ecodesign techniques evolved independently in areas of the world that have similar climates. Traditional building styles throughout the United States invariably exhibit practical ecodesign techniques because they had to meet local climate conditions before the widespread use of mechanical heating and cooling equipment.

Of the ecodesign techniques listed in Figure 6.2, **fireplace design, underground massing, internal zoning,** and **insulation** are the most important in northern climates to improve the solar-heating

Figure 6.2. *The Ecodesign Approach to Building Design: Design features that can be used to achieve natural climate control.*

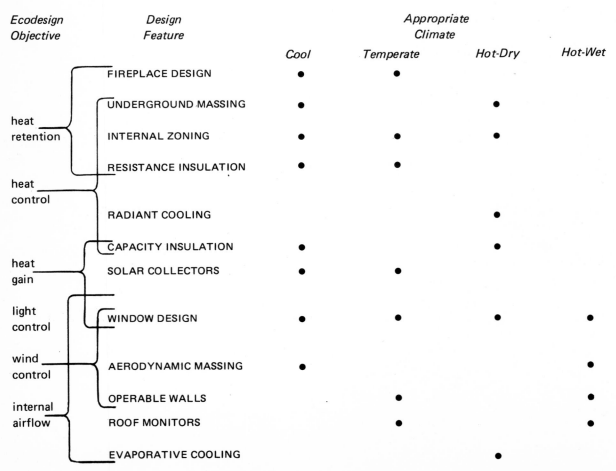

Ecodesign Objective	Design Feature	Appropriate Climate			
		Cool	Temperate	Hot-Dry	Hot-Wet
heat retention	FIREPLACE DESIGN	●	●		
	UNDERGROUND MASSING	●		●	
	INTERNAL ZONING	●	●	●	
	RESISTANCE INSULATION	●	●		
heat control	RADIANT COOLING			●	
	CAPACITY INSULATION	●		●	
heat gain	SOLAR COLLECTORS	●	●		
light control	WINDOW DESIGN	●	●	●	●
wind control	AERODYNAMIC MASSING	●			●
internal airflow	OPERABLE WALLS		●		●
	ROOF MONITORS		●		●
	EVAPORATIVE COOLING			●	

124

capacity of a house. These are discussed separately below. References for further reading are listed in Appendix I-A.

6.1.1 FIREPLACE/STOVE DESIGN

In areas where wood is available, fireplaces can be used for supplementary heating. With large-capacity solar systems, an efficient wood-burning fireplace/stove may be the only additional back-up heating element required.

The conventional opening fireplace does not of it-self provide an efficient means of heating: it increases the rate of ventilation or air change of a house—with most of the heat going up the chimney. The efficiency of fireplaces and stoves can be increased dramatically by the following devices:

Reflecting backwall and smoke shelf. The design of the firebox itself can be improved, as in the so-called Rumford fireplace design, to reflect more heat into a room by angling the sides of the firebox and by decreasing the depth, with a smoke shelf to increase the draft velocity.

Outside air at the firebox. Instead of consuming the oxygen of the room, a fire can be fed by outside air, thereby decreasing the draw of heated air from the house interior. Outside air should be ducted to the sides or front of the firebox through openings approximately as large as the chimney flue.

Recirculating air systems. The heat from the space around the firebox can be blown to other parts of the room or to other rooms, as in the Heatilator design—which was originally developed to cool the sheet metal construction of the firebox lining.

Recirculating liquid systems. Liquid heated in pipes at the back of the fireplace can be piped to water storage, and thus augment the temperature of water in solar heating systems.

Fireplace Designs

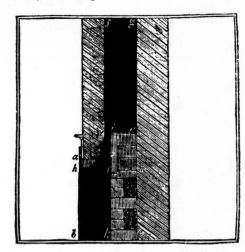

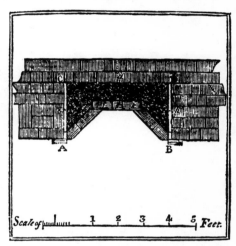

1798 Drawings by Benjamin Count of Rumford for improving heat reflectivity and draw of existing fireplaces by adding bricks as shown. (G. Curtis Gillespie, Rumford Fireplaces, 1906)

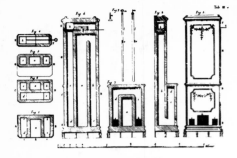

1775 Drawings by C. T. Cronstedts and F. Wredes for design of Scandinavian extended flue wood stoves. (B. Tunander, Kakelugnar, 1973)

Extended Flue through exposed fireplace masonry is sole heat source for remodeled farmhouse outside Helsinki, Finland. Marja Watson, Architect.

Firebox covers and oxygen inlet controls. The flow of air supplied to the fire can be reduced, as in a wood-burning stove, to create a slower and more efficient burning rate.

Extended chimney flues. The heat from the chimney flue itself can be recovered by extending the flue through the fireplace masonry in a labyrinthine pattern, as perfected in traditional Scandinavian fireplace/stoves.

Design of Fireplace	% Heating Effect
Ordinary Fireplaces	10-12
Ventilating Fireplaces	33-35
Common stoves without circulation of air (not recommended)	
Cast-iron, coal burning	83-90
Porcelain, burning wood,	87
Metal stoves, with circulation of air from room from the outside (recommended practice)	68-93
Heaters with pipes for circulation of hot air	63-80
Apparatus for circulation of hot water	65-90

Heating Efficiency of Various Fireplace Designs. Source: J. P. Putnam, The Open Fireplace. *(1880) and* Smithsonian Reports *(1873)*

6.1.2 UNDERGROUND MASSING

Placing a house partly or entirely underground has been proposed as a means to reduce heat loss in northern climates and could be considered in cold/dry regions. In temperate and more humid zones, exposure to the air and sun is desirable to maintain humidity control.

Underground massing of the building takes advantage of the moderating effect of the ground temperature below the frost line, and reduces the exposure of the building to cold winter wind. Waterproof insulation, available in rigid sheets, should be applied outside of the building walls and under the floors that are located below-ground, so that the heat-storage capacity of the masonry construction of the foundation walls and floors can be used to help moderate temperature extremes in the interior.

Earth-covered roofs have also been proposed to increase the insulation of the house, but here the added cost of structure to support wet earth and to resist sustained freeze and thaw action discourages most home builders. In a simpler method, "earth berms" can be used to partially cover exterior walls. On sloped sites this technique may have both cost and aesthetic advantages.

Underground Massing—Cold Climate. *Western Eskimo Housing built to support snow for winter insulation. (After Murdoch)*

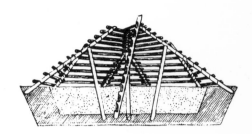

Underground Massing—Hot Climate. *Pit dwelling construction typical of North American Indian structures to support earth cover for sun protection and heat time lag in hot dry climates. (After Teit)*

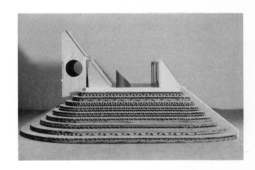

Project for solar house with earth-bermed side walls on three sides. Designer: Mac Godley.

T. Pedersen

Scanticon Student Housing near Aarhus, Denmark *with rooms built into southern slope of hill with earth covered roofs for added insulation. (Courtesy K. Friis and E. Moltke, Architects)*

127

Areas Where Underground Massing is Beneficial *for summer cooling and/or winter heating economy.*

1. Area of greatest advantage. The south-western end of this zone has less summer benefit because it is drier. Also, yearly temperature extremes are not so great. Northern portions of this zone, with cool summers, would need to use sun's heat to take summertime chill off a sunken living room, but wintertime benefits would be very positive.

2. This area has both summer and winter advantages. But due to high relative humidities, a sunken room in this zone would require some mechanical air-drying to prevent condensation on walls and floors.

3. Area where underground living offers only minor advantages and is not recommended for the following reasons: because climate above ground is pleasant and

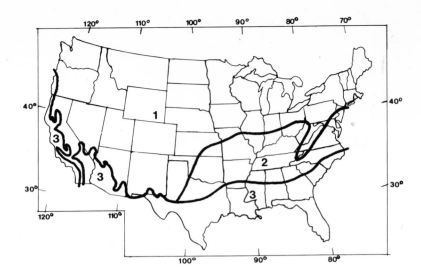

without great extremes; because the underground temperatures are not different enough to correct the above-ground climate, or because of the complications of extreme humidities. (Source: Dr. Paul Siple, House Beautiful Climate Control Project, 1949)

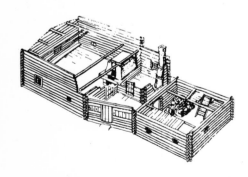

Internal Zoning—Cold Climate. *Traditional Finnish farmhouse plan (14th century) with many air locks and internal zones, each heated by a different fireplace. (N. Valonen, Zur Geschicte der Finnischen Wohnstuben, 1963)*

6.1.3 INTERNAL ZONING

The use of double doors, air locks, sunrooms and porches, are examples of "internal zoning" to reduce heat loss from opening doors and to reduce the number of rooms to be fully heated at one time.

Internal zoning is simply a matter of proper planning and can often be achieved by adding doors and rearranging spaces so that rooms are placed according to use and availability of sun, with the storage, service and little-used spaces located on northern exposures. The plans presented throughout this book show many ways of internal zoning. Of these, one of the most effective is the solarium, which can be used for heat-collection during sunny days and closed off to reduce the house heating requirement when there is insufficient sunshine.

Internal zoning permits the homeowner to set back the thermostat in unused zones, for savings of fuel in the range of 3 percent for each degree of setting reduction.

128

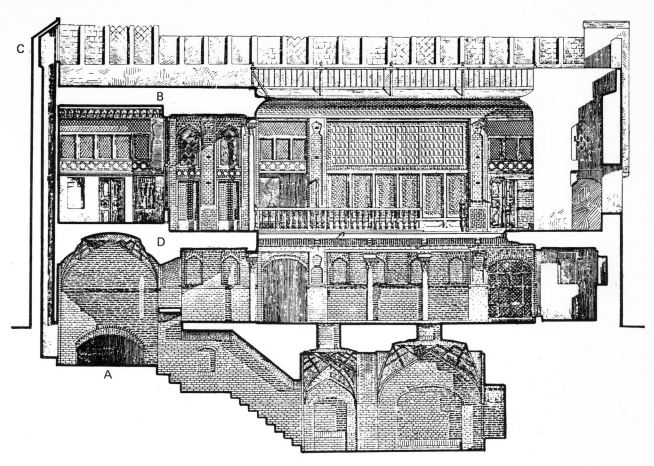

Second-floor interior, showing light wood and glass construction. (Photos courtesy of Jala Makzoumi)

Internal Zoning—Hot Dry Climate. *Traditional house, Bagdad, Iraq. One of the best examples of zoning for natural climate control. Underground and first-floor rooms are cool in summer due to heavy masonry construction (A). Roof terrace can be used for sleeping on summer nights (B). Fresh air inlet from wind scoops in roof (C) cool the air as it passes by masonry and wet clay jars at bottom of air shaft. Second story, built of light wood and glazing, is heated by sun during winter days (D), with heat lag through roof. (After D. Reuther)*

Wind scoops on roof terraces.

6.1.4 INSULATION

Adding insulation to reduce heat loss through windows, walls and roofs is the most economically practical method of energy saving. Increased insulation reduces the size of the mechanical equipment required and thus results in increased solar-heating efficiency for a given investment.

References listed in Appendix I-A have been written specifically for easy use by homeowners to determine the proper amounts of insulation for homes in each part of the United States.

Two terms are used in discussing insulation and

R38 (12 inches) attic insulation

double-glazed)

R19 (6 inches) Side wall insulation

Tightly sealed construction to reduce air infiltration

Insulated doors with weather-stripping

R22 (6½ inches) Under floor insulation over unheated basement or crawl spaces

Scaled down heating and cooling equipment

Insulation recommendations are by Owens-Corning Fiberglas Corporation and correspond approximately to current recommendation of the National Bureau of Standards. Insulation thicknesses recommended for a house located in Zone 1. "R" is a measure of thermal resistance. The higher the R, the higher the insulating value. (Professional Builder magazine)

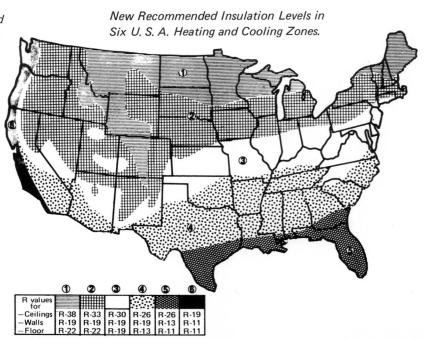

New Recommended Insulation Levels in Six U. S. A. Heating and Cooling Zones.

R values for	①	②	③	④	⑤	⑥
—Ceilings	R-38	R-33	R-30	R-26	R-26	R-19
—Walls	R-19	R-19	R-19	R-19	R-13	R-11
—Floor	R-22	R-22	R-19	R-13	R-11	R-11

Roofs of traditional Danish farmhouses designed to permit moderate snow build-up for added insulation, but steep enough to shed heaviest snow.

the heat transfer characteristics of building materials: the **resistance** to heat flow (the "U" or "R" value of a material, alone or in combination) and the **heat storage capacity.** Two walls, one a wood wall and the other of masonry, could have identical resistance insulation (their "U" values would be the same), but their thermal capacity would be quite different. As discussed previously, buildings with good heat-storage capacity, either in the construction of their floors, walls and roofs or in special heat storage units, perform much better than low-capacity construction in moderating the effect of wide temperature swings experienced in most climates. Even though more expensive in many parts of the United States, masonry construction may be justified in terms of comfort and reduced heating equipment requirements. The heat storage capacity in the building materials is especially useful in passive solar heating design to help prevent overheating. (High heat-capacity construction is counterproductive in hot-humid climates where night cooling relies upon natural ventilation only.)

Inadequate insulation accounts for snow melt pattern that shows roof joist construction.

6.2
House Plans Based on Ecodesign Principles

To show how ecodesign principles are applied to the basic shape and orientation of a house plan, we will outline the four distinct requirements that a house may be designed for: **minimum heat loss**; **maximum winter solar heat gain**; **minimum wind exposure** (to reduce heat loss), and **maximum natural ventilation** (Figure 6.3).

(1) Minimum heat loss. To reduce the heating energy requirement, a house should be designed to retain the heat efficiently that is generated within

131

the building. This can be best achieved if the initial design objective is to enclose the spaces required with a minimum amount of surface exposed to the outside.

The shape that ideally meets this objective is a hemisphere, for it provides the least external envelope for enclosed floor area. The igloo of the Arctic, the pit dwelling, and the earth lodge used by the aboriginal Indian tribes throughout North America are examples of such shapes found in early buildings. The same objective—to minimize heat loss—is also achieved by high insulation standards, partially underground placement of the house, snow and sod roofs, internal heat zoning, and compact planning, such as double-storied house construction.

Figure 6.3. *House forms based on Specific climatic conditions.*

Maximum Thermal Retention   *Maximum Solar Heat Gain*

(2) Maximum winter solar heat gain. Using a building's outside surface to gain solar heat leads from round or square-shaped designs to elongated plans that permit more surface area to be heated by the winter sun. This is achieved by increasing the part of the building that is exposed to the south—for passive solar heat traps or for active solar collectors on vertical or inclined wall or roof surfaces.

There is a limit, however, to which a compact and thermally efficient shape can be extended. Beyond a certain point, the heat losses through the increased wall area exceed the solar heat gains. Austin Whillier, one of the researchers associated with the Massachusetts Institute of Technology experimental solar houses, concluded that the limit to which a standard building shape with solar collectors could be extended was a length-to-width radio of 1.5 to 1, with the longer side facing south. Beyond this, heat loss could exceed the potential solar heat gain. The house plan shape could be extended lengthwise beyond this ratio if building costs were not considered and insulation were increased.

(3) Minimum wind exposure. On building sites that experience severe wind, the building shape may be dictated by the requirement of minimum wind resistance. This provides structural strength against wind forces and in northern climates reduces wind-induced heat losses.

132

The sides of a building exposed to cold winds lose heat at a faster rate than the other surfaces, the more so as the wind speed and the resulting "chill factor" increase. It is helpful, also, to locate the major openings of the building on the lee side of the prevailing cold wind so that heat losses through opening doors and window cracks are reduced.

The Indian hogan of the Dakotas represents an ideal shape for minimum wind resistance, if one assumes the winds are multi-directional. The sloping roofs of traditional houses with the low side facing the prevailing winter wind also illustrate an efficient response to severe wind conditions. Underground massing, protected courtyards and internal heat zoning are other design solutions for cold wind conditions.

(4) Maximum internal air flow. In hot-humid climates, ventilation and air movement are essential for comfort. In recent years, the use of mechanical air conditioning has led to house designs that neglect the natural cooling techniques of sun-shading and natural ventilation.

But even where mechanical conditioning is used, whether powered by conventional fuels or by solar heat, provision in the basic house design for natural cooling and ventilation can reduce the energy load on the house.

When the air inside a building rises and exhausts at the highest point, a pleasant natural ventilation and cooling effect can be achieved. The warm air that rises in the building and leaves at the top then can be replaced by cooler ground air. This "thermal chimney" effect works well even in the absence of outside wind if roof and wall openings are properly sized and located.

The Indian tepee makes ideal use of such devices for natural ventilation, controllable by adjusting the openings at top and bottom. The roof cupolas on traditional barns were developed to meet this requirement as well.

These idealized shapes show how building plans can be designed to meet specific climate requirements. However, all of the ecodesign objectives can be combined as needed to meet the climatic conditions of the building location. In each

Minimum Wind Resistance   *Maximum Internal Airflow*

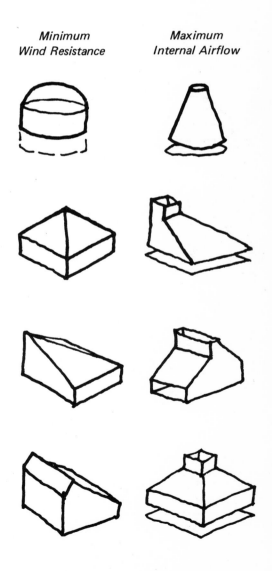

133

Figure 6.4. *House designs based on com-bined climatic conditions.*

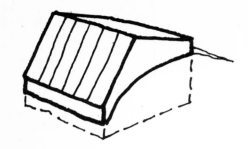

Cool Climate

Maximum thermal retention
Maximum solar heat gain
Minimum wind resistance

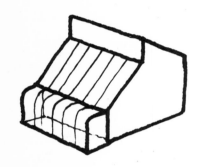

Temperate Climate

Moderate thermal retention
Moderate solar heat gain
Slight wind exposure (humidity control)
Moderate internal air flow

Hot Dry Climate

Minimum solar heat gain
Moderate wind resistance (dust)
Moderate internal air flow

climate, a wide range of designs can meet the same objectives, with the result that a house plan based on ecodesign objectives can be developed to respond to the condition unique to each climatic region (Figure 6.4).

Cool climates. Partly underground massing, designs that enable snow accumulation to stand against walls or on roofs, and internal heat zoning especially with "air-locks" at entry ways, all help to reduce heat losses in cool-climate houses. These solutions have been used for centuries in traditional dwellings throughout Northern Europe, Scandinavia and North America.

Temperate climates. In temperate climates, the humidity which builds up inside the building and in the building materials needs to be controlled by exposure to the drying effect of sun and wind. This usually argues against the underground massing that could be used in colder climates.

Greenhouses and other passive solar-heat devices can be used to advantage in temperate zones, while cooling needed for only a small portion of the summer can be provided by roof monitors or other ventilators which minimize additional energy requirements.

Hot-dry climates. Natural cooling and heating designs, interior courtyards (for sun and wind control), and partly underground placement of the building (for reduced heat gain in summer) all are appropriate for hot-dry climates where night temperatures fall well below day averages, even in summer. The glare and intensity of direct sunlight in hot-dry climates require sun controls at the windows, and in dry, desert areas, protection is needed against wind-blown dust and sand.

Hot-wet climates. The major objective in hot-wet climates is to maximize the effect of natural cooling by exposure to breezes. Walls with windows, screens and ventilating louvers will provide storm protection, insect control, privacy and variable light conditions. Interior courtyards and roof monitors can be used to produce natural chimney effects for ventilation. In some instances, a building may be raised to increase its exposure to the wind, as well as for insect and humidity control.

The generalized design recommendations illustrated here must be adjusted carefully to the specific conditions of building sites. This is the great opportunity in designing a home—to take advantage of the particular climate conditions at the building site to increase comfort by natural means. Ways in which local climate information can be used in siting a home are discussed in Chapter 8.

Although the remainder of this chapter focuses on the specific requirements of solar heating as a part of the house design, the examples are based on the ecodesign objectives to meet year-round climate conditions.

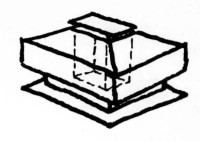

Hot Wet Climate

Maximum wind exposure
Maximum internal air flow

6.3
Solar House Design: Technical and Aesthetic Considerations

Solar heating makes economical sense in northern climates, where home heating costs are proportional to the severity of the winter. Therefore, the discussion here focuses on the design of houses with the medium-to-large solar collector areas that are required in cold climates. As we investigate how solar collectors can be placed on houses in northern climates in a pleasing and practical way, it will become obvious that in milder climates the application will be much easier.

Because of its size, the collector area needed and its placement on (or near) a building are the most critical factors involved in solar design. In northern climates, a costly and large area of solar collector is required to supply a substantial portion of a home's heating needs. Using even the best solar collectors available today, the required collector area may be as high as 40 percent of the building's heated floor space. With less-efficient collectors, the area would be even larger.

If the collectors are mounted on some adjacent structure or on the ground, the problem is removed from the design of the house, but the appearance of the collectors in the landscape still must be considered. And the collectors must be quite near the building for construction economy and heat efficiency.

135

Whether of a passive or active type, the design of solar heating in northern climates thus could be cumbersome and expensive if proper consideration is not made of the impact of the solar collector area on design. As a result, two rules of solar design should be followed.

First: **Use ecodesign techniques to reduce the heating requirements of the house, before considering solar heat gain.**

Second: **Use passive heating methods as much as is practical in the basic design and construction of the house,** such as windows for heat gain and masonry for heat storage.

By following these two rules, the collector area that is required to provide active solar heating can be brought down to a size that does not dominate the appearance and structure of a house. The remainder of this chapter outlines just what the various design limitations are.

6.3.1 OPTIMUM TILT AND ORIENTATION OF FLAT-PLATE COLLECTORS

If a solar collector is fixed in one position, as is normal for practical construction and maintenance reasons, the optimum angle is that which directly faces the average position of the sun during the winter season. The height of the sun varies with latitude, and the farther north the location is, the lower the sun appears—and the more critical is the shadowing effect of nearby buildings and trees.

For space heating, the optimum angle of tilt for a fixed collector can be calculated by adding about 15 degrees to the local latitude. Thus, at 42° N latitude, the optimum tilt would be 57°. A steeper tilt than latitude plus 15° is acceptable, particularly if there is reflection from water or snow, and in such a case it may be practical to use the south wall for the required collector area.

Other than this exception, the collectors used for space heating should be tilted no more than 10 degrees off the optimum angle. If combined solar

Snow melting approximately 9:00 AM after snowfall of previous night. Snow was completely clear of collectors less than half an hour later. If required, the collectors could be heated from storage to start the melting process.

136

	Latitude (Degrees N.)								
	24°	28°	32°	36°	40°	44°	48°	52°	56°
JAN	44	48	52	56	60	64	68	72	76
FEB	35	39	43	47	51	55	59	63	67
MAR	24	28	32	36	40	44	48	52	56
APR	13	17	21	25	29	33	37	41	45
MAY	4	8	12	16	20	24	28	32	36
JUN	½	4½	8½	12½	16½	20½	24½	28½	32½
JUL	4	8	12	16	20	24	28	32	36
AUG	13	17	21	25	29	33	37	41	45
SEP	24	28	32	36	40	44	48	52	56
OCT	35	39	43	47	51	55	59	63	67
NOV	44	48	52	56	60	64	68	72	76
DEC	47½	51½	55½	59½	63½	67½	71½	75½	79½

heating and cooling (or domestic water heating alone) is planned, then the tilt of the collectors should be approximately equal to the local latitude, to accommodate the **annual** variation in solar altitude.

The best orientation for solar collectors with respect to true north (in the northern hemisphere) is between south to 10°-15° west of south. The bias to the west of south is acceptable because collector efficiency increases with higher outside temperatures and afternoon air temperatures average 15 to 20 degrees F. higher than in the morning. Table II.8 (Appendix II) shows the reduction in percentage of daily solar radiation received on a collector as it varies from due south.

Small variations from the recommended angle certainly are permissible, but if every attempt is made to approximate the optimum angles of tilt and orientation, then the best use is made of any given collector.

Figure 6.5. *The tilt angles (degrees from horizontal) shown for the 21st day of each month for the various latitudes are optimum for a south-facing collector. Instead of adjusting the panels throughout the year, a compromise setting can be calculated for the months of the greatest projected use of the collector (varies depending on climate and installation). For the average optimum for a given latitude, sum the angles for each month of greatest usage (such as pool heating, space heating, etc.) and divide by the number of months. (Source: OEM Products, Inc.)*

6.3.2 ALTERNATIVE LOCATIONS

Alternative locations for solar heat collectors are diagrammed in Figure 6.6. In most cases, collectors are located high on a building to receive the best exposure. A pump or fan and a controller are required to circulate the heat from the collectors to heat-storage and to the building.

137

Figure 6.6. *Alternative locations for solar flat-plate collectors.*

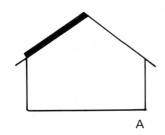

A

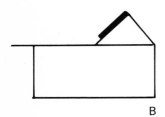

B

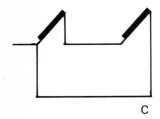

C

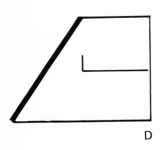

D

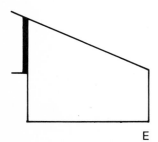

E

Alternative A, the most common roof installation type, usually has the best unobstructed exposure to the sun. Roof-mounted collectors also can serve as the finished roof and as insulation.

Alternative B also is roof-mounted, but is set back from the roof edge. This location may eliminate the view of the collector from the ground, and it could benefit from reflection gains from the roof surface. The bottom of the collector should be kept above the line of normal snow build-up, which is less likely to occur with Alternate A.

Alternative C, a "saw-tooth" arrangement of several rows of collectors, is the most common on large flat-roofed buildings. The raised roof portions also can serve as clerestory lights and ventilating roof monitors. The collector rows should be placed far enough apart to prevent any shading of one collector row by another.

Alternative D is a wall installation, appropriate in far-northern latitudes where the collector angle can be close to vertical and where large collector areas must be provided. As in similar "A-frame" designs, the full use of the interior floor space close to the angled wall may be limited due to insufficient headroom.

Alternative E shows solar collectors located in the vertical south wall—as in the 1949 Dover, Massachusetts solar house (Figure 1.8). A vertical collector does not receive as much direct sun as one placed at an optimum tilt angle, but there are compensating gains in reflectivity from the ground, particularly if there is snow cover. South wall installations are appropriate for high-rise buildings in northern latitudes.

Alternatives F and G use reflective surfaces to increase the amount of solar radiation to conventional, flat-plate collectors. Alternate "F" shows a reflective surface on the inside face of an adjustable flap or wall which can be dropped to rest on the ground or angled according to the solar altitude to obtain optimum reflection. Alternate G—the arrangement used in the Wormser Pyramidal Optics

System, (see Section 3.3.2)—places the collector and reflector within a transparent roof shield and thus minimizes weather-proofing concerns.

Alternative H, a ground-mounted collector removed from the building it serves, is appropriate for "retro-fitting" solar heating installations to existing dwellings which do not have existing roof or wall areas facing south. In northern latitudes the collectors also could be mounted vertically on a fence.

A possible advantage of ground-mounted collectors is that it is easier to adjust the collector's angle to follow the seasonal changes in solar altitude, as In **Alternative I**.

The solar houses shown in this book illustrate the wide variations that are possible within these nine alternatives. In the next section, the first and most common alternative—the roof-mounted collector—is examined to see how a large solar collector area may limit house design options.

6.3.3 ARCHITECTURAL FACTORS THAT LIMIT SOLAR COLLECTOR AREA

Even when a house is well-insulated and uses other passive methods of energy conservation, a large area of solar collectors is required in northern climates to supply a major percentage of the heating load. The use of more efficient collectors can reduce the total collector area required, but it may be more expensive to do so, at least until higher-performance collectors are commercially produced.

And because the collectors must be located on a building within certain tilt and orientation angles, there are restrictions on other design choices—such as for windows, balconies and greenhouses that also ideally would face the sun.

The problem whether solar collectors limit the house design can be approached by reversing the question: In what ways do the requirements of house design—its appearance, its function and its construction—impose practical limits on the solar collector area?

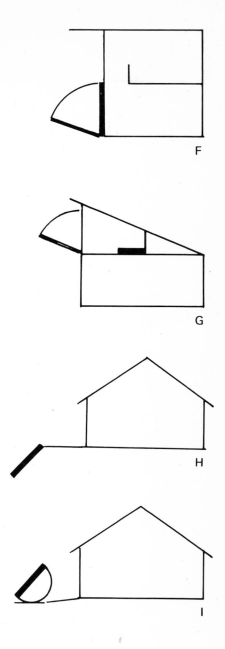

139

The question is important for several reasons. If the solar collector area required is too large to be attractive or practical, then the number of houses that can be built with (or converted to) solar heating will be extremely limited. In turn, the large market for solar heating needed to reduce manufacturing costs will not develop—at least not in housing.

In northern climates, with low-to-medium efficiencies typical of site-fabricated collectors, a collector area equal to 50 percent of the heated floor space or more is required to obtain any sizeable portion of solar heating. And yet, at present, site-fabricated collectors are the most economical to install, especially for owner-builders. More efficient collectors are factory-produced, but thus incur additional transportation, distribution and sales costs.

Thus the question: What **are** the limits of collector area **above which** their use on standard houses becomes impractical?

The following study is shown here to illustrate what percentage of solar collector might reasonably be incorporated into a house design.

A generally efficient house plan was selected, with a roof shape that could be used for solar collectors, and with plan choices for window, balconies and other design features on the south side. To focus the question, the following assumptions were made:

1. The length-to-width ratio is held to 1.5 to 1 because of heat loss considerations.

2. Design standards and dimensions of conventional house construction are assumed.

3. Flat-plate collectors (either liquid or air) of the types currently available are used.

4. The collectors are fixed in position at optimum angles for winter space heat in northern climates. (Although the house designs illustrated below show the roof slope with the collectors at a 60-degree tilt angle, a 10- to 15-degree variation would not alter the basic configurations.)

5. The first floor of the south-facing facade is left free of collectors for windows, doors, patios and greenhouse options.

Within these limits, options for locating the collectors are reduced to four alternatives (Figure 6.7).

Section A has the greatest portion of south roof covered with collectors. The roof which projects higher than in most conventional houses, could be used either as a clerestory monitor or as a closed attic space. There are no south-facing windows at the second floor. In this alternative, the collector area could equal up to 60 percent of the heated floor space contained in the house.

Section B eliminates the lowest of the three rows of collectors and thus makes the second floor wall available for windows and balconies, while retaining the raised roof profile. The collector-to-floor area ratio is 40 percent.

Section C has the same collector area as Section B, but with the projected roof profile eliminated, of-

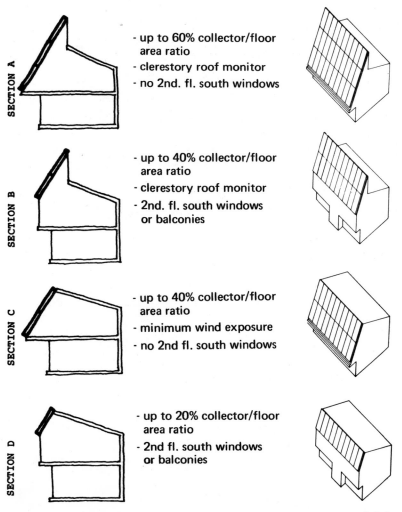

SECTION A
- up to 60% collector/floor area ratio
- clerestory roof monitor
- no 2nd. fl. south windows

SECTION B
- up to 40% collector/floor area ratio
- clerestory roof monitor
- 2nd. fl. south windows or balconies

SECTION C
- up to 40% collector/floor area ratio
- minimum wind exposure
- no 2nd fl. south windows

SECTION D
- up to 20% collector/floor area ratio
- 2nd fl. south windows or balconies

Figure 6.7. *Four section alternatives for solar collectors on a house used in the design study.*

141

fering the advantage of less building area exposed to wind and a more efficient ratio of envelope-to-enclosed space—but, like Section A, the second floor's south wall options are eliminated.

Section D has the least collector area—20 percent of the heated floor space, and while this plan holds few architectural constraints, the collector efficiency has to be nearly double that of those now typically available, to provide a major portion of northern heat requirements.

To see what variety of design can be achieved within the four sections illustrated in Figure 6.7, let us assume that any three of the sections could be combined in one house. Combining four sections in any one of three plan locations results in 40 unique alternatives, as shown in Figure 6.8.

The left half of Figure 6.8 shows the alternatives where the ratios of collector areas to heated floor-space is between 60 percent (one choice on the left)

Figure 6.8. *Solar House Design Study combining four sections and plan alternatives.*

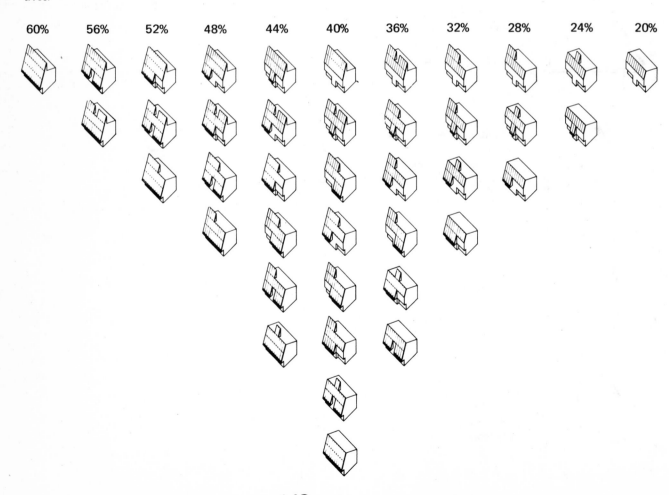

| 60% | 56% | 52% | 48% | 44% | 40% | 36% | 32% | 28% | 24% | 20% |

and 40 percent (eight alternatives in the middle column).

Although this study simplifies many features that make houses different from one another, it also illustrates that only below coverage ratios of 44 percent is there an adequate number of design alternatives to meet various site, climate and row-house requirements. In the example, there are 20 alternatives in the 36 to 44 percent coverage range, but only 10 alternatives in the 44 to 60 percent coverage range.

This study helps to make the point that the more efficient the collector, the greater the range of design choices that are possible—including south-facing windows and greenhouses. They themselves serve as heat traps, while providing natural lighting, ventilation and visibility, no matter what the climate (Figure 6.9). In any solar house design, the south-facing portion of a building thus is a "prime zone," to be used to maximum benefit for both passive and active solar-heat collectors.

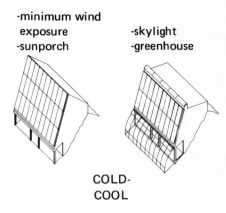

Figure 6.9. *Solar House Design Study: Alternatives.*

-minimum wind exposure
-sunporch
-skylight
-greenhouse

COLD-COOL

-roof monitor
-greenhouse
-outdoor court
-sundeck

COOL-TEMPERATE

-roof monitors
-outdoor courts
-balconies
-outdoor courts

TEMPERATE-WARM/HUMID

CHAPTER 7

SOLAR HOUSE DESIGN IN NORTHERN CLIMATES

The decision to choose solar heating today is one made for the future—in purely economic terms, to save fuel costs; in environmental terms, to conserve limited resources. The economic argument for solar heating is based upon the assumption that fuel costs will continue to rise, as they have in recent years, well above general inflation. From the economic point of view, the investment in solar heating is justified if it pays back the added solar installation cost by fuel cost savings within a reasonable period. From an environmental point of view alone, solar heating is justified because it reduces our dependence on non-renewable polluting fossil fuels.

From an environmental point of view, the best solar-heating installation is therefore the one that saves the most non-renewable energy—in short, the one with the largest solar-heating capacity. However, in economic terms, the best solar installation is the one which offers the highest return on the investment in solar-heating equipment—given current costs of installation, conventional fuel and construction financing.

As we shall see in this chapter, the solar approach most justified in economic terms varies according to climate, local fuel costs and the accuracy of assumptions made about eventual fuel cost rises.

Fuel cost escalation is critical in deciding which solar approach is best for a given climate, but at the same time it involves the most uncertainty. While fuel costs are certain to escalate, the rate of escalation is subject to unpredictable economic and political factors. There is a greater certainty about the future availability of sunshine as an energy source for house heating than any of the conventional fuels or of atomic power.

In choosing between different approaches to solar heating on the basis of current costs, solar alternatives which have a small initial installation cost may be more justified than the larger capacity systems. Various alternatives—from domestic water heating, window heat recovery, auxiliary solar heating, and medium-to-large capacity solar heating—are compared in this chapter in terms of their relative economic merit as affected by different factors of climate and fuel cost escalation. In making judgments about the economic merit of solar heating, however, it should be kept in mind that many assumptions are involved so that the conclusions should not be taken as either absolute or precise.

First, calculation methods of the heating energy required by a house and the potential heat contribution of solar equipment give approximate results only. Actual use of a house and a homeowner's own lifestyle can account for wide differences from the calculated heat requirement. And, while solar equipment manufacturers supply data about the performance of their products, test conditions may differ from actual use conditions.

Second, costs of solar installations vary according to local construction rates, the equipment used and the amount and type of financing available. For example, a self-help builder who can contribute his own labor for a solar installation saves not only on construction labor, but contractor's overhead percentages and the resulting finance charges as well. In addition, a variety of tax incentives currently being considered by many state legislatures will make solar heating more economically attractive.

Third, the cost of fuel varies widely in different areas throughout the United States, depending on local availability or price controls. And as mentioned, the rate of fuel cost escalation remains one of the most critical yet uncertain assumptions made in determining the comparative economic merit of different solar heating approaches.

145

To overcome these limitations, the comparisons reported here apply the same assumptions to all the solar heating approaches.

7.1 Six Solar Heating Alternatives

Six solar heating alternatives described in this section are compared with one another in terms of performance and cost, as installed on a 1200-square-foot three-bedroom house, which is based upon the ecodesign techniques and solar heating requirements discussed in the previous chapter (Figure 7.1).

Reducing the heating energy required makes sense in terms of energy saved per dollar invested, but the total amount of solar heat used by a well-insulated solar house is less than an identical but poorly insulated one. Thus, if solar heating installation costs and fuel savings are compared independent of insulation costs, the higher the heating energy requirement of the house, the better the cost payback of the solar installation will appear (Figure 7.2). However, the **combined** investment in both improved insulation and solar heat equipment is superior to solar heating alone. From an economic point of view, a homeowner therefore would invest **first** in practical ways to reduce the

Figure 7.1. *Basic Solar House Plan used in calculation in this chapter. The design combines the many ecodesign features discussed in the previous chapter.*

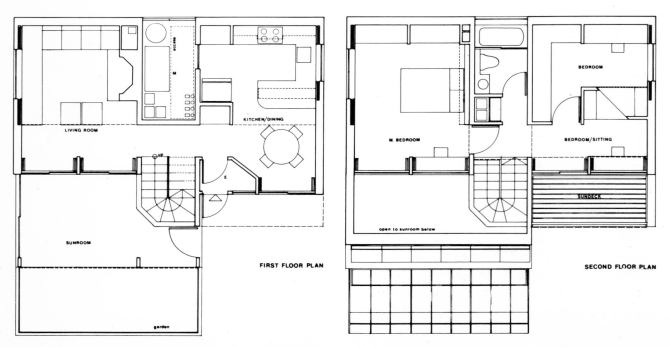

LIVING ROOM

KITCHEN/DINING

SUNROOM

garden

FIRST FLOOR PLAN

BEDROOM

M. BEDROOM

BEDROOM/SITTING

SUNDECK

open to sunroom below

SECOND FLOOR PLAN

heat loss of the house, thereby lowering the total amount of heating energy needed, and he **then** would compare various solar alternatives. For this reason, higher-than-average insulation standards are applied to the example house design used in this chapter, and they would be achieved by the following techniques:

Insulating controls for windows. The greatest amount of heat loss in standard house construction is through windows, which, even if double-glazed, lose five times as much heat as a well-insulated wall. Therefore, the first step to reduce heat loss is to use insulating shades or panels, as described in Section 3.1.

Increased wall and roof insulation. To improve wall and roof insulation is a second effective means of reducing heat loss in typical construction. One of the simplest ways to accomplish this within conventional practices is to use 2 x 6-inch studs for the exterior walls, instead of the typical 2 x 4s, and increase the wall insulation to 5½ inches in thickness. This, together with additional ceiling and roof insulation, adds to the construction cost, but in northern climates the expenditure is easily repaid in fuel savings within a very few years.

Reduced air infiltration losses. Once insulation standards have been improved, the greatest remaining source of heat loss is infiltration of outside air from opening doors, from cracks around windows, and through the wall construction itself. To reduce infiltration losses, air locks at outside doors, internal zoning, and other wind buffers are, as shown, incorporated into the house plan.

Compact planning. A compact double-storied plan, that can be subdivided into separate temperature zones and that provides air locks at entryways, can reduce the energy requirement significantly in northern climates. In addition, the fireplace also can be used in conjunction with many solar heating alternatives and should be located on an interior wall near the center of the house.

Model of Basic Solar House *with south side, available for various solar collector alternates, including collectors, windows, greenhouse and sun deck.*

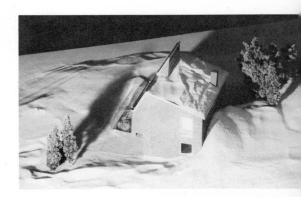

Model of Basic Solar House *with northwest protected by trees and roof designed to retain snow build-up.*

147

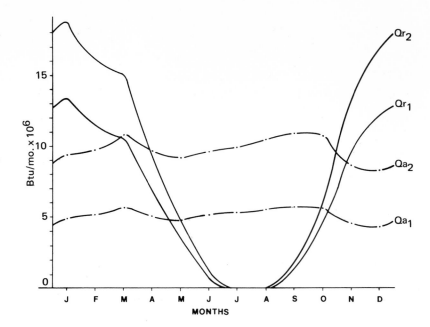

Figure 7.2. *The monthly heat demand of the example house for Denver, assuming conventional insulation (Qr₂) or high insulation standards (Qr₁). The comparative solar heat contribution is shown for 20% collector/floor area (Qa₁) or for 40% collector/floor area ratios (Qa₂). If solar heating is compared in terms of energy savings between the two insulation standards, solar heating would supply a greater amount of heat in the case with less insulation (Qr₂−Qr₁ below the Qa lines). But the total heat demand not supplied by solar is greater (Qr₂−Qr₁ above the Qa lines).*

Compact planning results in a more economical space enclosure compared to house plans with a larger amount of outside walls or roof area.

The combination of these ecodesign planning and construction techniques has the effect of reducing the total heating energy requirement by about 40 percent when compared to standard house construction. In a well-insulated house, the size of the heating system can be smaller than that required in a conventional house, thus reducing heating equipment costs to offset the cost of increased insulation. Lower temperatures from heat storage can also be used effectively if cold drafts are eliminated from such sources as basement floors, windows and entryways. And, by organizing the house plan into zones, only part of the house needs to be fully heated at one time—another saving in the total fuel requirement.

The house plan used in the example therefore is one that is energy-efficient in its planning and design. It has a major portion of its windows facing south. Heat from the sunroom can be allowed to flow into the house interior simply by opening interior door and windows. The same plan is easily adapted to any one of the six solar heating alternatives that we are comparing.

148

ALTERNATIVE A: SOLAR DOMESTIC WATER HEATING

A major portion of the year-round requirement for domestic water heating can be supplied by a small solar collector area (three collectors in the example calculation, for a total of 56 square feet of collector area). Solar domestic hot water equipment, now available from many manufacturers throughout the United States, imposes few if any restrictions on the building design.

The installation costs in the example, based upon current costs of good-quality solar equipment, are $900 above the cost of a conventional domestic hot water heater.

ALTERNATIVE B: WINDOW HEAT RECOVERY

The heat gain from solar-oriented windows, sunrooms, greenhouses and/or upper portions of the house has the effect of overheating the sunny side of a building while the colder side still calls for heat. However, direct window heat can be recovered and more evenly utilized by an air circulation system that removes the heated air and passes it through low-temperature rock storage, in effect cooling the house when overheated during sunny winter days and storing the heat for nighttime carry-over. Installation costs of windows can be considered part of the normal house construction and the rock storage unit can be built within typical foundations. The window heat recovery system in the example house is planned around the sun room/greenhouse which can gain solar heat without overheating the residence itself.

The installation costs used in the calculations that follow were estimated at $1200, and include an insulated rock-type heat storage unit within the sunroom foundation, a fan, dampers and controls, and some additional duct work.

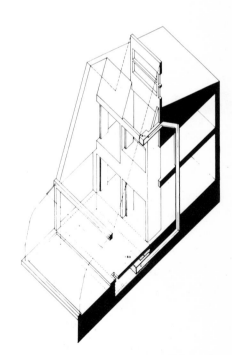

Greenhouse Heat Recovery System *returns warm air at top of sunroom to rock storage below.*

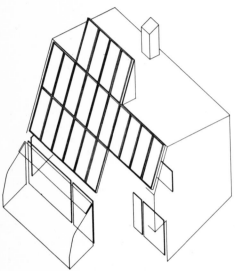

Basic Solar House, *showing various sub-systems of large-capacity solar space heating.*

Solar collector subsystems

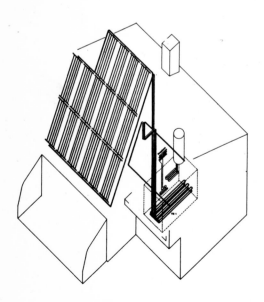

Collector to storage transport systems

ALTERNATIVE C:
AUXILIARY SOLAR HEATING

Auxiliary solar heating, like window-heat recovery, involves only a small added investment to achieve partial solar heating. As described previously in Section 5.1.5, auxiliary solar heating uses the same components as a solar domestic water installation, (Alternative A, above), adding only a few more solar panels to increase collection area (in the example, to 93 square feet) and a heating coil to pipe excess heat when available into the conventional space-heating system. Other than a slightly increased domestic hot water storage size, no long-term heat storage is involved, so that the installed cost and construction requirements are small. The control sequence used, whether to first supply domestic hot water with the excess to space heating, or the reverse, depends on engineering decisions related to climate and comparative fuel cost. In the calculations below, the first control sequence was chosen because the assumed electric fuel rate for the domestic hot water energy results in a higher unit cost for heat delivered than the oil fuel rate used for the space heating in the calculations.

The estimated installation cost for such an auxiliary system, including a domestic hot water heating capability, is the domestic hot water installation cost ($900), plus an additional $1100—which includes two more collectors, the auxiliary coil and a circulator with controls—for a total of $2000.

ALTERNATIVE D: AUXILIARY SOLAR HEATING
AND WINDOW HEAT RECOVERY

This option combines Alternatives B and C, to include domestic water heating, auxiliary space heating and a house heat recovery system. If a window-heat recovery system did not have the rock-type heat storage component, then to combine it with the auxiliary space heating system would be redundant—for both would provide space heating on sunny days only. However, with heat storage, the day-time heat recovered from the house can be carried over into nighttime hours, in effect permitting a better utilization of the heat gained both from the windows and from solar collectors.

The estimated installation cost thus is a combination of Alternates B and C, or $3200.

ALTERNATIVE E: SOLAR SPACE HEATING
WITH A RELATIVELY SMALL COLLECTOR AREA

In this option, the collector area (223 square feet) is held to less than 20 percent of the heated floor area, and, as shown in Figure 6.8, imposes little constraint on architectural design. The solar heat storage unit used in Alternate B is heated to a higher temperature from the increased collector area to achieve longer carryover. In the example calculations, the installed cost estimate of $5800 for this system over and above the cost of a conventional heating system includes Alternates A and B above, and the additional collectors and controls.

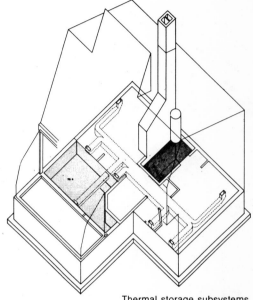

Thermal storage subsystems

ALTERNATIVE F: LARGE-CAPACITY SOLAR
SPACE HEATING

This option is the same as Alternative E, but with more collectors (36 percent of the heated floor area, or 427 square feet). Of the solar alternatives compared in the example, this option requires the largest construction cost but also contributes the largest percentage of solar heating.

The installation cost includes the same items as Alternative E, with the added cost for 204 square feet more collector area, or $8500 in all.

While cost reductions in solar installations are eagerly awaited, these are not included in the above estimates. The performance and cost of the solar equipment in the installation costs used in the economic comparison that follows represent "state-of-the-art" estimates, based on current technology.

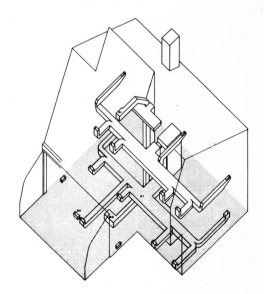

Storage to room distribution subsystems

151

The costs are relatively high compared to some claimed by other sources, but the solar system performance-efficiency assumed in the calculations also represents high quality solar equipment.

7.2
The Six Alternatives in Four Climates

An Economic Comparison

In this section, the relative economic merits of the six solar heating alternatives are compared in four northern locations, based on fuel savings as affected by different rates of fuel escalation.

To compare these variables, the same house plan is used in all the calculations, with construction costs and current fuel costs assumed to be equal in all four locations (even though in reality these factors vary considerably). The calculation methods are detailed in Appendix II.

Although, as mentioned, the house example has a smaller heating energy requirement than standard house construction, the energy saving due to high insulation standards is omitted from the economic comparison because the purpose here is to show the relative merit of the different solar alternatives **after** everything had been done to reduce fuel requirements by practical design techniques.

The six alternatives are compared in four cities representative of northern climates in the United States: Pittsburgh, Denver, Hartford, and Williston, North Dakota. Pittsburgh and Denver both are near the 40° north latitude, but have quite distinct winter sunshine characteristics due to differences in cloudiness, sky clearness and altitude. Williston, North Dakota, while farther north and with a much greater heating energy requirement than Pittsburgh or Denver, benefits from excellent winter sunshine which, as will be seen from the calculations, makes it as viable a location for solar heating as Denver. Hartford is included as a typical New England location, with a relatively high heating energy requirement, and with only moderate winter sunshine availability.

Figure 7.3 lists the heating load calculations of the example house in the four locations. Figure 7.4 summarizes the system variables used in calculating the performance of the six different

152

Location	Lat	Elev	t_0	DD	DHL	DHW	HTG	TOT
						Qr 10^6 Btu		
Hartford, CT	42	15	5	6235	35	13	83	96
Pittsburgh, PA	40	749	11	5053	33	13	67	81
Williston, ND	48	1877	-17	9243	47	14	123	138
Denver, CO	40	5283	3	5524	36	13	74	87

Figure 7.3. *Climate Design Variables used in the calculations.*

| | Domestic Hot Water | | | Space Heating | | | Installed | |
	CA	tank size	AUX	WA	CA	STO	Cost $	$/mo.
○ ALTERNATE A domestic hot water A	56	60					$900	$8
ALTERNATE B window heat recovery B				300		X	1200	10
ALTERNATE C auxiliary solar space C heat	93	80	X				2000	17
△ ALTERNATE D combined alternates D B and C	93	80	X	300		X	3200	28
ALTERNATE E large capacity solar E 20% CA/FA	56	60		150	223	X	5800	50
□ ALTERNATE F large capacity solar F 40% CA/FA	56	60		150	427	X	8500	74

solar approaches, together with installation costs shown as the added "solar premium" over and above conventional heating system costs. The "cost per month" shows the monthly mortgage payment on the added investment required for the solar installation, financed at 8½ percent for 20 years.

Figure 7.5 shows the six alternatives compared in terms of average monthly payback in fuel savings in the four climates, assuming fuel cost escalation rates from 0, 8, 12 and 16 percent. The average monthly payback shown is the total fuel saving over 20 years prorated monthly, after the finance charge is deducted.

Here, the negative numbers in the 0 percent fuel escalation rate column show that for the example taken, if conventional fuel costs do not increase, the solar investment in some cases does not pay back within the 20-year mortgage period. However, a projection of 8 to 10 percent fuel escalation repre-

Figure 7.4. *System Design Variables, where CA = net effective collector area; WA = net effective south window area; installed cost = incremental cost differential of solar installation minus conventional system cost; and $/mo = additional monthly mortgage payment for solar premium at finance charge of 8½% for 20 years.*

	Hartford					Pittsburgh					Williston					Denver				
	% sol	\% fuel increase				% sol	\% fuel increase				% sol	\% fuel increase				% sol	\% fuel increase			
		0	8	12	16		0	8	12	16		0	8	12	16		0	8	12	16
○ ALTERNATE A domestic hot water	11	4	21	40	72	11	3	19	36	65	8	5	25	46	81	15	7	29	52	92
ALTERNATE B window heat recovery	24	-2	10	23	45	21	-4	5	15	31	22	1	16	33	62	36	1	18	35	65
ALTERNATE C auxiliary solar space heating	18	-1	24	50	94	17	-3	17	38	75	14	1	27	55	103	25	1	28	57	106
△ ALTERNATE D combined alternates B and C	40	-4	31	69	134	37	-8	21	53	106	34	-1	40	83	156	58	1	43	88	164
ALTERNATE E large capacity solar 20% CA/FA	51	-24	15	57	127	44	-30	0	32	86	42	-20	24	71	151	74	-17	32	84	172
□ ALTERNATE F large capacity solar 40% CA/FA	70	-41	6	58	145	60	-49	-13	27	93	57	-37	18	76	176	95	-34	24	87	194

Figure 7.5. *Six Alternatives to Solar Heating: Average monthly payback over twenty years based on well-insulated 1200 SF house with various annual fuel cost increase projections. Monthly payback shown is net gain (or loss) after finance charge is deducted, at rate of 8½% for twenty years. No credit is taken for savings due to added insulation. Domestic Water Heating compared to electric heating at 4.5¢/kWh. Space Heating compared to oil heating at 42¢/gallon.*

sents the consensus of both private and government forecasts.

In comparing the payback results, it can be readily seen that the order of economic merit of the six alternatives does not reflect their relative initial cost. The relative merit of the alternatives also varies according to climate and assumed fuel cost escalation. The large-capacity solar heating, **Alternative F,** is among the poorest of the six choices in economic terms **if fuel costs do not increase,** even though it may rank highest in "environmental merit" by greatly reducing the reliance on non-renewable and polluting fuels.

One result shown in Figure 7.5 is surprising but telling: Alternatives A, B, and C—which individually rank low with fuel-cost increases above 8 percent—become in combination as **Alternative D** economically the most justified option in all of the climate locations considered.

These results, in graphic form in Figure 7.6, show the approximate crossover points of economic merit of various alternatives as a function of changing fuel escalation rates. For example, in Denver **Alternative D** is the best choice of all the alter-

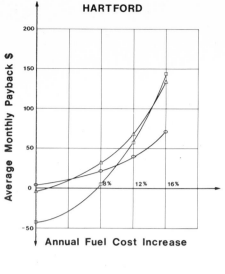

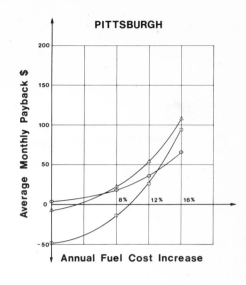

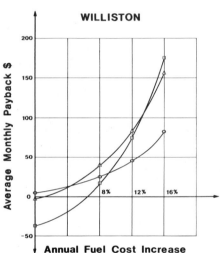

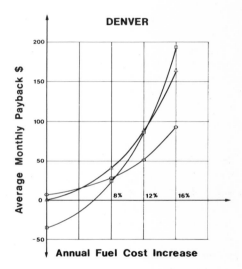

natives if the fuel cost increase is between 5 to 12 percent per annum. In Hartford, it is the best choice at fuel cost increases between 5 and 14 percent.

What this shows in effect is that if partial solar heating can be achieved by the Alternative D installation cost of $3200—say between 34 percent (Williston) to 58 percent (Denver)—then any added investment for increased solar heating capacity will be economically justified only if the annual fuel cost rise is above 12 percent. Otherwise the added investment would have diminished returns. This is shown in Figure 7.7, which, **based on the assumptions made in the example,** shows the monthly payback relative to the percent of solar capacity.

Figure 7.6. *Average monthly payback of three solar heating alternatives as a function of the rate of annual fuel cost rise.* ○ = *System A,* △ = *System D,* □ = *System F.*

155

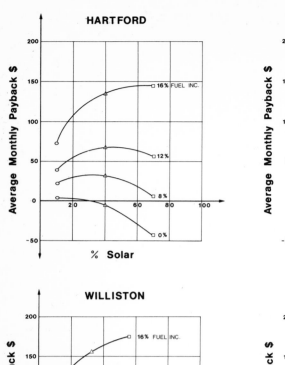

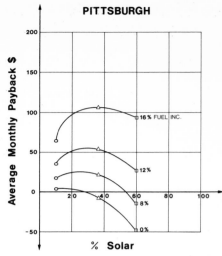

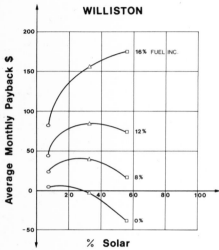

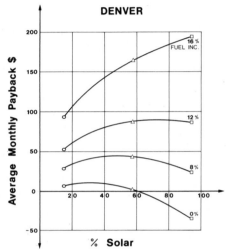

Figure 7.7. *Average monthly payback of three solar heating alternatives as a function of the percentage of the total heat requirement supplied by the solar installation.* ○ = *System A,* △ = *System D,* □ = *System F.*

INTERPRETING THE RESULTS OF THE EXAMPLE CALCULATION

The calculations are based upon the heating energy requirement of a house of the size and type shown in Figure 7.1, which is energy-efficient in its design and construction. By excluding the fuel savings achieved through ecodesign features, including high insulation standards, the monthly payback due to the solar installations appears to be less than if compared to a house built to conventional insulation standards.

The economic calculations assume the solar installation costs indicated, as well as specific fuel costs and mortgage rates. The solar design calculation methods given in Appendix II enable the

156

mathematically inclined reader to make estimates based on other climate and cost assumptions.

All of these assumptions were made to represent the typical case for solar heating alternatives. Variations from these assumptions would, of course, give different results. Actually, as we have seen in this chapter, solar equipment is only part of the added investment to make a house energy-efficient. It gives the best total result when combined with an ecodesign approach to basic design and construction. Thus, to properly evaluate the total added investment, one could add the energy savings achieved from energy-efficient design and planning, most of which can be achieved with little added construction cost, as represented in Figure 7.8. If these fuel savings were combined in the economic analysis and compared with the conventional house plan, the total payback of the investment would be greatly increased. However, the real purpose of the limited comparison made in this chapter is to illustrate the economic merit of various approaches to solar heating relative to one another.

Installation and financing costs vary with individual circumstances. Improvements in solar

Figure 7.8. *Added construction costs (representative) to reduce heating and cooling requirements of a house (approximately 30-40% reduction): (1) Where air conditioning is required. (2) Cost combined with feature No. 2. (3) Insulation in addition to typical insulation standards. (Source: Fitch Creations)*

Feature	Cost (Additional)
1. Heat pumps for heating and cooling[1]	$300
2. Exterior walls clad with polystyrene foam sheathing	250
3. R-11 (3½-inch) sidewall insulation	
4. Perimeter insulation around concrete floors[2]	
5. Four-inch batt insulation at crawl space floors	40
6. Eight-inch blown ceiling insulation[3]	40
7. All windows double-glazed	100
8. Thermal break aluminum windows with storm sash	200
9. Caulking around all window and door frames	20
10. Insulated (solid core) front door, fully weatherstripped	
11. Wood storm/screen door combination at front entrance	
12. Sliding glass door (to deck) has tempered, insulated glass	50

Feature	Cost (Additional)
13. Skylights are double-domed	40
14. Hot water heater thermostat set at 120°	
15. Caulk sill between floor system and wall panels	
16. Insulated attic access door	5
17. Wind-powered attic ventilating turbine	50
18. Ceiling-mounted bathroom heaters	50
19. Removable metal covers for fireplace openings	5
20. Rough-in holes for plumbing and wiring caulked and insulated	10
21. Pipes and ducts are insulated	
22. Interiors painted off-white (improved lighting)	
23. Automatic flow control shower heads	1
24. Water-saving toilets	
Total	$1161

Figure 7.9. *Solar house with auxiliary solar heating and window heat recovery.*

Figure 7.10. *Solar House with large capacity solar heating. Jespa Enterprises, Old Bridge, NJ, 1976.*

equipment design or cost reductions due to government subsidies will make large-capacity solar heating more attractive economically. Other ways in which the installation cost of large-capacity solar heating might be lowered—including "do-it-yourself" construction—are discussed in the next chapter.

Although these limitations should be kept in mind, the calculations do show that in the almost certain event that fuel costs increase, some sort of solar energy for house heating **is economically justified in any northern climate.** Domestic water heating and auxiliary space heating are economically attractive even if fuel-cost rises are limited to 4 and 8 percent per year. Larger capacity installations will become justified if equipment costs are lowered if the rate of financing a solar installation is reduced (such as in a low-interest loan program) or if fuel costs increase above 10 percent per year—which many energy specialists take to be a real prospect.

In any event, no matter what the fuel cost escalation rate may be, a middle-range solution presents itself: an **incremental approach** to solar design in which a house is built with only partial or auxiliary solar installation (Alternates A through D) at first, but with space left to add a large-capacity system in the future (Alternates E and F) as the economic variables change in favor of increased solar heating.

In this way, the plans can be based on a justified economic investment (according to one's own circumstances) and aimed towards a house that is environmentally sound as well.

CHAPTER 8

BUILDING A SOLAR HOUSE

Building a solar house is no ordinary enterprise, but most often is an effort to fulfill life-long hopes to create a home that is both economically and environmentally sound. At any point along the way—in choosing a building site, in developing a design, in selecting a builder and in obtaining financing—there are pitfalls that can quickly dim these hopes.

While such pitfalls accompany any house construction project, careful planning is even more important in solar house building, where construction techniques and solar equipment may be new and unfamiliar to local builders, thus resulting in costs higher than in conventionally heated houses. Because of this, several points should be followed carefully in planning a solar house project:

1. Allow sufficient time. It takes time to find a site, to develop a house plan, to obtain financing and building permits, and to select a builder. Building a solar house may take longer than conventional building if the construction materials and the solar equipment are not standard items. Time should be allowed to locate the best materials and to obtain competitive prices for them and for labor. Time-scheduling is particularly important for owner-builders who are able to work on their house only evening and weekend hours and who are not completely familiar with all aspects of the construction they are undertaking.

2. Obtain complete budget estimates. Because a solar house project involves added costs for building materials and equipment, the budgeting of one's investment in construction should be carefully anticipated. Experienced home builders normally provide cost estimates for all work that is shown on the plans. These costs can be itemized for various solar alternatives that the owner wishes to consider, so that adequate financing can be secured before construction is begun.

3. Properly site the building. Siting a building is the first and often the most important decision in construction. The place of a building on the land can, in itself, achieve fuel savings by gaining exposure to winter sun or to summer breezes. Factors related to selecting a building site for a solar house are detailed below in Section 8.1.

4. Develop an appropriate solar house design. Whether one uses pre-engineered plans or a custom design for a house, it should be suited to local climate requirements and construction methods. The approach to solar heating that is best for a particular homeowner also will depend upon the appearance and type of house desired, as well as on the amount of financing available for construction. How these factors may lead to an appropriate choice of solar heating method is summarized below in Section 8.2.

5. Select appropriate construction methods. Construction methods will greatly influence the project's cost. Self-help or owner-built construction is one of the most common ways to reduce building costs, and some solar heating systems can be installed by owner-builders.

Factory-produced solar equipment, while generally more costly than owner-fabricated solar units, may be justified on the basis of their higher performance and durability, and the manufacturers may themselves provide recommended installation details and instructions.

Whatever the construction method, however, the solar installation must be carefully coordinated with the house construction process, as discussed below in Section 8.2.

160

Building development transforms the natural setting of the landscape. A building can do so in a positive manner, contributing to the support of vegetation, water and wildlife habitat. The building itself can be relieved of its energy demands by the natural protection against wind and sun that is available from nearby trees and land forms.

Just as there are examples of ignorant and abusive land development, conservation planning in many cases has created and preserved areas that otherwise would not naturally survive. This has been achieved by reforestation, soil replenishment, irrigation, flood control, shelterbelts and windbreaks, and erosion control.

8.1
Site Planning

Ecodesign site Planning Objectives.
(Source: Solar Dwelling Design Concepts, U.S. Department H.U.D., 1976)

OBJECTIVES:	COOL	TEMPERATE	HOT ARID	HOT HUMID
	Maximize warming effects of solar radiation. Reduce impact of winter wind. Avoid local climatic cold pockets.	*Maximize warming effects of sun in winter. Provide shade in summer. Reduce impact of winter wind but allow air circulation in summer.*	*Maximize shade late morning and all afternoon. Maximize humidity. Provide air movement in summer.*	*Maximize shade. Maximize air movement.*
Position on slope	Low for wind shelter	Middle-upper for solar radiation exposure	Low for cool air flow	High for wind
Orientation on slope	South to Southeast	South to Southeast	East-southeast for P.M. shade	South
Relation to water	Near large body of water	Close to water, but avoid coastal fog	On lee side of water	Near any water
Preferred winds	Sheltered from North and West	Avoid continental cold winds	Exposed to prevailing winds	Exposed to prevailing winds
Clustering	Around sun pockets	Around a common, sunny terrace	Along E-W axis, for shade & wind	Open to wind
Building Orientation*	South to Southeast	South to Southeast	South	South, toward prevailing wind
Tree forms*	Deciduous trees near bldg. Evergreens for windbreaks	Deciduous trees nearby on west. No evergreens near on south	Trees overhanging roof if possible	High canopy trees. Use deciduous trees near building
Road orientation	Crosswise to winter wind	Crosswise to winter wind	Narrow; E-W axis	Broad channel. E-W axis
Materials coloration	Medium to dark	Medium	Light on exposed surfaces; dark to avoid reflection	Light, especially for roof.

*Must be evaluated in terms of impact on solar system.

161

Traditional Block Island Houses *well situated in landscape, with porches oriented to summer breeze and windbreaks against average 30 mph winter wind.*

The natural cycles that exist in mutual dependence in the landscape are now the familiar topic of ecology, which is defined by H. T. Odum as the "biology of the environment." The land, its topography and vegetation, fulfills many functions in the cycle of nature: it cleans the air, it holds moisture, it creates zones for productive plants, insect and animal life. If natural land is disrupted by construction and is not restored, the ecological role it serves often is lost forever.

Just as a house by its setting in the landscape can symbolize our relation to nature, a house in a community can reinforce social values. By grouping houses, spaces can be created which strengthen the unique quality of a neighborhood.

While this opportunity is most obvious in the design of new housing neighborhoods, a house in an existing community should be designed to be in keeping with the surrounding buildings. This is particularly important in solar house design, since with the required solar collectors a building's style and size may appear out of scale with its surroundings and objectionable to the neighboring community.

The style of building that is traditional in a particular region can offer useful guidelines on how a house design can fit conditions of local climate, site and community. It may suggest how a solar house design can evolve out of traditional building styles. An example of how both the natural setting and traditional house styles of Block Island, Rhode Island established the basis of a passive solar house design there is shown in the accompanying illustrations.

The relation of climate to building design was discussed in Chapter 6; in this section the same climate factors—solar radiation, sunlight and

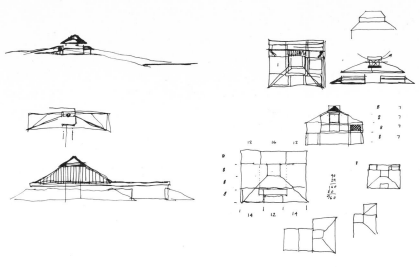
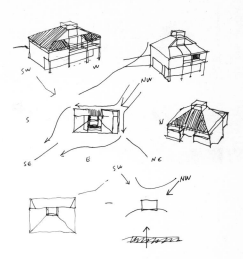

shading, wind and air flow, and precipitation and humidity—are reviewed in terms of site planning decisions.

8.1.1 SOLAR RADIATION

Solar energy is the source of heat gain, natural illumination, and bacteriological and humidity control.

By adjusting the building's siting, the potential heat gain in cool periods can be increased (by proper exposure to the sun), or the undesirable ef-

Passive Solar House, Block Island, RI. Design sketches, showing development of house design in landscape, with porches located to break prevailing northwest winter wind and to catch summer breeze from southwest. Separate loft zone above is for views of ocean, and natural light and ventilation and winter solar heat gain, ducted to basement masonry storage and house distribution system. Donald Watson, AIA, Architect.

View from northeast, direction of winter storm winds.

View from northwest, direction of prevailing winter winds.

View from west, direction from predominant view of inland lake on the site.

View from southwest, direction of prevailing summer breezes.

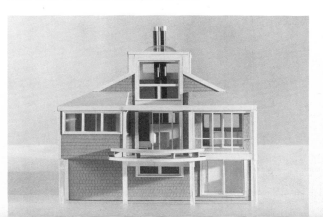

fects of heat gain in warm periods can be mitigated (by shading from surrounding trees). Therefore, the possible conditions for sunlight and shading should be considered as presented by surrounding topography, vegetation and buildings.

When planning a solar house, a careful check should be made of the December sun angles to determine whether windows or solar collectors would be shaded by nearby terrain, buildings, evergreens, fences and the like.

Deciduous trees to the east, south or west of a site may provide the perfect method of sun control, shading the building in summer and exposing it to winter sun when the leaves are down. However, a dense forest of trees south of the collectors may, during November, December and January, cast an undesirable shadow on the collector area. If the tree branches are fairly sparse, then their shading effect can be tolerated; otherwise the dense branches could be thinned. Obviously evergreen trees would cast a fairly dense shadow on the collector area—enough to make the solar heating impractical.

To work well, solar collectors should have a minimum of six hours per day of unobstructed sun-

Figure 8.1. *Magnetic Variation from True North. (1965 Coast and Geodetic Survey, U.S. Department of Commerce)*

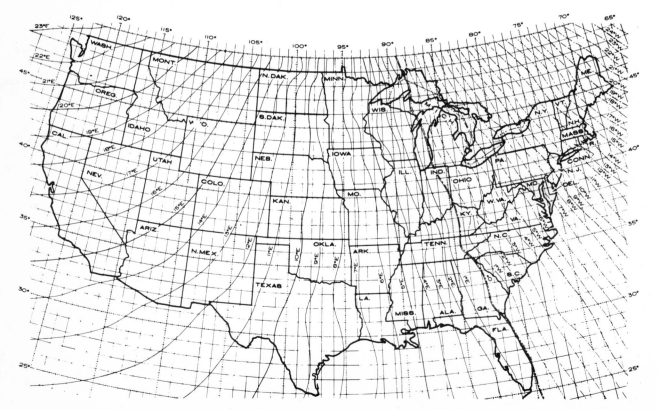

shine. If sun angles cannot be directly observed during the winter at the building site, they can be estimated by reference to Table II.5 in Appendix II. Snow melt patterns or spring blooming sequences also might provide clues to which parts of a site receive most favorable solar radiation.

The direction of south should be established for siting the solar collectors by reference to **true** north, rather than magnetic north (Figure 8.1). Precise compass variations or declinations can be obtained from local land surveyors. Since the magnetic pole shifts somewhat each year, only recent survey maps should be used.

Figure 8.2 shows an easy method of finding true south at a particular site. Siting the North Star on a clear night also is quite simple and is accurate within a few degrees. Local newspapers may list the time of solar noon (half-way between sunrise and sunset) for any given day. True south can therefore be determined by the shadow cast at solar noon.

The use of solar heating in city areas present uncertain prospect of shadows cast by taller buildings erected in the future nearby and to the south.

The only way this problem will be resolved is by zoning regulations with "sun rights," which might set a limit to the size of a building near existing solar installations. In some cities in California building ordinances have been established already to provide such safeguards.

8.1.2 WIND AND AIR-FLOW

Of all the climatic factors, the local winds are most affected by specific site features. Whether the design objective is to minimize wind resistance (as in exposed, northern locations) or to maximize breezes (as in hot-humid zones), analysis of winds at the site itself can be extremely helpful before settling on the building location.

Prevailing winds in the winter season are constant enough to justify providing wind protection in the house design and landscaping.

In the summer, prevailing breezes can establish the best position for porches and window openings for natural ventilation. In some regions, dust or rain

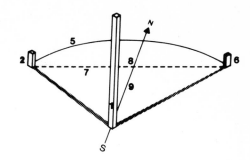

Figure 8.2. *Finding True North-South (after Vetruvius). Materials: five-foot-long wood staff, two small stakes, string, pointed stick.*

Procedure:

1. *Drive the five-foot-long staff into the ground in an open area.*
2. *In the morning, scratch a mark at the end of the staff's shadow and place a wooden stake at this point.*
3. *Tie a string loosely to the staff.*
4. *Stretch a string to this stake, and at this point, attach the string to a pointed stick.*
5. *Draw an arc on the ground with the pointed stick from this stake to the other side of the staff.*
6. *Place another stake where the late afternoon shadow touches the arc.*
7. *Draw a straight line between these two stakes.*
8. *Find the halfway point along this line, then draw a line from this point to the staff.*
9. *This meridian line indicates a true north-south line, with the staff being south.*

(Source: Bachert/Snooks, Outdoor Education Equipment, *Interstate Printers and Publishers)*

165

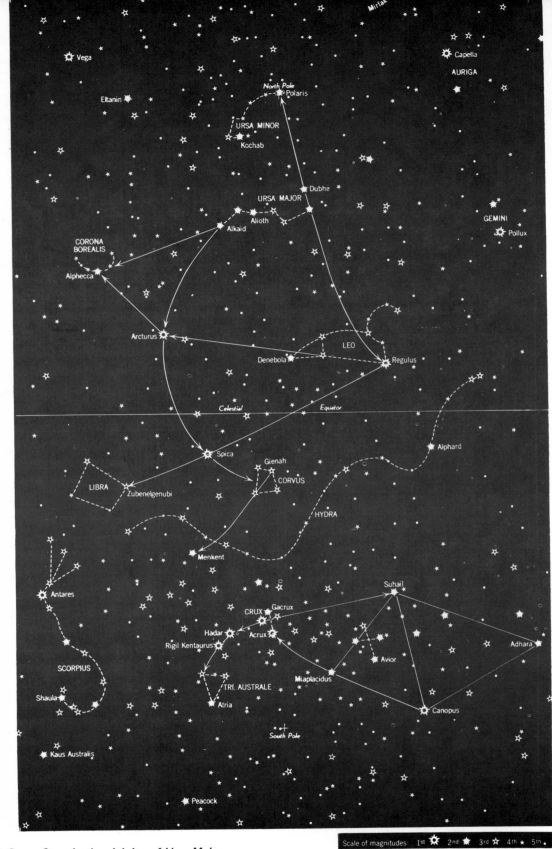

Finding the North Star. *Stars in the vicinity of Ursa Major (the big dipper). (U.S. Navy Hydrographic Office. Thanks to suggestion of W. A. Shurcliff)*

storms require special protection devices. The pattern of storm winds can often be determined at the site by evidence of "rain shadows"—differences in vegetation growth on the lee side of wind-protected landscape features.

Data on the prevailing winds, available from local airports or weather stations, may be sufficient for initial site planning and design considerations. The regional wind directions then can be confirmed at the site by informal analysis of wind patterns at various times of the year. Strong wind effects at potential building sites also may be deduced from natural evidence—such as wind damage on trees or land.

Studies of natural air-flow effects upon building sites, carried out by researchers at the Texas A & M Research Station, show various conditions by which adjacent vegetation can affect air flow through or around buildings (Figure 8.3).

8.1.3 PRECIPITATION AND HUMIDITY

Rain, snow and humidity patterns at the site should be analyzed to assure the protection of both building and site.

Evaporation of humidity in and around a building is desirable, and can be encouraged by air flow and sun exposure, both of which would be adversely affected by very dense foliage.

It is essential to analyze the impact of a building plan on local ground water conditions to maintain proper drainage or rainfall away from the building.

Windbreaks near a building can reduce its exposure to snow and rain. Snow build-up patterns typical of a given building site may be revealed by tree damage. Branches of evergreens may be faded or dried just above the average snowline, due to reflected solar radiation, or may be broken due to freeze and thaw action.

Solar collectors should be located so that they are not likely to be covered by drifting snow during heavy storms. If they are close to the ground, as on a fence or south wall, there is the chance that several feet of snow would cover the bottom of the collectors—a condition that may also occur with certain roof configurations. By allowing the free flow of

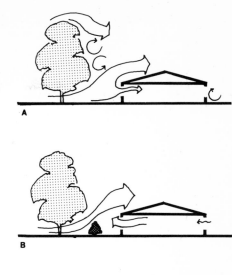

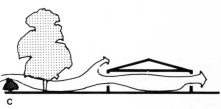

Figure 8.3. *Effect of Outside Wind Breaks, Trees and Hedges on Natural Ventilation. Large tree 20 feet from building creates Venturi effect (A) with only partial ventilation entering window due to upward air flow at building; (B) with negative pressure at window due to location of hedge nearby; (C) with full cross-ventilation created by placement of the hedge on the lee side of the large tree. (After R. White, Effects of Landscape Development on Natural Ventilation, Texas A & M University, 1954)*

167

Design of Windbreaks. *Wind velocity at instrument stations 16 inches above the ground in 15 mph wind blowing at right angles to three types of windbreaks: (1) A 16-foot high board fence of 33% density; (2) a dense belt of green ash, 290 feet wide; and (3) a thin, rather open cottonwood belt, 165 feet wide. The velocities are given in percentages of wind velocities in an open field nearby.* (After J. Stoeckeler, Yearbook of Agriculture, *1949)*

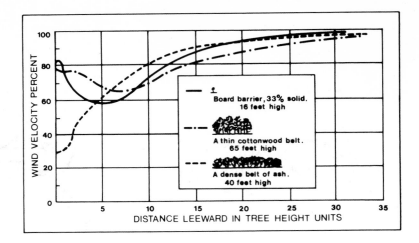

wind under the bottom of a collector, snow drifting and build-up can be reduced.

The **Site Planning Checklist,** below, reviews the items that should be considered in siting a solar house.

Site Planning Checklist

1. Determine local zoning or subdivision planning requirements. Building location may be limited by property line setback, site coverage and building height restrictions.

2. Determine property deed restrictions, covenants or subdivision design requirements. Review of architectural design may be required in planned residential developments.

3. Determine status of site in terms of future development and property values. Local or state zoning plans may indicate future development of area by roads, commercial development, flood zone or other ecological zoning districts, etc. Adjacent properties, although unbuilt at present, may be developed in future, affecting views and, if nearby, shading the building site.

4. Determine subsoil characteristics of site. Rock outcroppings or ledge may need special foundation construction. If in-ground sewage system is required, local and state codes must be followed in size and placement of the drainage field. (A successful soil percolation test should be a pre-condition of a building lot purchase.) If a well is required for water, local experience with well

168

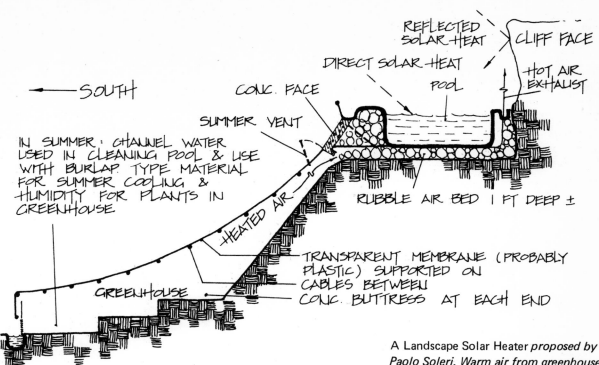

SOUTH →

REFLECTED SOLAR HEAT — CLIFF FACE

DIRECT SOLAR HEAT

CONC. FACE

POOL

HOT AIR EXHAUST

SUMMER VENT

IN SUMMER: CHANNEL WATER USED IN CLEANING POOL & USE WITH BURLAP TYPE MATERIAL FOR SUMMER COOLING & HUMIDITY FOR PLANTS IN GREENHOUSE

HEATED AIR

RUBBLE AIR BED 1 FT DEEP ±

GREENHOUSE

TRANSPARENT MEMBRANE (PROBABLY PLASTIC) SUPPORTED ON CABLES BETWEEN CONC. BUTTRESS AT EACH END

A Landscape Solar Heater *proposed by Paolo Soleri. Warm air from greenhouse created by transparent membrane is used to heat rock storage beneath swimming pool. (Solar-Oriented Archi-tecture, AIA Research Corporation and Arizona State University)*

depths should be sought. Well location must be placed upland and away from leaching field. The house construction itself must rest on sound, un-disturbed soil free of clay or silt. (If a soil sample mixed in a bottle of water does not settle after several hours, a high percentage of clay may be present in soil, requiring special foundation de-sign.)

5. Determine surface topography. A building site should be graded so that water will drain away from the building. Existing water courses should be maintained or corrected. Water drainage to adjacent property by new construction is prohib-ited by code in most locations. Swampy land or other low land may result in standing water and insect breeding part of the year. Steep building sites require special construction of foundations and access.

6. Determine access for electrical and water or sew-erage service as required.

7. Determine direction of true south and shading characteristics on building site from nearby trees and buildings.

Ecological Site Planning, *Sea Ranch, CA.*
Housing planned to fit particular site
conditions of sun and wind. Houses
located to protect and be protected by
existing land forms and established trees.
Behavior of wind over obstacles was
studied to determine most suitable
angle of roofs if housing were placed to

windward side of hedgerows and had to
provide its own protection. The houses
were subjected to wind-tunnel studies,
whose results influenced the final
designs. Sod roofs were added on some
of the structures. (Photos courtesy of
Esherick, Homsey, Dodge & Davis, Architects and Planners)

*Sunroom, with protected courtyard
behind fence.*

*Detail of fence with top to direct wind
away from protected courtyard.*

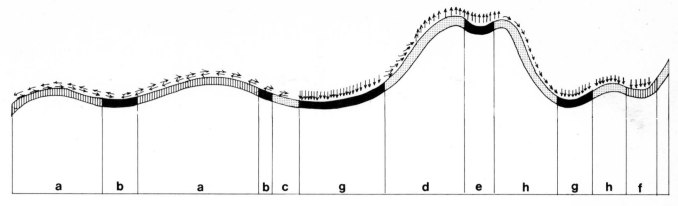

| a | b | a | b | c | g | d | e | h | g | h | f |

(a) Normal over moist soil
(b) Normal over wet soil
(c) Normal over dry soil
(d) Warmer over dry soil
(e) Warmer over wet soil
(f) Colder over moist soil
(g) Colder over wet soil
(h) Colder over dry soil

Effect of Local Topography and Vegetation on Microclimate. *(After Odum, Fundamentals of Ecology)*

8. Determine direction of local prevailing winds, as appropriate for winter wind protection devices and summer cooling designs.

9. Determine the aesthetic qualities of the landscape, views, vegetation and landform. Place the building so that it preserves the natural state of the best areas of a site, such as its hilltops or clearings.

8.2 Designing and Building

The choices involved in building a solar house can be made manageable when undertaken as a sequence of decisions, each of which will be discussed separately:

1. **Select a solar heating approach** that fits the local climate and your financial and home-ownership expectations.

2. **Consult with professionals** experienced in solar design and engineering.

3. **Develop a house plan** to fit your needs and the solar heating approach that you prefer.

4. **Select solar equipment** appropriate to the approach you have selected, based on cost, performance and operational requirements.

5. **Choose a construction method** that assures quality building, and a solar installation within a realistic budget and time schedule.

8.2.1 SELECTING A SOLAR HEATING APPROACH

This book has presented many approaches to solar heating—to help the reader understand the advantages and disadvantages of various alternatives.

These alternatives are summarized in the accompanying chart in terms of climate, house type, construction method and financing.

Summary: 1. Passive Systems: Solar Windows

CLIMATE

Hot Dry: Recommended for use with other passive systems; must be protected against summer sun to prevent overheating.

Hot Wet: Acceptable if summer ventilation fully operable; shading, insect screening and storm protection also required. Ventilating roof monitor recommended.

Temperate: Recommended for use with other passive and active systems; both undesired heat gain and heat loss must be considered. Greenhouses may be fully solar-heated.

Cool: Recommended for use with other active systems; insulation against nighttime heat loss required. Use of ventilating skylights may eliminate need for air conditioning.

HOUSE TYPE

Existing House: Add shading and insulating devices to improve suitability of windows; insulating draperies the best first investment in improving energy efficiency of existing houses.

Existing Apartment: Options may be limited to interior insulating shades and draperies. Skylights added to roofs for light, air and view can also be used for winter day heat.

New House (detached): East, south, and west windows can be used for winter heat gain; south windows preferred for ease of control against summer overheating.

New Apartments: Most windows should face south; balconies can be used for summer shading.

172

CONSTRUCTION METHOD

Owner-Built: Standard sizes of insulated glass can be purchased for installation in site-built frames (also with insulating systems such as Bead-wall). Otherwise use high quality, well-insulated windows with self-flashing mounting flanges.
Greenhouses can be purchased as kits or fabricated from re-used window sections if well installed to prevent air leakage around frames.

Built for Sale: Solar-oriented windows can usually be included in normal construction cost and sale price; conventional building plans can be improved in window orientation, internal zoning and heat flow without adding to construction cost.

Custom-Built: Views can be coordinated with solar windows. Internal zoning recommended to create green-house or sunrooms.

FINANCING METHOD

Short-Term Investment: Solar windows recommended because of low initial cost; interior temperature swings or insulating controls that require manual operation may not be acceptable to next buyer.

Long-Term Investment: Effective insulating panels or draperies recommended, even though more costly to install, for considerable long-term savings.

2. Passive Systems: Collector/Storage Building Elements

CLIMATE

Hot Dry: Recommended for near full-capacity heating and (with Skytherm -type systems) cooling.

Hot Wet: High thermal mass in structure not desirable in this climate.

Temperate: Thermal capacity desirable, with controls against overheating.

Cool: Thermal capacity necessary; insulation against heat loss required.

HOUSE TYPE

Existing House: Difficult to install in existing houses.

Existing Apartments: Difficult if not impossible to install.

| New House (detached): | Adequate wall and roof areas are available for effective arrangement of passive elements. |

| New Apartments: | Reduced wall and roof areas limit options; glass-covered masonry collector/storage walls well suited to multi-storied construction. |

CONSTRUCTION METHOD

| Owner-Built: | Several masonry block systems can be easily installed by self-helpers; Drumwalls easily installed; Skytherms currently being used in self-help projects. |

| Built for Sale: | Passive systems may be unfamiliar to house-buying public; interior temperature swings and insulating devices may be unacceptable to buyers. |

| Custom-Built: | Suitable in order to make necessary design adjustments to climate, site and to owner's lifestyle. |

FINANCING METHOD

| Short-Term Investment: | Unfamiliar passive systems may limit resale of house. |

| Long-Term Investment: | Because of specific nature of design and use, passive systems with collector/storage building elements are best suited to long-term investment (custom design, single ownership). |

3. Active Systems: Flat-Plate Collectors

CLIMATE

| Hot Dry: | Only domestic hot water or auxiliary space-heating systems (active) are required, with appropriate passive design. |

| Hot Wet: | Domestic hot water heating, auxiliary space heating, pool heating and heat pump systems most practical. Solar-powered cooling may become practical in future. |

| Temperate: | Auxiliary space heating (including domestic hot water heating) recommended, with window-heat recovery system. Heat-pump system practical if air conditioning is required. Single glass collectors and site-fabricated collectors are sufficient. |

| Cool: | Large-capacity solar heating recommended in |

174

sunny, cool locations. Well-fabricated and efficient collectors are required. Air systems avoid problems of freezing.

HOUSE TYPE

Existing House: Requires acceptable location and orientation of collectors, usually on special frame support on existing roof or ground.

Existing Apartment: Roof area may be available for small collector area (recommended for domestic hot water heating).

New House (detached): Ideal for proper sizing and orientation of required collector area.

New Apartments: May be limiting in available area for collectors. Single large collector area, which supplies several units, may be practical.

CONSTRUCTION METHOD

Owner-Built: Site-built collectors must be carefully made, especially to prevent air leakage, condensation damage and glass breakage. Air collectors and water-trickling collectors commonly used for low initial cost.

Built for Sale: Liquid systems commonly used because of flexibility of installation and availability. Even if initial installation is small (domestic hot water or auxiliary space heating), space should be left for enlargement of system in future.

Custom-Built: Ideal for proper integration of collectors into house design and construction, adapted to specific sites.

FINANCING METHOD

Short-Term Investment: Domestic hot water heating and auxiliary space heating have shortest payback period.

Long-Term Investment: Uncertainty of future fuel availability and its cost warrants consideration of large-capacity systems over the long term.

4. Active Systems: Advanced Solar Collectors

CLIMATE

Hot Dry: Not necessary for space heating. Clear sky conditions make focusing collectors effective (for high-temperature applications).

Hot Wet:	May be required for solar-powered cooling applications. Not necessary for heat pump installations.
Temperate:	Diffuse sky conditions and medium temperature requirements favor flat-plate collectors.
Cool:	High-performance collectors may be required to reduce collector area needed.

HOUSE TYPE

Existing House:	High-performance collectors may be required if only limited collector area available.
Existing Apartment:	Flat roofs may provide good areas for tracking and reflecting collector designs.
New House (detached):	Not necessary if proper space available for flat-plate collectors.
New Apartments:	High-performance collectors may be required if only limited collector area available.

CONSTRUCTION METHOD

Owner-Built:	Honeycomb heat trap and other reflecting collectors can be built by self-helpers. However, patent use rights may be required.
Built for Sale:	Advanced collectors not yet cost-effective in the built-for-sale market.
Custom-Built:	May be appropriate to suit special requirements of design or structure.

FINANCING METHODS

Short-Term Investment:	Advanced collectors not yet sufficiently available to be cost-effective for short-term payback in residential application.
Long-Term Investment:	A long-term investment analysis may show that advanced collectors are cost-effective over the long term.

5. Active Systems: Storage

CLIMATE

Hot Dry:	Active systems require storage sized for only one day carryover, because of high frequency of sunny winter days.
Hot Wet:	Large storage capacity not required because of low heat demand.
Temperate:	Storage can be sized to available collector

area; near 100 percent solar heating possible, although smaller capacity is more justified in current economic terms.

Cool: More than two days carryover not practical due to large storage size required with current sensible heat storage methods.

HOUSE TYPE

Existing House: Generally difficult to install required storage volume due to limited space, except outside the house. Smaller, latent heat-storage methods may solve this problem.

Existing Apartment: Difficult, if not impossible, to install required storage.

New House (detached): Recommended to incorporate storage in house foundation or basement.

New Apartments: Party walls and masonry structure can be used as low-temperature (passive) storage mass. Low heat loss (compared to detached dwellings) results in reduced storage volume requirements.

CONSTRUCTION METHOD

Owner-Built: Rock storage requires on-site labor, therefore is cost-effective for self-helpers. Liquid storage systems require plumbing skills.

Built for Sale: Slab-on-grade construction may favor rock-type in-foundation storage enclosure.

Custom-Built: Any storage type can be properly incorporated in custom design.

FINANCING METHOD

Short-Term Investment: Small storage system or use of construction mass (masonry walls, etc.) for storage, most cost-effective for low initial investment.

Long-Term Investment: Larger investment in full storage capacity with proper controls is justified over the long term.

6. Active Systems: Distribution

CLIMATE

Hot Dry: Active systems of heat distribution (fan operated) recommended to control heat imbalance. Nighttime regenerative cooling of rock storage possible in summer.

177

Hot Wet: Warm-air distribution systems give most flexibility for humidity control and air cooling options.

Temperate: Any distribution system applicable. High supply/low return air distribution appropriate.

Cool: Any distribution system applicable. High supply/low return air distribution can be used only if usual cold drafts at windows, entries and stairs are eliminated.

HOUSE TYPE

Existing House: Existing hydronic (baseboard) can be used only with solar collector-heat pump combination to increase delivery temperature. Existing warm-air distribution ducts can be used if large enough (sized for air conditioning).

Existing Apartment: Generally difficult to use existing distribution systems, except as noted above for existing houses.

New House (detached): Any distribution system can be used. Warm-air system recommended for utilization of lower temperature from storage.

New Apartments: If central heating plan is used, long distribution runs may require hydronic system.

CONSTRUCTION METHOD

Self-Help: Air distribution systems are usually easiest to install, but must be air-tight and well insulated. Liquid systems require plumbing skills.

Built for Sale: Any distribution system can be used, although warm-air distribution is recommended as noted above under New House (detached). Air supply registers must be carefully located to avoid low-temperature air drafts.

Custom-Built: Same consideration applies as noted above for built-for-sale construction. Special requirements of natural convection in double-height rooms can be met with careful design of distribution system.

FINANCING METHOD

Short-Term Investment: Warm-air distribution systems recommended, with active solar systems, offering greatest flexibility for future re-sale or system improvements (air cleaners, humidity controls, cooling).

Long-Term Investment: Same as above.

178

8.2.2 CONSULTING WITH PROFESSIONALS

A prospective homeowner should keep informed of local building experience with the various solar-heating methods and with technical developments in solar equipment.

Publications prepared by government agencies to help homeowners become informed about energy conservation and solar energy are listed in Appendix I-A. In addition, some state agencies and universities have public information and extension services to help homeowners who are interested in practical approaches to energy conservation.

There may be solar installations that you can visit in your area. A number of universities have built prototype homes as energy experiments, and builders throughout the United States are now completing houses as part of the U. S. Department of Housing and Urban Development's solar demonstration program.

Appendix I-B contains a list (and illustrations) of a representative selection of solar houses that are built or are under construction at this time, some of which are open for public inspection.

While many states require that an architect or engineer prepare the building plans, in most states this is not required for private residences. However, professional architects and engineers who have experience with solar design can help in designing a house within budget and schedule limitations and evaluating the technical merits of the solar equipment alternatives.

Architects, and the mechanical engineers who work with architects on house designs, charge for their services in one of two ways—as a percentage of the building construction cost from 5 to 15 percent (depending upon the scope of services required) or an hourly consulting basis (typically from $15 to $30 an hour).

The percentage of construction cost basis is the normal arrangement in cases where an architect provides full services—which include initial site analysis, design and materials specification, contract negotiations with a builder, and verification of construction work as it progresses.

However, an hourly consulting arrangement with an architect may be suitable if the home-builder wishes only to take advantage of professional expertise for a limited number of questions—as might be the case with solar design applications.

For example, a home-builder may have a basic plan already in mind and may simply need advice on how to improve its energy efficiency and its adaptability to a solar installation. Many architects are willing to work on an hourly consulting basis to enable an owner-builder himself to more easily carry out the organization of the project, including the construction.

Before selecting an architect or other professional consultant, you should interview several firms to learn of their previous experience and capability in the solar field and select the one best suited to work with you. Determine an architect's previous experience in solar design, whether he or she has the time available to devote to your project, what is the fee arrangement, and how important proximity to the site might be during construction.

The architects and designers of the projects shown in this book are listed in Appendix I-C. Local professional societies may also be able to provide an up-to-date list of architects or engineers who are qualified to practice in your area and who are experienced in solar design.

8.2.3 DEVELOPING A HOUSE PLAN

The house designs discussed in this book show a variety of plans and the solar systems that can be used throughout the United States, illustrating that solar heating can be used to practical advantage without dictating only one particular system or plan type.

In beginning the search for a house plan that is appropriate to your particular location, your life-style and construction budget, the essential point (made throughout this book) is first to reduce the total heating requirement by applying ecodesign principles in the basic design. Then one can select a combination of passive and active solar heating that fits one's budget and one's long-term plans for the house. The previous chapter showed that even if a large-capacity solar heating system is not installed at first, space should be left for it to be added in the future (Figure 8.4).

A house plan that is appropriate to one's needs and that takes advantage of ecodesign principles can be developed even with houses that are severely limited in size and cost. In fact, ecodesign principles encourage building solutions that are, by definition, economical in shape and size.

Even in early planning stages, the requirements of the solar equipment need to be considered, whether for immediate or future installation. The criteria for assuring the proper coordination of house design with solar equipment are summarized here in the **Building Design Checklist.**

Building Design Checklist

1. Determine local or state building codes that apply to the building design.

2. Design building to be compatible with local and regional building styles, to suit landscape and neighborhood setting.

3. Use materials that are compatible with conventional building technology.

4. Use passive solar and ecodesign approaches to reduce size of active and back-up heating systems.

5. Provide adequate space on structure or near-by ground for installation, servicing and replacement of present or future solar collectors.

6. Provide adequate space for installation, servicing and replacement of heat storage unit.

7. Provide adequate space in house interior for installation of collector storage and distribution piping or ducts, with service access to controls.

8. Provide proper access width and head clearance in all interior spaces where solar equipment is installed.

Figure 8.4. *Owner-Built Solar House Design Development.*

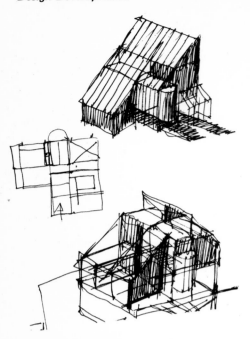

Figure 8.4A. *First sketches, starting with approximate arrangement of plan and large collector/roof area.*

8.4 B & C. *Later sketches, still with large roof area available for collector options.*

9. Avoid shading of collector by other collectors or by adjacent building structure, chimneys, etc.

10. Allow three-foot clearance of chimneys and flues above adjacent collectors or building roof structure within 10 feet (or as required by applicable codes).

11. Maintain integrity of building structure in locating access holes for pipes or ducts. Allow for differential movement of materials in design of water-tight penetrations of building envelope. Provide for additional weight of collectors and collector mounting in structural calculations.

12. Avoid use of plastics in building interiors that might be exposed to flame in a fire. (Expanded plastics used for insulation should be protected by fire-resistant coatings.)

13. Avoid use and placement of materials that might be subject to accident hazard. (If the collectors are mounted close to the ground, such as to form a fence around a swimming pool, then the cover sheet of the collector should be plexiglass or a polycarbonate to eliminate the hazard of glass breakage. Alter-

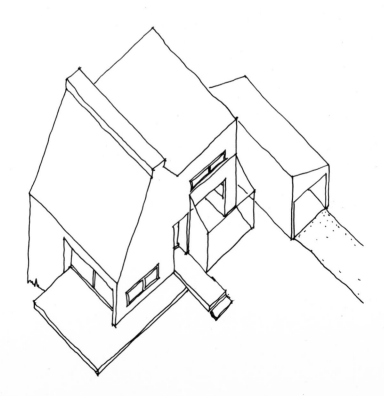

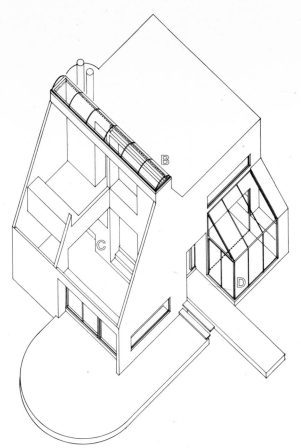

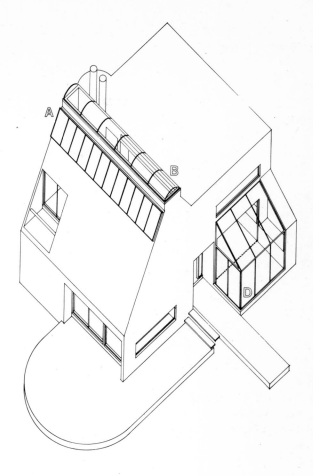

8.4D. *Final design drawings, with only small collector area (A) envisioned to reduce initial investment in construction. Skylight (B), central fireplace (C) and greenhouse (D).*

8.4E. *Alternate design for large capacity system (below).*

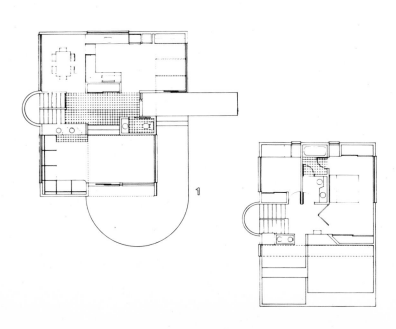

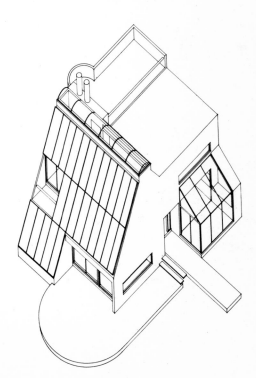

8.4F. *House as built, with initial solar domestic water heating system, leaving roof area available for enlarged solar system in future.*

natively, a wire screen could be placed over glass covers. This may also be desirable in areas where there are severe hail storms or the threat of vandalism.)

14. In the placement of solar collectors: avoid blocking desirable views; consider the ground-shading caused by high building structures to avoid shadows on nearby gardens or play areas; consider undesirable reflections from collectors on nearby patios, etc.

15. In placing collectors or storage outside a building: avoid blocking access for servicing

184

building, septic field (maintain minimum distance of 10 feet), or sewer line (minimum distance of 3 feet).

16. If collectors are placed on the ground or on flat roofs, install with sufficient clearance at the base of the collectors to avoid rain-splashed dirt and snow accumulation.

17. If the heat storage unit is placed underground in areas of high ground water, precautions must be taken against flotation in event that tank is emptied.

8.2.4 SELECTING SOLAR EQUIPMENT

Once one has a solar approach in mind and an appropriate house plan, solar equipment can be selected on the basis of its cost, performance and durability.

Solar collectors are the essential component in active solar heating, while heat-storage devices may be used in passive or active systems. Collector and storage units are the only parts of a solar heating installation that are new to home builders. Special application pumps and controls are being developed to suit the operating requirements of solar systems, but these are not unfamiliar to the house construction trades.

HOW TO EVALUATE A FLAT-PLATE SOLAR COLLECTOR

The climate and the design and intended use of the house will dictate in part what collector type should be used.

Many solar collector designs now are being marketed throughout the United States, each with its own claims about durability and performance, and one is often left with a confusing picture of their comparative advantages. Yet performance eventually will determine the cost-effectiveness of a solar installation.

The final choice of a collector, however, may be decided by factors other than cost and efficiency,

185

due to other advantages that apply for a particular house.

For example, some collectors can be easily installed by owner-builders themselves. Or one collector may be more suitable for a given house design due to its size or its appearance. Or a manufacturer in a particular area may be ready to supply solar engineering, installation and servicing.

In most cases, however, to make the best possible selection for a particular building, one should compare collector designs. The following discussion gives general criteria for evaluation but meanwhile bear in mind that many manufacturers now are developing improved collector designs, and mass marketing potentials will tend to reduce costs substantially, as well as establish industry-wide quality controls.

Manufacturers' literature should be examined carefully in terms of the following factors:

Durability. Solar collectors are now available that carry warranties against defects, provided use and service conditions are followed. This is the best guide to the buyer as to durability.

Liquid collectors usually carry five-year warranties, and air collectors for up to ten years. The normal service life of a well-made collector actually might exceed twenty-five years. However, warranties usually apply only to the parts supplied by the manufacturer. The installation workmanship itself should be guaranteed for at least one year by the building contractor.

The way a collector is installed may be the cause of failure—rather than the collector itself—so the manufacturer's recommendations must be followed carefully.

All parts of a building are subject to severe stresses of temperature, wind, snow and hail, and to deterioration due to air pollutants. A solar collector should be designed and built to last for the life of a building—at least well beyond the mortgage period on which financing is based. Although collectors should be accessible for easy inspection and servicing, only minimal replacement of parts during the life of the building is normally acceptable to the buyer.

(Above and left) *placing absorber sheets in vertical south wall covered with 1½-inch foamglass insulation. Two-inch opening at base of insulated wall is for air return manifold.*

Owner-Installed Air Collector System: White solar house, Norwich, VT, 1975. Performance results of this collector installation are reported in A. O. Converse, "The Assessment of Solar-Heated Buildings" (July 1976), Thayer School of Engineering, Dartmouth College.

(Below) *Installing fiberglass double glazing, Kalwall Sun-lite cover sheets over absorbers.*

Completed installation.

The following factors (discussed in greater detail earlier), affect the durability of the collector construction itself:

1. If it is exposed to the sun, yet the heat is not removed by the collector-to-storage circuit, temperature in the collector may rise to 350° F. or higher. (This might happen during construction, when the collectors are mounted on a building but not yet in operation, or during power outages.) Therefore, all materials in the collector, including the insulation, must be able to withstand such high temperatures.

2. Metals exposed to the temperature changes typical of exterior building surfaces will expand and contract, and this can cause stress within the collector or along the connections between many collectors. The collector design, therefore, must allow some movement between parts. This is especially critical in the cover plate design, because glass or plastic changes dimension at a rate different from the metal enclosure or wood structure.

3. Glass that is custom-cut on the job is subject to cracking at weak points in the edges. Thus, to minimize edge stresses, glass should be rounded or sanded before being set in place.

4. Some plastics used for cover sheets will sag considerably after one or two years of use. They also may be subject to degradation from ultraviolet light.

5. The black paint or selective coating used on the absorber plate—the most sensitive part of the collector—is subject to deterioration under conditions of excess dust, moisture or chemical pollutants. Some manufacturers' selective surfaces are covered by warranty. Others have been successfully applied to copper and withstood in-use conditions for fifteen years or more. Selectively surfaced aluminum coatings have been developed only recently.

6. Absorber plates made with pipes attached to a sheet may be subject to separation cracks due

to an inadequate bond, rendering the absorber plate relatively useless. Spot-welded jointing is most likely to suffer separation, so in well-designed collectors the pipes are nested within an insert in the absorber plate and joined by continuous soldering.

7. The two parts of a collector that may break or fail under use are the cover sheet (due to vandalism or accident) and the absorber plate and manifold connection (due to improper installation or corrosion). Thus a collector should be be designed so that either the cover sheet or the entire collector can be replaced or serviced without removing adjacent collectors.

Cost. At present, collector costs vary enormously, and cost reductions may be anticipated as companies go into high-volume production. Collector efficiencies can also be improved when collector designs are developed for factory production under quality-control conditions.

Collectors often are compared on the basis of square-foot costs. Selection of a collector on this basis can be misleading, the real criterion of comparison being the installed cost in relation to heat delivered.

Collectors also vary considerably in their construction details. The mountings and edge construction of some have to be custom-built, while others are supplied ready for direct attachment to any finished building surface. Collectors that are easy to install, of course, will have a lower on-site labor cost.

To compare collectors, therefore, one must first establish the total installed cost—including all connections, insulation, roof flashing and finishing materials. The installed cost is often quite a bit more than the stated manufacturer's cost.

Here a judgment should be sought from a builder as to what the comparative labor cost might be between various collectors, based on ease of installation. Once the total installed cost is determined for the entire collector area, one can calculate the installed cost per square foot of **usable** collector area—that is, the absorber itself, rather than the overall collector area. (The usable absorber

Figure 8.5. *Comparison of Installed Collector Costs (representative): Calculated for a 1500 SF house, 46,000 Btu/hr. DHL, 70 degrees F. temperature differential (degree day), collector area to supply 50% annual space heating requirement.*

	Collector A	Collector B	Collector C	Collector B with heat pump
INSTANTANEOUS EFFICIENCY	32%	45%	62%	
OVER-ALL EFFICIENCY	26%	36%	50%	46%
COLLECTOR AREA REQUIRED	900 S.F.	640 S.F.	480 S.F.	520 S.F.
COLLECTOR/FLOOR AREA RATIO	60%	43%	32%	35%
COLLECTOR COST/ S. F. INSTALLED	$6.25	$9.00	$11.50	$11.69*
TOTAL COLLECTOR COST INSTALLED	$5625	$5760	$5520	$6079

*$1400 added for heat pump and its controls = $2.69/SF additional cost.

Liquid storage tanks. Source: E. Pickering Stanford Research Institute.

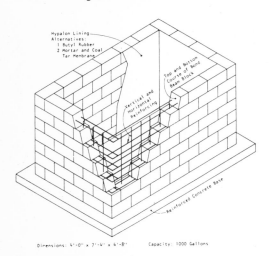

A. *Reinforced concrete block tank.*

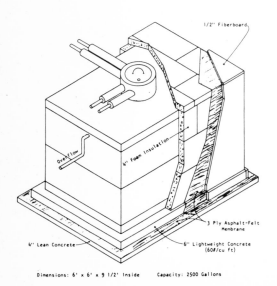

B. *Precast sectional utility tank.*

area may be 10 to 15 percent less than the overall collector size, due to the edge and frame detail.)

The heat delivered by the collector for a typical winter month under the climate conditions that prevail in the area can be determined from manufacturer's literature or by calculation methods described in Appendix II.

A collector whose factory cost is higher than another still may be much more cost effective in terms of equivalent amount of heat delivered, as shown by the example tabulation in Figure 8.5.

Whether one selects manufactured collectors or chooses instead to fabricate them at the building site depends upon the design, the construction budget and the performance one expects to obtain.

Site-fabricated collectors may be 30 to 50 percent less efficient than a good-quality factory-produced collector. As a result, to obtain comparable results, a much larger collector area is required, and economies (based on the total installed cost for heat delivered) may not be large.

However, at present some site-fabricated collectors cost less than one half the average cost of manufactured collectors, and in many circumstances, this initial economy in installation is crucial. Thus, even if the site-fabricated collectors take more area and perform less efficiently, they may be appropriate, particularly in less demanding, temperate climates.

190

Performance. The technical aspects of collector performance were discussed in Chapter 4. Established collector manufacturers now are providing data, based on performance tests, that give the output of their solar collectors for different operating conditions. These performance tests often are run under different conditions of solar radiation, wind speed and flow rates. The U. S. National Bureau of Standards, therefore, has proposed standard conditions for uniform testing, to provide adequate comparison of collector performance. Once adopted by solar equipment suppliers, these performance comparisons then will be much easier.

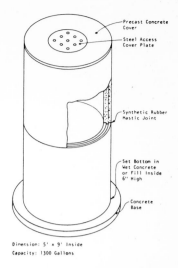

C. Tank assembled from precast concrete storm drain sections.

HEAT STORAGE CONTAINERS

Storage containers often can be built as part of the house basement construction. If the system uses air-type collectors and the rock storage volume is large, on-site construction of the storage bin in practically the only solution.

For a liquid-type collector and storage system, commonly available metal storage tanks from 1500 to 2500 gallons may be the most economical choice. The storage bin for liquid can also be built within the masonry foundation, provided that proper structural reinforcement is placed under it to spread the heavy load over a sufficiently large soil-bearing area. Various methods of constructing storage containers are shown in the accompanying illustrations on pages 190-192.

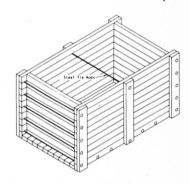

D. Rectangular wood tank.

Rock storage. When installing rock storage, the insulation envelope should be tightly sealed against air leakage, and rock size and type should conform to engineering design requirements. However, leeway should be allowed to use rock sizes that are economical and available nearby.

There may be great difference in cost between washed gravel and construction-grade "trap rock." The latter may be one half the cost—but it requires cleaning at the site. Because rock is delivered by the truckload and easily dumped directly into the storage bin, a grating can be constructed as part of

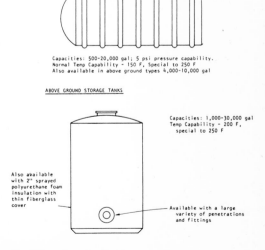

UNDERGROUND STORAGE TANKS

Capacities: 500-20,000 gal; 5 psi pressure capability.
Normal Temp Capability - 150 F, Special to 250 F
Also available in above ground types 4,000-10,000 gal

ABOVE GROUND STORAGE TANKS

Capacities: 1,000-30,000 gal
Temp Capability - 200 F,
special to 250 F

Also available
with 2" sprayed
polyurethane foam
insulation with
thin fiberglass
cover

Available with a large
variety of penetrations
and fittings

E. Fiberglass tanks.

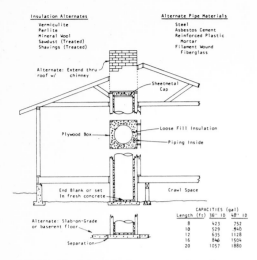

Insulation Alternates
Vermiculite
Perlite
Mineral Wool
Sawdust (Treated)
Shavings (Treated)

Alternate Pipe Materials
Steel
Asbestos Cement
Reinforced Plastic
Mortar
Filament Wound
Fiberglass

Alternate: Extend thru roof w/ chimney

Sheetmetal Cap

Plywood Box

Loose Fill Insulation

Piping Inside

End Blank or set In fresh concrete

Crawl Space

Alternate: Slab-on-Grade or basement floor

Separation

CAPACITIES (gal)		
Length (ft)	36" ID	48" ID
8	423	752
10	529	940
12	635	1128
16	846	1504
20	1057	1880

F. *Vertical tank in house construction.*

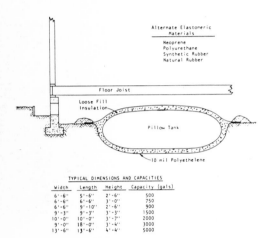

Alternate Elastomeric Materials

Neoprene
Polyurethane
Synthetic Rubber
Natural Rubber

Floor Joist

Loose Fill Insulation

Pillow Tank

10 mil Polyethelene

TYPICAL DIMENSIONS AND CAPACITIES			
Width	Length	Height	Capacity (gals)
6'-6"	5'-6"	2'-6"	500
6'-6"	6'-6"	3'-0"	750
6'-6"	9'-10"	2'-6"	900
9'-3"	9'-3"	3'-3"	1500
10'-0"	10'-0"	3'-7"	2000
9'-0"	18'-0"	3'-4"	3000
13'-6"	13'-6"	4'-4"	5000

G. *Elastomeric pillow tank in crawl space.*

the dumpway to allow the rock to be washed as it is removed from the truck. Dirt and dust that does accumulate in the storage area may settle to the bottom and be harmless, but filters are necessary to keep dust out of the house air system and the collectors themselves.

Liquid storage. Corrosion and rusting can occur when metal containers are used for water storage. Steel tanks usually are the least expensive, but precautions are necessary to prevent corrosion. Rust- and corrosion-inhibitors can be placed in the water, but many of these are toxic and could leak to contaminate the potable water supply.

Because of the leak possibility, all the fittings and heat exchangers in water storage systems must be installed so that they can be replaced. For large exchangers, this means that there must be enough room outside the tank to remove it entirely. If the tank is metal, it may have to be replaced or repaired, so its insulation must be removable as well.

Storage containers can be located outside a building, above or under the ground, and this is often the only option in fitting solar heating to existing houses. But the distance between collector-to-storage and storage-to-house should be as small as possible, to minimize cost as well as heat losses in the connecting piping.

Underground storage must be well insulated and protected against moisture and ground water. If it is a metal tank, it should be placed in soil that drains well, and not be too close to the drainage field of a septic system. An empty tank, too (when first installed or when repaired) may be dislodged by flotation under high ground-water pressure.

The storage container should be easily accessible from above in case it must be removed. Thus a permanent structure, such as a patio or porch, should not be placed above it. Special structural provisions must be made, also, if it is located where vehicles might drive over it.

The collector cost represents only part of the total installed cost of a solar heating system. There are the additional controls, dampers, valves, fans, pumps required to use solar heat efficiently, and, of course, the heat storage unit.

The number of nationally recognized companies that manufacture solar equipment is growing, some with representatives and distributors in every part of the United States. Small solar specialty companies which manufacture, install and service their own equipment may be cost-competitive with larger companies, due to their smaller distribution, transport and handling costs.

The first guideline to follow in evaluating solar equipment suppliers is to seek complete information. The informed buyer of any appliance or equipment used in houses can make his or her own judgment, provided essential information is accurately represented. It is, therefore, not surprising that the highest-quality collectors are also those that are the most completely described in manufacturers' catalogs. Appendix I-D contains a listing of solar equipment manufacturers.

Solar equipment that is purchased must be coordinated with the parts of the heating system built on the site and with the house structure itself. Solar equipment selection and its integration into construction are reviewed in the **solar system checklist,** below.

Collector to Storage Heat Exchanger approximately 10 feet long, fabricated for insert into storage tank. Tank location should allow inspection and removal and repair of heat exchangers.

Solar System Checklist

1. Solar collector must be designed to meet all stresses of conventional building materials: wind loads, hail and icing, freezing, differential temperature movement, condensation, sunlight (ultraviolet) degradation, and corrosion from airborne pollutants.

2. Manufactured collectors must be designed to meet all stresses of transport and construction before system operation: vibration, uneven loading, and heat build-up in stagnant no-flow conditions.

3. Differential settlement of storage foundation should be considered in the design of structural support and fittings.

4. Insulate collectors, piping, ducts and storage to prevent heat loss from system and undesired overheating of building interior.

(Checklist continued on page 196)

Owner-Installed Storage System: Lipsey house, Aspen, CO, 1976. A pebble bed storage is heated by air collectors. Above the pebble bed, a water pond is heated by air passing under it in its return passage to the collectors and acts as a low-temperature radiant floor system. The system provides a high storage capacity, but with limitations of control over response time. (Photos courtesy of Ron Shore)

A. *Main supply duct across bottom of storage bin placed within insulated foundation construction.*

B. *Main supply duct on left and across inside wall in foreground. Slots in plywood wall for return air flow.*

C. *Boxed and screened openings from main supply duct to pebble bed.*

D. *Concrete block partitions to support floor above pebble bed. One boxed opening (as shown in C above) for each section.*

E. *Foamed-in-place insulation over pebble bed.*

194

F. *Metal decking to provide support for water pond. Space left above insulated pebble bed to serve as air passage to heat water pond radiant floor.*

G. *Metal decking corrugations topped with concrete for flat surface in preparation of waterproofing.*

H. *Waterproof water pond made of continuous 1/8 inch butyl rubber sheeting.*

I. *Second layer of metal deck to cover water pond.*

J. *Pond cover topped with concrete and concrete reinforcement in place.*

K. *Finish of concrete slab.*

Harry Teague

Lipsey house near completion.
Water storage containers to be placed
in front of second story window.

5. Provide means of servicing and replacement of system components without removal of adjacent building material or equipment. Liquid collector systems should include means of easy removal of entrapped air by draining or purging (non-freezing air vents required). Air collector systems should include means of easy inspection and replacement of filters.

6. Provide means of easy inspection and testing of solar collectors, solar collector fluid and system controls. Liquid systems should be pressure-tested at 120 psi for one hour at time of installation. Refer to manufacturers instructions for other installation and servicing requirements, as applicable.

196

8.2.5 CHOOSING A CONSTRUCTION METHOD

The bottom line, the installed purchase price, still is the major concern of most people who contemplate using solar heating. Ultimately the building contractor who undertakes the responsibility of installing and servicing a heating system determines its price to the homeowner. The many items involved in a solar installation and representative prices for them are shown in Figure 8.6 (page 198).

At present these installation costs are higher than they will be if mass-produced and package-type installations are marketed, and if solar heating gains widespread acceptance for use in houses. The Solar Heating and Cooling Demonstrations Act, passed by Congress in 1974 and which now accounts for the funding of many solar house demonstrations throughout the United States, is based on the premise that such economies will occur if solar heating reaches a wider market.

To reduce solar installation costs, one might look for economies in any one or several of these approaches to solar building construction: pre-engineered plans, one-contract installation, site-fabricated systems and self-help construction.

Pre-engineered plans. Because solar heating for houses is a relatively new development, each project requires both design and engineering that matches a solar equipment system to the house's particular energy demand, the building layout, the construction, and the local climate.

The design fee for preparing these building plans and heating equipment specifications, whether borne by the equipment supplier or the purchaser, must therefore be considered part of the cost of a solar system. In addition, because every solar house up to now has been new to the building trades involved, and has required custom-fabricated collectors, storage or other mechanical equipment, the labor costs have been high to include the "learning time" of installers who have not been familiar with solar heating systems previously.

To overcome the additional costs involved in custom design and installation, builders and house

Pre-Engineered Solar House Plan proposed by Acorn Structures, Inc.

197

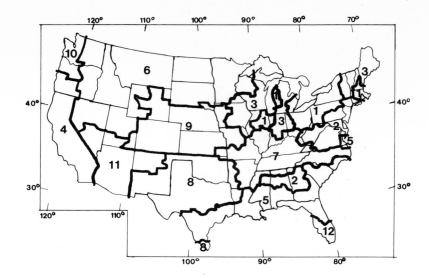

Climatic zones as listed in Figure 8.6 below. There are wide variations within each zone due to differences in altitude.

Figure 8.6. *Approximate collector and storage tank sizes and costs required to provide the heating and hot water needs of a 1500 square foot home with energy supplied and annual dollar savings. Installation costs shown include back-up heating system. As described in Chapter 7, the large-capacity systems represented on this chart may not be as cost-effective as smaller capacity installations in some locations. (Source:* Solar Life *and Energy Research and Development Agency)*

Climatic Zone	Percent of Energy Supplied by Solar	Collector Area, Square Feet	Storage Tank Capacity, Gallons	Representative Cylindrical Storage Tank Dimensions		Energy savings, Millions of Btus	Comparison with oil[2]		Comparison with electricity			Range of Solar Costs for a 1,500 Square Foot Home Including Backup System
				Diameter, Inches	Length, Inches		Equivalent gallons	Dollar savings	Equivalent Kilowatt Hours	Dollar Savings at Indicated Cost	Cost per KWh	
1	71	800	1,500	48	200	67.9	757	303	19,900	995	5¢	$8,000-$16,000
2	72	500	750	42	138	54.9	612	245	16,000	720	4.5¢	$5,000-$10,000
3	66	800	1,500	48	200	82.0	914	366	24,000	960	4.5¢	$8,000-$16,000
4	73	300	500	48	78	41.8	466	186	12,200	488	4¢	$3,000-$ 6,000
5	75	200	280	42	60	33.8	377	151	9,900	347	3.5¢	$2,000-$ 4,000
6	70	750	1,500	48	200	98.9	1,103	441	29,000	1,015	3.5¢	$7,500-$15,000
7	70	500	750	42	138	50.6	564	226	14,800	518	3.5¢	$5,000-$10,000
8	71	200	280	42	60	39.0	435	174	11,400	399	3.5¢	$2,000-$ 4,000
9	72	600	1,000	48	132	74.6	832	333	21,900	767	3.5¢	$6,000-$12,000
10	58	500	750	42	138	46.5	518	207	13,600	272	2¢	$5,000-$10,000
11	85	200	280	42	60	43.7	487	195	12,800	512	4¢	$2,000-$ 4,000
12[1]	85	45	80	20	63	16.7	186	74	4,900	196	4¢	$ 450-$ 900

[1] Includes only hot water needs.
[2] 65% furnace efficiency at 40¢/gallon

manufacturers are developing pre-engineered solar houses. These often are available as stock plans, or as packaged houses in which the entire building and solar equipment are delivered as pre-finished building sections for assembly at the site. These pre-engineered plans and building packages, familiar in conventional house construction, therefore can be expected to make solar homes more economical.

One-contract installation. Potential cost reductions also can be realized by "one contract" installations of solar heating packages, in which all the components are engineered to fit a particular house, and are installed and serviced under a single contract.

Some solar equipment manufacturers already supply many or all of the components for solar domestic hot water heating under such an arrangement, which is also usual for the installing of conventional heating and air-conditioning systems in houses. The same trend may develop in solar space-heating installations as well.

The advantages to the homeowner or builder are obvious. It eliminates multi-source purchasing, assures that all parts are compatible and assigns responsibility for the installation and servicing to qualified specialists in solar heating.

There are also substantial cost reductions available to one-contract suppliers who purchase all the required plumbing and heating equipment in volume, and it is hoped, these economies could accrue to the homeowner.

Site-fabricated solar heating systems. The ultimate price of a manufactured item must include not only materials and labor costs, but transportation and distribution charges as well—and these often account for a two- to three-fold increase in the cost of equipment and supplies.

Most of the solar demonstration projects currently funded by the United States government use solar equipment that is factory-produced. The premise here is that manufacturing costs will decrease with large volume production and marketing.

However, until such mass production of solar equipment actually results in lowered market-place costs, it is often more economical to assemble solar

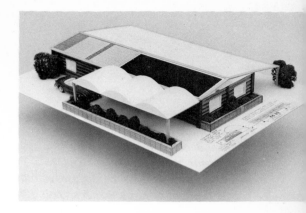

Modular Solar House Plan for trailer delivery proposed by Fred Rice Productions.

Kit House for site assembly by owner. Shelter-Kit Incorporated, Franklin, NH. Various options can be combined to include large solar-oriented windows, as shown.

199

heating systems at the site from building components that are already mass-produced and available locally from building supply houses.

Examples of this already discussed include using insulated glass panels and metal roofing sheets for collectors, concrete pipe sections for heat storage containers, and foil-faced rigid insulation for reflecting/insulating panels.

The economy of solar heating systems such as the water-trickling collectors and site-fabricated air-type systems lies in the use of readily available stan-

Figure 8.7. Summary of Methods for Self-Help Construction. *The construction method best suited to the owner/builder depends upon one's level of involvement, time and construction skills. One or several of these methods may hold advantages for one's particular situation.*

CONSTRUCTION METHOD	Local Materials Low Transport Cost	Local Technology High Transport Cost	Factory Technology Low Transport Cost	Factory Technology High Transport Cost	Variety of Design	Easily Changed	Advantages	Disadvantages
1 INDIGENOUS Local materials, scavenged or re-used	●				●		ecologically sound local adaption lowest cost	greatest construction time
2 CONVENTIONAL Materials as stocked and marketed. Trade skills.		●			●		self-helper learns trade skills	requires construction time and skills
3 RATIONALIZED Marketed materials, design coordinated for compatible assembly		●				●	uses available stock; competitive prices	connectors not yet available; requires technical development
4 ON-SITE PREFAB Conventional shop assembly of panel components. Trade skills.			●		●		self-helper participates in shop fabrication	mutual self-help only
5 PREFAB COMPONENTS Partial kit, structural, core or skin components.				●			speed in assembly and flexibility; owner can finish interior construction out of weather	high transport cost or incompatibility of other systems
6 PREFAB KIT Total components delivered for on-site assembly.				●		●	total package delivery, factory to owner	flexibility of components, good delivery system and volume required

dard building components. Additional ways to improve the performance of these field-assembled solar systems therefore will find a ready market.

Examples of products that could be developed to improve site-assembled solar installations include a selective black coating that can be applied to collectors at a building site, gasketing or flashing materials that permit easy attachment and replacement of glass for roof-mounted collectors and replaceable linings for liquid thermal storage tanks that can be inserted into a basement foundation container.

Self-help construction. At least 10 percent of the homes in the United States are built by owner-builders, often working after hours and weekends to complete all or part of their houses on a do-it-yourself basis. Many of the solar houses in use today have been so built by their owners, who by their labor contribution have lowered the cost of the solar installation. Pre-engineered building and solar heating packages, which can be easily assembled at the building site, can also be the best construction aid to an owner-builder.

A self-helper can save 15 percent or more on construction costs by organizing the purchase of materials and the labor tasks for the separate trades involved in house construction.

In addition, some building tasks can be competently done even by relatively unskilled owner-builders, although the time schedule for construction should be amply extended. As noted earlier, some solar heating ideas, such as air-type systems, readily lend themselves to owner construction.

The accompanying illustrations on pages 187, 194-95, 201 and 202 show various solar installations by owner-builders.

Site-Fabricated Solar Collector. *Construction sequence photos: An inventive use of standard construction materials in constructing a built-in air collector. Zuber Solar House, Pataskala, OH. Joseph Kawecki, designer.*

Installing the first panels. Firring strips serve as spacers for insulation and provide foothold for installers.

Air space between reflective foil insulation and collector glazing created by painted metal strips, normally used as corner beads in interior drywall construction.

Completion of glazing (using Kalwall fiberglass panels) with space at top and bottom of collectors for external manifold.

Eames house, Groton, CT (1976). An owner-built house with an air collector and storage system. Donald Watson, AIA, Architect.

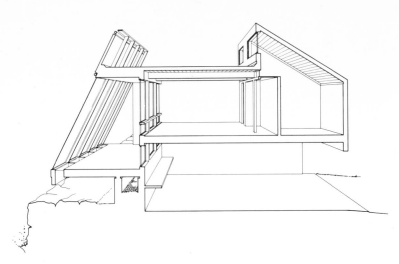

Section through greenhouse and bedroom. Placement permits views of the ocean through the greenhouse. Small rock storage area for greenhouse heat recovery.

Model mock-up to assure proper sizing and layout of air ducts.

Model of completed house. Small liquid collectors for domestic water heating are adjustable from roof deck.

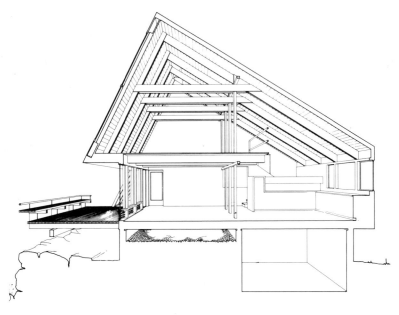

Section through living room-kitchen. Rock storage beneath for several days' carryover.

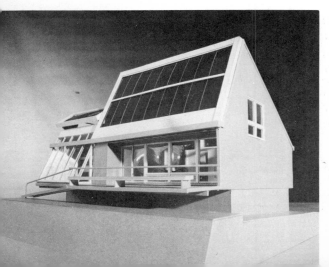

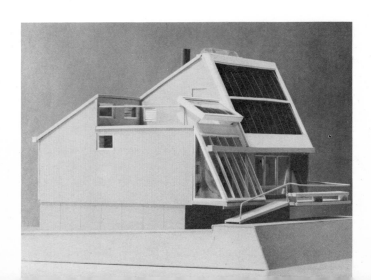

Construction of concrete foundation, showing insulation applied to outside below grade and to storage lining. (Construction photos courtesy of Garvey Blanc)

Placing the rock in storage.

Wood flooring with fiberglass insulation between concrete and wood plate.

Plywood sheathing over 2 x 6 wood wall construction.

Tilting up the end walls.

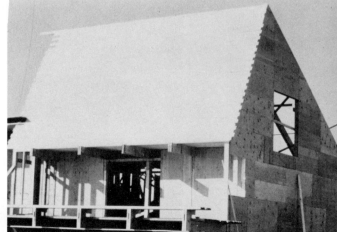

Wood roof decking before insulation and collectors are applied.

203

ACKNOWLEDGMENTS

If the reader has stayed with the narrative this far, through parts that are technical and detailed, perhaps I might add some personal notes, to place this book in perspective and to acknowledge the many individuals who contributed to it.

I was introduced to the realistic potential of solar heating by Everett M. Barber, Jr., who embarked with me on the design of the Westbrook, Connecticut house in 1972. Both of us, in turn, owe our gratitude to the owners of this house, Clarence and Ruth Frank, who with us patiently suffered the doubts and construction delays involved in putting into operation one of the first solar houses in New England since the MIT solar experiments fifteen years earlier.

At the time of construction of the Westbrook house there were no solar collectors being produced commercially in the United States. They had to be fabricated in a make-shift shop, with the selective surface applied to the copper sheets by being dipped—one end at a time—in used oil barrels, which were the only containers available to us for the chemical application. The collectors went on the roof, assembled at the site, with as many people documenting and reporting the installation as were working that day.

The many individuals who have built their own solar houses will sympathize with the somewhat fitful amateurism that accompanies beginning solar projects—often sustained only by the enthusiasm and hope that it will all work when the solar system goes together.

Since that time, in continuing with many solar house designs in the past four years and in writing this book, I have been in extensive contact with

Westbrook, CT. December, 1973.

solar designers, builders, manufacturers and home-owners throughout the United States. There is hardly a recommendation in this book for which I am not indebted to these individuals, who contributed the benefit of their experience and, as shown in many of the illustrations, documentation of their projects.

In Appendix I that follows, I have listed as accurately as possible these individuals who are researching, designing and building solar houses today. The appendices are thus offered as resources to the reader who wishes to take the step of building a solar house. I hope the path will be easier, due to the efforts conveyed in this book.

If the reader does build a solar house, he or she will find, as I did, that although the project may be the first in a particular part of the country, it is not undertaken in isolation. There is a growing number of solar enthusiasts throughout the U. S. willing to share their increasing knowledge. The work of all of us who are currently active in solar heating rests upon the efforts of many years by pioneers who

205

were developing solar concepts even before there was any energy crisis to underscore the importance of their work. Some of their work is described in this book and many continue to contribute to solar research: George and William Keck, Maria Telkes, Hoyt Hottel and the others who took part in the MIT experimental houses, Raymond Bliss and Eleanor Donovan, Harold Hay, John Yellott, Harry Thomason, Henry Mathew, Eric Farber, and George Löf.

To these ladies and gentlemen and to the many others who contributed to this book, I am indebted for their example and help. I regret only that I have not been able to describe more fully and accurately all of the current solar developments. I alone am responsible for any misinterpretation and errors in the text.

Some of the illustrations in this book have appeared in two previous books on solar heating, **Design Criteria for Solar Heated Buildings** which I co-authored with Everett Barber, Jr., and **Innovation in Solar Thermal House Design** which I prepared for the AIA Research Corporation under a research subcontract sponsored by the U. S. Department of Housing and Urban Development and the National Bureau of Standards, whose support is gratefully acknowledged.

I would like to end with a special expression of gratitude to my colleagues Everett Barber, Jr. and Fred Broberg, whose engineering expertise is reflected throughout this book, and to John Yellott, for reviewing the final manuscript. Robert Page and Robert Haisley prepared the illustrations, except as otherwise credited. Cathy Hopkins and Trent Armbruster typed the manuscript from nearly illegible script. My wife Marja not only kept the family functioning during the extended preparation of this manuscript but as an architect contributed to many of the designs shown in this book. We thus join in conveying this book to the sunshine kids of tomorrow, two of whom are mentioned in the dedication.

ADDITIONAL REFERENCES

1 Solar Periodicals

Solar Age
Solarvisions, Inc.
Route 515, Box 288
Vernon, NJ 07462
(1 year $20; monthly)

Solar Energy Digest
P.O. Box 17776
San Diego, California 92117
(1 year $28.50; monthly)

Solar Energy Journal
c/o W. H. Klein
International Solar Energy
    Society
12441 Parklawn Drive
Rockville MD 20852
(quarterly, with $15.00 yearly
    membership)

Solar Engineering
8435 North Stemmons
    Freeway
Suite 880
Dallas, TX 75247
(1 year subscription $10)

Solar Life
Newsletter of Solar Energy
    Institute of America
Box 9352
Washington, DC 20005
(with $15.00 yearly
    membership)

2 Publication Lists

Alternate Energy Sources
and related subjects
(enclose self-addressed
stamped return envelope
with request for publication
list)

AIA Research Corporation
1735 New York Avenue, N.W.
Washington, D.C. 20006
(Solar publications for
 architects)

Brace Research Institute
McGill University
Ste. Anne de Bellevue
Montreal, Canada
(self-help construction
technologies, including solar,
for developing countries)

**Environmental Action
Reprint Service**
2239 East Colfax Avenue
Denver, Colorado 80206
(reprints of solar-related
    articles)

New Alchemy Institute
Box 432
Woods Hole, MA 02543
(hydroponic farming, various
solar-related devices for crop
drying, etc)

Rural Housing Alliance
Dupont Circle Building
1346 Connecticut Ave., NW
Washington, DC 20036
(self-help and mutual aid
housing construction methods
and organization)

Vita Publications
3706 Rhode Island Ave.,
Mt. Rainier, MD 20822
(self-help construction
technologies)

3 Information on U.S. Government Solar Demonstration Programs

ERDA Technical
Information Center
Box 62
Oak Ridge, TN 37830
(solar publications)

National Solar
Information Center
Box 1607
Rockville, MD 20850
(data center for solar
information)

To be placed on mailing list,
indicate principal interest:

( ) Architects/Designers/
Planners (Private)
( ) Building Contractors
( ) Builder Developers
( ) Career Public Officials
( ) Educational Institutions
( ) Elected and Appointed
Public Officials
( ) Engineers (Private)
( ) Financial Community
( ) General Business Firms
( ) General Public
( ) Institutions
( ) Legal Community
( ) Marketing Community
( ) News Media
( ) Oil and Natural Gas Co.
( ) Public Libraries
( ) Public Utility Co.
( ) Realty Co.
( ) Solar Equipment Manufac-
turers and Suppliers
( ) Trade/Professional
Associations

For Builder/Developers—
HUD Solar Demonstration
Program:
Announcements of grants
awarded on a competitive basis
approximately once each year
to qualified builder/developers
only, to demonstrate solar
installations on houses built-
for-sale or rental (**not** privately
owned residences). Letterhead
request for information to
HUD Division of Energy, Room
8158, U.S. Department of
Housing and Urban Development, Washington, DC 20410.

For Solar Equipment
Manufacturers—
Announcements of funding
for innovative efforts on
systems, subsystems and
components that promise
breakthroughs in performance,
cost or ease of application.
Research will be conducted
leading to designs for collectors, storage units, cooling
units, instrumentation, heat
exchangers, controls and other
subsystems. If interested send
letterhead request to Marshall
Space Flight Center, National
Aeronautics and Space
Administration, Huntsville,
Ala. 35812.

4 Additional References

Climate Information: United States

1. **Regional Climatic Analysis
and Design Data** (1950).
Sun, wind, and rainfall
data of twelve regions of
the United States with appropriate house design
response. $15.00 from
Xerox University Micro-
films, Ann Arbor, MI 48106.

2. **Climatic Atlas of the
United States.**
$4.25 from Superintendent
of Documents, U.S. Government Printing Office, Washington, DC 20402.

3. **Home Winterization
   Manual.**
   Energy Conservation Paper
   28 (price information not
   listed). Office of Low Income
   Winterization Programs,
   Federal Energy Administration, Washington, D.C.
   20461.

4. **In the Bank . . . Or Up the
   Chimney? A Dollars and
   Cents guide to Energy-
   Saving Home Improve-
   ments (1975).**
   $1.70. Superintendent of
   Documents. U.S. Govern-
   ment Printing Office, Wash
   ington, D.C. 20402.

5. **Living With The Energy
   Crisis** (1973).
   25¢. Small Homes Council-
   Building Research Council,
   University of Illinois, 1 East
   St. Mary's Road, Cham-
   paign, Illinois 61820.
   (Energy conservation tips
   for the home owner—
   emphasis on insulation)

6. **Save Energy: Save Money**
   (1974).
   (Price information not
   listed.) Institute on Energy
   Conservation Office of
   Economic Opportunity,
   Washington, D.C.

7. **Retrofitting Existing
   Housing for Energy
   Conservation: An
   Economic Analysis** (1974).
   $1.35. Calalog No.
   C13.29:2/64. Superintend-
   ent of Documents, U.S.
   Government Printing
   Office, Washington, D.C.
   20402.

8. **Your Energy-Efficient
   House: Building &
   Remodeling Ideas.**
   (Anthony Adams). $4.95.
   Garden Way Publishing,
   Charlotte, VT 05445.

**Solar Product Directories
and Technical Manuals**

9. **Calalog of Solar Heating
   and Cooling Equipment.**
   (ERDA—75).
   Catalog No. 052-010-
   00470-1. $3.80 from
   Superintendent of Documents. U.S. Government
   Printing Office, Washington, DC 20402.

10. **Solar Products and
    Services.**
    Sent with $15 yearly mem-
    bership from Solar Energy
    Institute of America, Box
    9352, Washington, DC
    20005.

11. **How to Design and Build a
    Solar Swimming Pool Heater.**
    Copper Development
    Association, Inc., 405 Lexing-
    ton Ave., New York, NY 10017.

APPENDIX I-B

SOLAR HOUSES IN THE UNITED STATES

The solar houses listed in this section have been selected from hundreds of examples built or under construction and illustrate the many approaches to solar heating discussed in this book, including passive and owner-built houses. Those built as builder's model homes or under the U. S. government solar demonstration program may be open to inspection—information about visiting hours is obtainable from the addresses listed. The completion of demonstration projects dated 1977 has not been confirmed.

Private houses should not be visited without prior permission of the owner. Include stamped self-addressed return envelope with any inquiry to them. In the cases noted, descriptive literature is available at costs that will be stated by the sources.

For more complete descriptions of solar heated buildings, see **Solar Heated Buildings—a Brief Survey** (periodically updated), $9.00, from W. A. Shurcliff, 19 Appleton Street, Cambridge, MA 02138. The solar houses built under the HUD Solar Demonstration Grant Program are described in **Solar Heating and Cooling Demonstration Program: Cycle 1,** $1.15 from U.S. Government Printing Office, Washington, D. C. 20402. Order No. 023-000-00338-4.

Corrections and additions are invited from solar house owners who would like to be listed in future printings of this book.

ALABAMA

Huntsville

Marshall Space Flight Center (NASA) Solar Test House (1974)
Huntsville 35807
Project manager: J. W. Wiggins
Liquid collectors with tedlar cover sheet; summer cooling with LiBr absorption chiller.

Moody

Solar House (1977)
Builder: Michael White
Spectrum Development Corporation
P.O. Box 146
Leeds, AL 35094
House built for sale, air system. Recipient HUD solar demonstration grant.

ARIZONA

Cordes Junction

Arcosanti (1972 to present)
Cosanti Foundation
6433 Doubletree Road, Scottsdale 85253
An extensive series of dramatic structures including communal facilities, residences and workshops, based on Architect Paolo Soleri's concepts of "Arcology"; air systems; greenhouse and other passive climate control devices; newsletter available.

Sedona

Sanders House (1975)
L-41 Chapel Vista, Sedona 86336
Designer/owner/builder: E. R. Sanders
Site-fabricated air system; regenerative cooling of storage for summer.

Sedona

Wagoner House (1975)
Red Rock Loop Road, Sedona 86336
Designer/owner/builder: R. G. Wagoner
Site-fabricated air system; retrofitted to existing residence; storage installed in existing crawl space.

Sun City
(near Phoenix)

Sun City House (1976)
10440 Wheatridge Drive
Builder: Del E. Webb Construction Co.
Solar engineer: D. I. Aaland
House built for sale; liquid system; LiBr absorption cooling.

Tucson

Meinel House (1973)
Owner/engineers: Aden and Marjorie Meinel
c/o Helio Associates
10121 Catallena Highway
Tucson 87515
Adobe wall, one-story residence, 300 S.F., vertically placed air collectors; outside storage bin with 1000 water-filled plastic bottles (gallon milk containers); regenerative cooling mode.

Tucson

University of Arizona Environmental Research Laboratory Solar Test House (1974)
Tucson International Airport 85706
Engineer: J. Peck and others
Air-type collector with four layers of copper screen absorber (photo below).

Tucson

Decade 80 Solar House (1975)
Sponsored by: Copper Development Association
405 Lexington Ave.
New York, NY 10017
Architect: M. A. Kotch
1800 S.F. liquid collector; LiBr absorption cooling; news release available.

Yuma

Hansberger Apartments (1975)
699 Avenue B, Yuma 85364
Owner/designer: E. L. Hansberger, Jr.
Liquid system; Rankine engine cooling.

ARKANSAS

Ozark Mountains
Newton County

Heliothermic Mountain Cabin (1975)
Architect: James Lambeth
South-facing glass; interior mass for storage
(masonry floor and fireplace); summer shading and
natural ventilation (photo below).

CALIFORNIA

Atascadero

Skytherm Southwest Test House (1973)
7985 Santa Rosa Rd.
Engineer: Phil Niles and Harold Hay
Architects: K. Haggard and J. Edmiston
California Polytechnic State University
San Luis ebispo, CA 93401
1140 S.F. residence, fully monitored for live-in
experimental evaluation of Skytherm system;
"Research Evaluation of a System of Air Condition-
ing," available from National Technical Evaluation
Center, Springfield, VA 22151. Order # PB243498,
$10.00. (See Figures 3.12-3.14)

El Cajon
(near San Diego)

Energy Systems Inc. Solar Houses (1973-present)
Vista del Colinas, El Cajon
2400 Euclid Avenue, San Diego 92021
Developer: Caster Development Corporation
634 Crest Drive
El Cajon, CA 92021
Architect: J. Flotz
Custom-built houses; liquid systems.

El Toro

Project SAGE House (Solar Assisted Gas Equip-
ment) (1975)
A project of Southern California Gas Company
810 South Flower St.
Los Angeles, CA 90017
Project director: V. Fione
Liquid collectors retrofitted to existing garden
apartments; brochure available.

Kentfield
(San Francisco)

Jeffrey House (1975)
Kentfield Hills, Marin County
Engineering: Interactive Resources
39 Washington Avenue
Point Richmond, CA 94801
Water-trickling collector, glass tube cover assembly.

San Diego

Vincente del Sol (1976)
San Diego Country Estates, San Diego
Owner/architect: Charles LeMenager
Engineer: J. Schultz
Liquid collectors, water-to-air heat pump; night
radiation cooling.

San Diego

Solar Housing Demonstration (1977)
Naval Complex, San Diego
Department of Defense Solar Residential Demon-
stration Project
Architect: Ezra D. Ehrenkrantz and Associates, P.C.
Various liquid and air systems on existing military
family housing.

Santa Clara

Solar Houses (1976-1977)
A project of the City of Santa Clara
Project manager: Robert R. Mortenson
1500 Warburston St.
Santa Clara 95050
Houses built for sale; solar installation to be owned
by public utility company, leased to home owner;
liquid system; recipient HUD solar demonstration
grant.

Selma

Self-Help Enterprises Solar Houses (1976-77)
Director: Robert Marshall, Self Help Enterprises
220 South Bridge St.
Visalia, CA 93277
Five houses with "Skytherm" heating and cooling
system; recipient of HUD demonstration grant.

Twenty-Nine Palms

Solar Housing Demonstration (1977)
Naval Base, Twenty-Nine Palms
Department of Defense Solar Residential Demon-
stration Project
Architect: Ezra D. Ehrenkrantz and Associates, P.C.
Multi-unit solar DHW installation on existing mili-
tary family housing.

COLORADO

Solar Housing Demonstration (1977)
U.S. Air Force Academy
Department of Defense Solar Residential Demon-
stration Project
Architect: Ezra D. Ehrenkrantz and Associates, P.C.
Air collectors with various storage media for exist-
ing military family housing (photo below).

Aspen

Lipsey House (1976)
Architect/owner/builder: William Lipsey
Box 3202
Aspen 81611
Consultant: Ron Shore
Air-type collector; combined rock storage with
water storage under concrete radiant slab; see illus-
trations on pages 194-196.

Boulder

Bushnell House (1974)
502 Ord Drive, Boulder 80303
Engineer/designer/owner: R. H. Bushnell, P.E.
Air collectors on ground to heat existing residence.

Boulder

West Pearl Condominium (1975)
2000 5th Street, Boulder 80302
Builder: Kinetics Construction
608 Pearl St.
Boulder 80302
Engineer: R. H. Bushnell, P.E.
Four-story unit condominiums; air-type wall-
mounted collectors; rock storage.

Boulder

Solar Housing (1977)
1814 19th Street, Boulder
Owner: Dorothy and Donald Stonebraker
3361 Vista Drive
Boulder 80302
Architect: Joint Venture, Inc.
Apartment Condominiums; compound parabolic
collectors; baseboard heating; recipient HUD solar
demonstration grant (photo below).

Octavio Figueroa

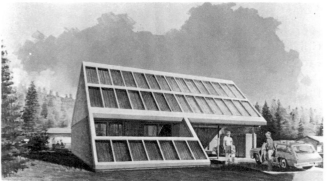

Colorado Springs

Phoenix House (1974)
5925 Del Paz Drive, Colorado Springs 80918
A joint project of Colorado Springs, the Phoenix
Corporation and the National Science Foundation
Project director: D. Jardine
                   P.O. Box 7246
                   Colorado Springs 80933
Architects: The Design Group
Liquid system; heat pump; data sheet available.

Colorado Springs

Jackson House (1974-1976)
1066 E. Woodman Rd., Colorado Springs 80918
Designer/owner/builder: R. H. Jackson
Water-trickling collector, subsequently changed to
closed liquid system in 1976.

Denver

Cherry Creek Solar Residences (1974)
419-421 St. Paul St.
Architect: Crowther Solar Group
Remodeled townhouses; air and liquid collector
systems, existing coal bin used for storage container; data sheet available.

Ft. Collins

Colorado State University Solar Houses (1974 to
present)
Fort Collins 80521
A project of the Solar Energy Applications Lab and
the National Science Foundation
Project managers: D. S. Ward and G. Löf
Three identical houses to test liquid, air, and evacuated-tube collectors; first house with liquid collectors; LiBr absorption cooling; report "Design and
Construction of a Residential Solar Heating System,"
available from National Technical Evaluation Service. Order document no PB 237042; see Figure
1.10.

Snowmass
(near Aspen)

Shore House (1974)
Designer/owner/builder: Ron Shore
                         Box 238
                         Snowmass 81654
Water-trickling nesting-type collector; large storage
capacity; descriptive literature available; see Figure
4.4.

CONNECTICUT

Groton

Eames Residence (1976)
Juniper Point Road, Groton 06340
Owner/builder: Court Eames
Architect: Donald Watson, AIA
Engineer: F. N. Broberg, Jr., P.E.
Air-type collector storage; liquid collectors for
DHW; greenhouse, heat recovery; see illustrations
on pages 202-203.

Guilford

Barber Residence (1974-77)
Guilford 06437
Engineer/owner: E. M. Barber, Jr., c/o Sunsearch
                       669 Boston Post Road
                       Guilford 06437
Architect: C. W. Moore, Associates, (now Moore,
                     Grover, Harper) with Richard Oliver
Designed for liquid system; house heat recovery in
rock storage under radiant concrete floor; see
Figure 5.1.

New London

Solar Housing Demonstration (1977)
NAVSU Base, New London
Department of Defense Solar Residential
Demonstration Project
Architect: Ezra D. Ehrenkrantz and Associates, P.E.
Liquid systems retrofitted to existing military family
housing; one single-family house and one row house
unit.

DELAWARE

Newark

Solar One (1973)
A project of the Institute of Energy Conversion,
University of Delaware, Newark 19711
Project directors: K. Böer, M. Telkes, K. O'Connor
Architect: H. M. Weese
Photoelectric cells for electricity, air system for
space heating; eutectic salt phase-change heating
storage; see Figure 5.28.

Rehoboth Beach

Pyramidal Optics Solar House (1976)
Owner/developer: John Jankus III
                      Box 389-AA
                      Hockessin 19707
Engineer: Wormser Scientific Corporation
Model Home; pyramidal optics installation; heat pump.

DISTRICT OF COLUMBIA

Washington, D. C.

Thomason Solar Homes (1959 to present)
Engineer & owner: Dr. H. E. Thomason
                      6802 Wasker Mill Rd., S.E.
                      Bethesda, MD
Several Thomason solar homes; water-trickling collectors; Solaris system; publication list available; see Figure 5.11.

FLORIDA

Gainesville

University of Florida Solar Test House (1955 to present)
Project of Solar Energy Conversion Laboratory
University of Florida, Gainesville 32611
Project director: Eric A. Farber
Early and continuing example in use of solar heating and cooling; descriptive literature available.

Homosassa

Sugarmill Woods Solar House (1976)
Sugarmill Woods Residential Community
U. S. Highway 19, Homosassa
Builder/developer: Punta Gordo Developers
Architect: Burt, Hill Associates
Model Home; liquid collectors LiBr absorption cooling; see Figure 5.25.

St. Petersburg

Solar DHW Retrofit (1977)
A project of the City of St. Petersburg, Department of Housing and Redevelopment, 4 Fourth Street, Room 604, St. Petersburg 33731
Project director: Edmund J. Boyle
Retrofit of solar DHW system on existing two story apartment, single bank of collectors serving four apartments; recipient HUD solar demonstration grant.

GEORGIA

Atlanta

Solar House (1976)
Builder: Hooker-Barnes
          400 Colony Square, Suite 1920
          Atlanta 30361
House built for sale; liquid collector and storage system; recipient HUD solar demonstration grant.

Dacula

Solar House (1977)
Tanner Road, Dacula
Architect/builder: Winford Lindsay
                        1100 Plaza Dr., Suite 5
                        Lawrenceville 30245
Built for sale; liquid system; recipient HUD solar demonstration grant.

Shenandoah
(near Atlanta)

Solar House (1977)
Builder: Peachtree Homes, Inc.
          Box 2436
          Peachtree City 30260
House built for sale; liquid system with LiBr absorption cooling; recipient HUD solar demonstration grant.

HAWAII

Honolulu

The Hawaiian Energy House
A project of the Department of Architecture, University of Hawaii (Manoa), Honolulu 96822
Sponsored by State of Hawaii, Hawaii Housing Authority and University of Hawaii Office of Research Administration.
Architect and project director: James E. Pearson, AIA
Solar domestic water heating; natural ventilation design; data sheet available.

ILLINOIS

Batavia
(near Chicago)

Fermilab House (1976)
21B Sauk Circle, Fermilab Villabe, Batavia 60510
Engineers: H. Hinterberger and J. O'Meara
Builders: Fermilab Solar Energy Club
        Fermi National Accelerator Laboratory
        P.O. Box 500
        Batavia 60510
Liquid collectors on ground outside existing house; storage in collapsible plastic bag in crawl space; report available.

Carlyle

Jantzen House (1975)
Box 172, Carlyle 62231
Designer/owner/builders: Mike and Elen Jantzen
Vacation house; skylight with operable reflectors used as collectors, two 100-gallon water tanks exposed to sun on interior used as storage; greenhouse and other solar applications; photo and drawing shown.

Eureka

Eureka Solar House (1975)
Sun Systems, Inc., Box 155, Eureka 61530
Engineer: Y. B. Safdari, President, Sun Systems, Inc.
Liquid system.

Vernon Hills
(near Chicago)

New Century Townhouses (1976)
Saratoga Court, New Century Town
Developers: Urban Investment and Development
        Co., (Marvin J. Richman, Vice President)
        845 N. Michigan Avenue, Suite 800
        Chicago 60611
Four townhouses, evacuated-tube collectors, heat pump; recipient of HUD solar demonstration grant; see Figure 1.11.

KANSAS

Leawood
(near Kansas City)

Solar House (1977)
12803 Pembroke Circle, Leawood
Builder: Koehler Building Co., Kansas City
Air system.

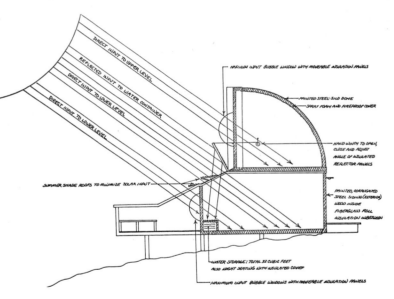

KENTUCKY

Solar Housing Demonstration (1977)
Fort Campbell
Department of Defense Solar Residential Demonstration Project
Architect: Ezra D. Ehrenkrantz and Associates, P.C.
Various solar-assisted heat pump installations (air-to-air and water-to-air) on existing row house units for military family housing.

LOUISIANA

Solar Housing Demonstration (1977)
Fort Polk
Department of Defense Solar Residential Demonstration Project
Architect: Ezra D. Ehrenkrantz and Associates, P.C.
Liquid systems on existing garden apartments, detached and row house units for military family housing.

New Orleans

Solar Housing Demonstration (1977)
Naval Complex, New Orleans
Department of Defense Solar Residential Demonstration Project
Architect: Ezra D. Ehrenkrantz and Associates, P.C.
Various flat-plate and advanced collectors on existing row house units for military family housing.

MAINE

Blue Hill

Stookey Residence (1977)
Fairwinds, Blue Hill 04615
Owner/builder: Noel Stookey
Designers: George and Noel Stookey
Site-fabricated air system on addition to existing house.

MARYLAND

Solar Housing Demonstration (1977)
Andrews Air Force Base
Department of Defense Solar Residential Demonstration Project
Architect: Ezra D. Ehrenkrantz and Associates, P.C.
Air, liquid and advanced collectors on existing row house units for military family housing.

Gaithersburg

National Bureau of Standards Solar Test House (1975)
An experimental house on the grounds of National Bureau of Standards
Project director: Dr. J. Hill, National Bureau
of Standards
Building 226, Room B504
Washington, D.C. 20234
Various types of liquid collector and storage systems; LiBr absorption cooling; fully monitored for experimental purposes.

MASSACHUSETTS

Acton

Acorn Model Solar House (1976)
Route 2A, Acton
Project director: J. Bemis, President, Acorn Houses
P.O. Box 250
Concord 01742
Experimental model for precut, pre-engineered house; liquid collector system.

Marlboro

Diy-Sol, Inc. House (1974)
29 Highgate Road, Marlboro, 01752
Designer/owner: F. Rapp, President, Diy-Sol, Inc.
Existing house retrofitted with air-type wall-mounted collector; storage in 750 gallon water tank; publications list available.

Waltham

Solar Heat Corporation House (1976)
Owner: M. Hyman, Solar Heat Corporation,
Waltham
Architect: Massdesign, Inc.
Large 1200 S.F. liquid-type collector; large 16,000 gallon storage system; photo below.

Weston

Saunders House (1960)
15 Ellis Rd., Weston 02193
Engineer/owner: N. B. Saunders
South wall glazing as collector; massive construction used as storage; publication list available.

217

MICHIGAN

Kalamazoo

American Timber Homes Solar House (1977)
Builder: Lion Enterprises
      321 East Vine Street
      Kalamazoo 49001
Architect: Donald Watson, AIA
Packaged solar house built for sale; auxiliary system with sunroom window heat recovery; recipient HUD solar demonstration grant; see drawing below.

MINNESOTA

Bloomington

Equinox Solar House (1976)
9948 Nesbitt Circle, Hyland Hills, Bloomington
Builder: Marvin H. Anderson Construction
      8901 Lyndale Avenue
      South Bloomington 55420
Engineer: Honeywell Corporation
House built for sale; liquid collectors, double-glazed with AR coating on glass; recipient HUD solar demonstration grant; see photo below.

Honeywell Corp.

Esko
(near Duluth)

American Timber Homes Solar House (1977)
Builder: Glen Koski, Red Barn Realty, Esko 55733
Architect: Donald Watson, AIA
Packaged solar house built for sale; liquid system; greenhouse with rock storage under for house heat recovery; recipient HUD solar demonstration grant.

Rosemount
(near St. Paul)

Oroborus, South (1974)
Experimental project of University of Minnesota
Project director: D. R. Holloway, School of
                   Architecture
                   University of Minnesota
                   Minneapolis 55455
Architect: J. Ilse, 7177 Arrowhead, Duluth 55811
Water-trickling collector; sod roof.

MISSOURI

Poplar Bluff

American Timber Homes Solar House (1977)
Tomaro Oaks Development
Builder: Oscar Wren, Jr., President
      Tomaro Oaks, Inc., 1 Tomaro Trail
      Poplar Bluff 63901
Architect: Donald Watson, AIA
Packaged solar house built for sale; liquid system with solar assisted heat pump; greenhouse with rock storage under for house heat recovery; recipient HUD solar demonstration grant.

MONTANA

Browning

Solar Houses (1976-1977)
A project of the Black Feet Tribe.
Self-help housing project; air system; recipient HUD solar demonstration grant.

NEBRASKA

Lincoln

Volume Collector/Heat Pump Demonstration House (1976)
An experimental project at the University of Nebraska
Project director: Prof. Richard C. Bourne
                    Department of Construction Management
                    University of Nebraska
                    Lincoln 68505
Translucent roof in attic space to provide supply air to air-to-air heat pump; report available.

NEW HAMPSHIRE

Bedford
(near Manchester)

Tyrrell House (1975)
Owner: R. Tyrrell
Designers: TEA, Inc.
Collector: Glazed masonry wall with beadwall insulation system; earth-bermed east, north and west walls; see Figure 3.7.

NEW JERSEY

Blackwood

Solar Houses (1976-1977)
Korman Corporation, Jenkintown PA 19046
Architect: Richard G. Guenzel, Korman Corp.
Two houses built for sale, liquid systems, recipient HUD solar demonstration grant.

Mt. Laurel
(near Camden)

Evans House (1976)
Hartford Road, Mt. Laurel
Owner/developer: E. Evans, Tri-Valley
                             Construction Co.
Architect: M. B. Wells
Air system.

Northfield

Solar House (1976)
Bay Avenue, Northfield
Builder: C. Chas. Bieber
              8201 Lagoon Drive
              Margate 08402
Architect: Donald Watson, AIA and Marja Watson
House built for sale; auxiliary solar heating, sun room with window heat recovery system; see drawing below.

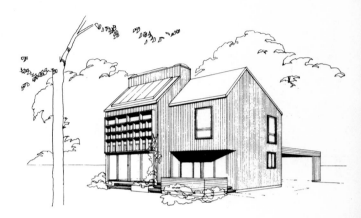

Old Bridge

Jespa Enterprises Solar House (1976)
Builder: Jespa Enterprises
              Box 11
              Old Bridge 08857
Architect: Donald Watson, AIA
House model built for sale; air system; liquid collectors for DHW; recipient HUD solar demonstration grant; see Figure 7.10.

Princeton

Kelbaugh House (1975)
Pine Street, Princeton 08540
Architect/owner: D. Kelbaugh
Glazed masonry wall collector/storage system; greenhouse; see Figure 3.8.

Shamong Township

Homan House (1975)
Tuckerton Road, Shamong Township
Owner/builder: R. Homan
Engineer: H. Thomason
Architect: M. B. Wells
Water-trickling collector; Thomason Solaris system; sod roof. See illustrations next page.

219

Homan House, Shamong Township, NJ.

Robert Perron

Robert Perron

NEW MEXICO

Albuquerque

Solar House (1976)
5808 Cambria Road, NW
Taylor Ranch Subdivision, Albuquerque
Project of Southern Union Gas Company and the
Dale Bellamah Corporation, Builders.

Corrales
(near Albuquerque)

Zomeworks Solar House (1971)
Designer/owner/builder: Steve Baer
                    Box 712
                    Albuquerque
Drumwall installation with reflectors; publications
list available; see Figure 3.9.

Las Cruces

Casa del Sol (1976)
A project of New Mexico State University
Interstate 25, Las Cruces
Project director: R. San Martin
Architects: Dean and Hunt Associates
            NMSU Mechanical Engineering
            Department
Liquid system; LiBr absorption cooling.

Santa Fe

Terry Residences (1975-1976)
Owner: Karen Terry, 636 Camino Lejo
        Santa Fe 87501
Architect: David Wright
Two houses, one for resale; skylights with insulating
controls used as collectors; massive adobe construction insulated on exterior and water-filled
drums used as storage.

Santa Fe

Van Dresser House (1958)
1002½ Canyon Road, Santa Fe
Designer/owner: P. Van Dresser
Adobe building remodeled for solar heating; air
system; data sheet available.

NEW YORK

Gardiner

Stevenson School Solar House (1976)
Project director: L. Rhoades, Riverside Dr.,
                        Gardiner
Designers: DAWN Associates, Jerome Kerner
            Box 66
            Phoenicia 12464
Glass-covered masonry wall system on small house;
high insulation standards.

Hamburg

Solar House (1976)
Innovative Building Systems, Inc.
69 Delaware Avenue
Hamburg 14075
Architect: Burt, Hill Associates
House built for sale; liquid collector with heat pump;
recipient HUD solar demonstration grant; see
drawing next page.

220

Solar House, Hamburg, NY.

Hopewell Junction

Ramage House (1976)
Beekman Road, Hopewell Junction 12533
Designer/owner: R. Ramage
Solar engineer: AHEAD Co., West Hurley, NY
Air system; regenerative cooling; liquid collectors
for DHW.

New York City

519 East 11th Street Apartments
Owner/builder: 519 East 11th St. Tenant
                      Association
Consultants: Travis Price (Solar design)
                    Tom Grayson (Installation)
                    448 E. 85 St.
                    New York City 10028
A self-help mutual-aid retrofit installation of liquid
collectors for DHW for renovated apartments; con-
struction improved for high insulation standards.

NORTH CAROLINA

Solar Housing Demonstration (1977)
Fort Bragg
Department of Defense Solar Residential
Demonstration Project
Architect: Ezra D. Ehrenkrantz and Associates, P.C.
Liquid collectors and vertical fin reflectors installed
on east/west roofs of existing military family
housing for side by side comparison with south-
facing optimum-tilt installation.

Octavio Figueroa

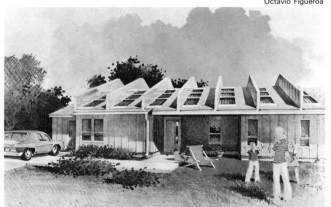

NORTH DAKOTA

Grand Forks

Solar Housing Demonstration (1977)
Grand Forks Air Force Base
Department of Defense Solar Residential
Demonstration Project
Architect: Ezra D. Ehrenkrantz and Associates, P.C.
Various liquid systems, existing townhouse units of
military family housing, including one collector
installation on a vertical end wall.

OHIO

Beallsville

Raven Rocks House (1977)
Owner/builder: Warren Stetzel, Rt 1
                      Beallsville 43716
Architect: Malcomb B. Wells
Self-help construction; partly underground; solar
windows, greenhouses and wind energy systems.

Cleveland

The Sun House (1974)
A project of Bob Schmitt Homes,
13079 Falling Water, Strongville, 44136
Skylight with insulating controls used to heat central atrium, storage in masonry floor construction;
fireplace and heat pump back-up; news release
available.

College Corner
(near Oxford)

Moore House (1976)
7384 Buck Paston Rd., College Corner 45056
Architect/owner: Fuller Moore
Water-trickling collector, later changed to owner-devised variation of nesting collector using thin copper foil as the upper absorber sheet; in-ground storage outside residence; descriptive literature available. (Illustration opposite.)

Columbus

Ohio State University Solar House (1974)
Ohio Exposition Center, Columbus
A project of Ohio State University with Homewood Corporation
Project manager: C. F. Sepsy, Ohio State University
Department of Mechanical
Engineering
Architect: G. M. Clark
Liquid system; LiBr absorption cooling; report available.

Dublin

Solar House (1977)
Builder: Building Industry Association of Central Ohio
(Charles Ruma, Chairman)
5898 Cleveland Avenue
Columbus, Ohio 43229
House built for sale; air system; recipient HUD solar demonstration grant.

Mansfield

Zaugg Solar Houses (1975-76)
Marion Avenue, Twin Lakes Golf Course
Richland County 44903
Designer/builders: T. Zaugg and J. Zaugg
Two houses; one water-trickling system, the other an air system; data sheets available.

OKLAHOMA

Tulsa

Solar Houses (1976-1977)
A project of the Creek Nation Housing Authority, Highway 75, Okmulgee, OK
Existing houses retrofitted with liquid systems; recipient HUD solar demonstration grant.

Wagoner

Engle House (1975)
Rt. 2, Box 57, Wagoner
Architect: A. Lower
Liquid system. See illustration below.

OREGON

Ashland

Solar House (1977)
Architect/builder: Vincent Oredson
236 East Main St.
Ashland 97520
Liquid system, greenhouse with insulating panels; recipient HUD solar demonstration grant.

Coos Bay

Mathew House (1967)
Designer/owner/builder: Henry Mathew
Box 768
Coos Bay 97420
Site-fabricated liquid collectors on roof ridge, reflectors on roof; performance documentation by University of Oregon (Prof. John Reynolds); publication list available.

Engle House, Wagoner, OK.

Opposite: Moore House, College Corner, Ohio.

Eugene

Solar Energy Resource Center (1975)
1565 Agate St., Eugene 97403
A project of the University of Oregon
Project managers: B. Beers-Green and J. Mele
Liquid system retrofit on existing residence.

Gladstone

Boleyn House (1976)
17610 Springhill Pl., Gladstone 97027
Owners/co-designers: Doug and Emily Boleyn
Architects: R. Hansen and D. McClure
Project assistance and funding by Portland General
Electric; liquid system; descriptive literature
available.

PENNSYLVANIA

Lewisburg

Barraclough House (1975)
1 Beck St. Lewisburg 17837
Designer/owner/builder: R. Joseph Barraclough
Air system.

Mt. Holly Springs
(near Harrisburg)

Slyder House (1974)
Engineer/builder/owner: J. Slyder
Water-trickling collector mounted on shop and in-
ground water storage outside house.

Philadelphia

Solar Townhouse Retrofit (1977)
A project of the Department of Engineering,
University of Pennsylvania
Project manager: A. E. Paddock
                 Towne Building (D-3)
                 Philadelphia 19174
Liquid system on roof of existing three story town-
house; recipient HUD solar demonstration grant.

Philadelphia

Solar DHW Retrofit (1977)
A project of Drexel University
Project directors: D. C. Larson and C. W. Savery
                   Drexel University
                   Philadelphia 19104
Retrofit solar DHW systems to existing multi-family
housing; collectors mounted on flat roof; recipient
HUD solar demonstration grant; report available.

Schecksville
(near Allentown)

**Pennsylvania Power and Light Experimental
House Project** (1974)
Project director: R. Romancheck,
                  PP&L, 901 Hamilton Mall
                  Allentown 18101
Fence-mounted liquid collectors; waste heat
recovery systems.

Stoverstown
(near York)

Lefever House (1954)

Designer/owner/builder: H. R. Lefever
                        P.O. Box 457
                        Spring Grove 17362
Vertical wall air-type collectors, no storage except
thermal capacity of house construction.

RHODE ISLAND

Jamestown

Solar Homes One Prototype (1975)
Lawn Avenue, Jamestown
Designer/builder: S. Dickinson and M. Smith
                  Solar Homes, Inc.
                  2 Narragansett Avenue
                  Jamestown 02835
Project built for sale; Thomason system; heat pump.

Little Compton

Eddy House (1976)
Designer: Travis Price
Addition to existing house; air system; greenhouse;
liquid collectors for DHS system.

SOUTH CAROLINA

Charleston

Solar Housing Demonstration (1977)
Naval Weapons Station, Charleston
Department of Defense Solar Residential
Demonstration Project
Architect: Ezra D. Ehrenkrantz and Associates, P.C.
Various flat-plate and advanced collectors on exist-
ing garden apartment units of military family
housing; see drawing below.

Octavio Figueroa

Columbia

Yacht Cove Development Solar Houses (1977)
John J. Kruse, President
Cambridge Development Group
Yacht Cove Road, Columbia 29210
Engineer: Wormser Scientific Corporation
Pyramidal optics installation in four condominium
townhouses; solar assisted heat pump system;
recipient HUD solar demonstration grant; see
Figure 3.24.

Greenville

USDA ARS House (1976)
Builder: Heliothermics, Inc.
        10 Delores Street
        Greenville 29605
Project manager: H. F. Zornig,
                  Agricultural Research Service
                  U.S. Department of Agriculture
Experimental prototype; translucent attic roof
serves as collector for rock storage; recipient HUD
solar demonstration grant.

TENNESSEE

Knoxville

University of Tennessee Solar House (1976)
Alcoa Highway, Knoxville
Project funded in part by TVA; liquid system; additional solar-oriented windows; performance to be
compared with identical unit with ACES system;
see Figure 5.22.

TEXAS

Solar Housing Demonstration (1977)
Sheppard Air Force Base
Department of Defense Solar Residential
Demonstration Project
Architect: Ezra D. Ehrenkrantz and Associates, P.C.
Fixed and tiltable collectors installed on existing
carports for military family housing; see
drawing below.

Octavio Figueroa

Arlington
(near Dallas)

Discovery '76 Solar Test House (1976)
Project of College of Engineering and
School of Architecture
Grant from Texas Electric Service Company
Project director: G. W. Lowery
Architect: Todd Hamilton, AIA
Demonstration house; Northrup Tracking Collector;
heat pump; LiBr absorption cooling.

J. Busse

Austin

Solar House (1977)
West Lake Hills, Austin
Builder: Lamar Savings Association
P.O. Box 1566
Austin 78701
Architect: Thomas Leach
Roof shape designed as air-foil for increased natural ventilation; Northrup concentrating collectors on ground detached from house; LiBr absorption cooling; drawing below.

Dallas

Solar Houses (1976-77)
Builder: W. Brown Custom Builders
1200 Preston Road
Dallas 75230
Houses built for sale; liquid systems; recipient HUD Solar demonstration grant.

Lubbock

Solar House (1977)
Builder: Gordon Deering, Jr.
3303 67th Street
Lubbock 79413
House built for sale; air system; recipient HUD solar demonstration grant.

San Antonio

Solar Houses (1976-77)
Builder: San Antonio Ranch, Ltd.
720 Travis Park West
San Antonio 78205
Three houses built for sale; liquid collectors with double-glazing AR cooling; LiBr absorption cooling; recipient HUD solar demonstration grant.

UTAH

Stansbury Park
(near Salt Lake City)

Terracor Demonstration House (1977)
C. Bruce Miller, President, Terracor-Utah
529 E. South Temple, Salt Lake City 84102
Architects: David Rohobit, Environmental Design Group and Crowther Solar Group
House built for sale; air system; recipient HUD solar demonstration grant. Photo below.

VERMONT

Brookline

Grassy Brook Village, Inc. (1977)
Builder: Richard D. Blazej
Box 39
Newfane 05345
Engineer: Dubin-Mendell-Bloome Associates
Architect: People/Space Co., Inc.
Liquid collectors in single bank detached from condominium housing; recipient of HUD solar demonstration grant. See drawing next page.

Grassy Brook Village, Inc.
Brookline, VT.

Hinesburg

Solar Retrofit (1975)
Owner: Douglas Taff
       Hinesburg 05461
Consultant: Garden Way Laboratories
Retrofit of 200-year-old farmhouse (once the home of U.S. President Chester A. Arthur) for DHW; collectors on east-west sloping roof with south-facing reflector.

John Franklin Smith

Norwich

White Residence (1976)
Architect/owner: C. S. White Jr., Banwell,
            White & Arnold, Inc.
Consultants: TEA, Inc.
Site-fabricated wall-mounted air collectors and rock storage system; wood stove and electric heating back-up; see illustrations on page 187.

Quechee

Quechee Energy House (1976)
A project of the Terrosi Construction Company, Quechee
Designer: Blue/Sun Ltd.
Engineering: Grumman Aerospace
Liquid collectors; solar-assisted heat-pump system.

Warren

Dimetrodon Condominium (1976)
Rt 1, Box 160, Warren
Designer/builders: Dimetrodon Corporation
Water-trickling collector with Thomason-type storage system.

Wilder
(near Hanover)

Wilder House (1976)
Designer/builder: CHI Housing
               68 S. Main St.
               Hanover NH 03755
Consultants: TEA, Inc.
Wall-mounted air collector, rock storage system;
well-insulated construction.

Windham

Solar House (1975)
Architect: People/Space Co., Inc.
Air collectors; large movable reflectors; movable
insulating panel on interior of south window;
rock storage.

VIRGINIA

Solar Housing Demonstration (1977)
Fort Belvoir
Department of Defense Solar Residential
Demonstration Project
Architect: Ezra D. Ehrenkrantz and Associates, P.C.
Liquid systems retrofitted to existing military family
housing units. Drawing below.

Octavio Figueroa

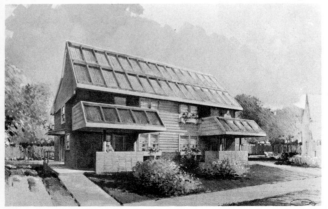

Alexandria

Solar House (1977)
615 S. Royal Street, Alexandria 22314
Builder: T. Rust
        210 S. Payne Street
        Alexandria
House built for sale; liquid system.

Hampton

NASA Technology Utilization House (1977)
NASA Langley Research Center
Project director: C. E. Kirby and others
Architects: Forrest Coile and Associates with
              Charles W. Moore and Associates
Experimental house with high insulation standards;
liquid system; heat pump; waste-water heat-
recovery system.

Virginia Beach

Solar Houses (1977)
Builder: Sir Galahad Company
         3929 Forest Glen Road
         Virginia Beach 23452
Two houses, built for sale; liquid system; recipient
HUD solar demonstration grant.

WISCONSIN

Milwaukee

Project Access: Solar Retrofit (1977)
A project of the University of Wisconsin, Milwaukee
53201
Project director: John Shade, School of
                     Architecture
Retrofit of existing dwelling, including many energy
conservation techniques; air system for space
heating; liquid collectors for DHW system; recipient
HUD solar demonstration grant; report available.

Rice Lake

American Timber Homes Solar House (1977)
Builder: William Burdich
        Route 2
        Birchwood 54517
Architect: Donald Watson, AIA
House built for sale, packaged solar house; air
system; separate rock storage for greenhouse heat
recovery system; recipient HUD solar demonstration grant. Drawing below; see also next page.

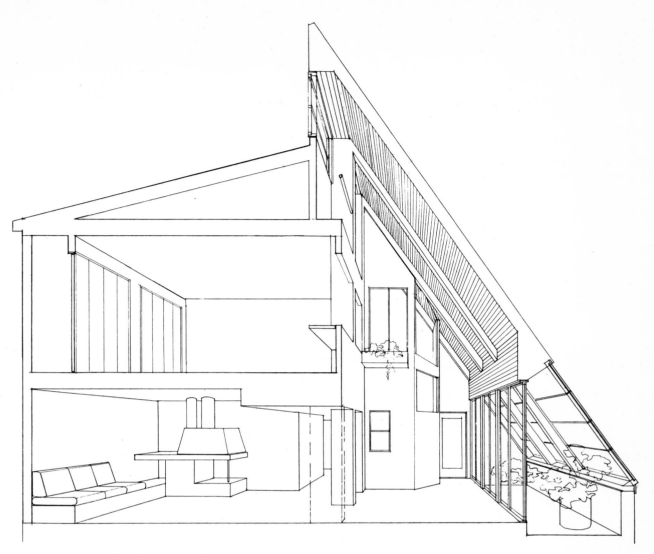

Interior perspective, Rice Lake house.

Summit

Solar House (1977)
Builder: Herbert B. Zien
         4450 North Oakland Avenue
         Milwaukee 53211
House built for sale; air system and air-to-air heat pump; recipient HUD solar demonstration grant.

Wild Rose

Kruschke House (1975)
Route 2, Wild Rose 54981
Designer/owner/builder: D. Krushke
Greenhouse used as collector; 25 steel drums filled with water exposed to sun used as storage; wood stove back-up system; report available.

SOLAR DESIGNERS, ARCHITECTS & ENGINEERS

The list includes solar designers, architects and engineers whose work is illustrated or referenced in this book and others who may be available as consultants to home builders. Inquiries to those listed should include a stamped, self-addressed return envelope.

For a more complete listing of architects and engineers with experience or interest in providing solar heating design services, see "List of Professionals Active in the Design of Solar-Heated Facilities," from AIA/Research Corporation, 1735 New York Avenue, N.W., Washington, DC 20006.

Architect TAOS
   (Bill Mingenbach)
Box 1884
Taos, NM 87501

Aronin, Jeffrey Ellis, AIA
389 Woodmere Boulevard
Woodmere, LI, NY 11598

Banfield, White and Arnold,
   Architects
2 West Wheelock St.
Hanover, NH 03755

Bridgers and Paxton,
   Consulting Engineers
213 Truman St. N.W.
Albuquerque, NM 87108

Brill, Kawakami, Wilbourne,
   Architects
77 Main St.
Cold Spring-on-Hudson, NY
   10516

Broberg, Fred N., P. E.
269-2 Grove Beach Road
Westbrook, CT 06498

Burt, Hill & Associates,
   Architects
   (Robert Rittlemann)
610 Mellon Bank Bldg.
Butler, PA 16001

Cook, Jeffrey, Architect
3627 Camino Sin Nombre
Scottsdale, AZ 85253

Crowther Solar Group
2830 East Third Avenue
Denver, CO 80206

Dadi Associates,
   Consulting Engineers
36 Woodland Street
Hartford, CT 06105

DAWN Associates
   (E. Eccli and J. Kerner)
Box 66
Phoenicia, NY 12464

Dubin-Mindell-Bloome,
   Associates
389 Woodmere Boulevard
Woodmere, LI, NY 11598

Ehrenkrantz, Ezra D. and
   Associates
   (William Meyer, Solar
   Projects Manager)
19 West 44th St., 18th Floor
New York, NY 10036

Fraker, Harrison, Architects
24 S. Nassau Street
Princeton, NJ 08540

Giffels Associates Architects
243 West Congress
Detroit, MI 48226

Haertling, Charles A.
1722 14th Street
Boulder, CO 80302

Hamilton, Todd, AIA
3883 Turtle Creek Blvd., Suite
712
Dallas, TX 75219

Hill and Harrigan, Consulting
Engineers
909 Whalley Avenue
New Haven, CT 06515

Joint Venture, Inc., Architects
(Phil Tabb)
1406 Pearl Street
Boulder, CO 80302

Kaptur, Hugh M. AIA
& Associates
600 E. Tahquitz-McCallum
Suite E
Palm Springs, CA 92262

Kawecki, Joseph
269 Cliffside Drive
Columbus, OH 43202

Keck, George F. and William
612 North Michigan Avenue
Chicago, IL 60611

Kelbaugh, Doug, Architect
Pine Street
Princeton, NJ

Lamar, Dick, AIA
201 Woodrow St.
Columbia, SC 29205

Lambeth, James, AIA
1891 Clark
Fayettesville, AR 72701

Levinson, Lebowitz, & Zapra-
vaskis, Architects
15 W. Highland Avenue
Philadelphia, PA 19811

Lipsey, Bill
Box 3203
Aspen, CO 81611

Lower, Alan, Architect
Suite 900
National Foundation Life
Building
Oklahoma City, OK 73112

Massdesign Architects and
Planners
18 Brattle Street
Cambridge, MA 02138

Medlin, Richard Larry
College of Architecture
University of Arizona
Tucson, AZ 85721

Minges Associates, Profes-
sional Engineers
The Exchange
Farmington, CT 06032

Moore, Fuller
7348 Buck Paxton Rd.
College Corner, OH 45056

Moore, Grover, Harper,
Architects
Essex, CT 06426

More-Combs-Burch Architects
3911 E Exposition Avenue
Denver, CO 80209

Pearson, James E. AIA
Dept. of Architecture
University of Hawaii
Manoa, Honolulu, HI 96822

People/Space Co.
259 Marlborough Street
Boston, MA 02116

Pinney, Neil, AIA
Earth/Life Systems Design
136 13th St.
Seal Beach, CA 90740

Price, Travis
Sun Harvester Corp.
729 7th Avenue
New York, NY 10019

REDE Research and Design
Institute
(Ronald Beckman)
Box 307
Providence, RI 02901

Reynolds, John, Architect
1858 University Street
Eugene, OR 97403

Shore, Ron, Solar Consultant
Box 238
Snowmass, CO 81654

Speilvogel, Lawrence G.,
Consulting Engineer
Wyncote House
Wyncote, PA 19095

TEA Associates, Inc.,
Designers
Church Hill
Harrisville, NH 03450

Watson, Donald, AIA
Box 401
Guilford, CT 06437

Wells, Malcomb B. Architect
Box 183
Cherry Hill, NJ 08002

Wormser Scientific Corporation
88 Foxwood Road
Stamford, CT 06903

Wright, Dave
c/o General Delivery
Sea Ranch, CA 95497

Yellott Solar Engineering
Laboratory
9051 N 7th Avenue
Phoenix, AZ 85013

Zoe Works, Architects
70 Zoe Street
San Francisco, CA 94107

Zomeworks (Steve Baer)
Box 712
Albuquerque, NM 87103

SOURCES OF SOLAR HEATING EQUIPMENT

1. SOLAR COLLECTORS

Companies are listed which manufacture solar collectors for distribution nationally (or, as noted, regionally). Names of local distributors are available from manufacturers. A stamped, self-addressed return envelope enclosed with your inquiry is a courtesy to companies, especially to small ones, which are often unprepared for volume inquiries.

This list is representative only, drawn in part from directories by ERDA (October 1975) and by **Professional Builder** magazine (June 1976). It includes those companies which have technical data available, backed up by performance test results. No endorsement of these products listed should be implied.

This list does not include manufacturers of other solar system components, such as heat exchangers, controls, or heat pumps. The advice of a qualified professional engineer is recommended for equipment selection and system design.

The U. S. Environmental Research and Development Agency (ERDA) periodically evaluates solar equipment for use in government demonstration projects. The results of these evaluations and a more complete listing of entries in the solar equipment manufacturing field is available on written request to ERDA Technical Information Center, Box 62, Oak Ridge, Tennessee 37830. (Also see Appendix I-A4, items 9 and 10). A list of companies that are members of the Solar Energy Industries Association (a private organization) is available for $2.00 from Solar Energy Industries Association, Inc., 1001 Connecticut Avenue, NW, Washington, D.C.

Solar Collectors: Space Heating—Air-Type

Contemporary Systems, Inc.
(John C. Christopher)
68 Charlonne Street
Jaffrey, NH 03452 (Regional)

Crimsco, Inc.
(Leo LoMaglio)
5001 E. 59th St.
Kansas City, MO 64130

International Solarthermics
    Corporation
P.O. Box 397
Nederland, CO 80466

Kalwall Corp./ Solar
    Components Div.
(Scott Keller)
Box 237
Manchester NH 03105

Rocky Mountain Sheet Metal
(Don Erickson)
5010 Cook St.
Denver, CO 80216
(Regional)

Solar-Aire
(Jerry Knips)
1611 9th St.
White Bear Lake, MN 55110
(Regional)

Solar Energy Products Co.
121 Miller Road
Avon Lake, OH 44012
(Regional)

Solaron
    (George Löf)
4850 Olive Street
Commerce City, CO 80022

Sun Stone
(Glenn F. Groth)
Box 941
Sheboygan, WI 53081
(Regional)

Sunwall, Inc.
(Ronald J. Gramm)
Box 9723
Pittsburgh, PA 15229
(Regional)

Sunworks, Division of
    Enthone Inc.
(F. C. Perry)
Box 1004
New Haven, CT 06508

Solar Collectors: Space Heating—Liquid-Type

Ametek, Inc.
(John Bowen)
1 Spring Avenue
Hatfield, PA 19440

CSI
(L. H. Sallen)
12400 49th Street
Clearwater, FL 33520
(Regional)

Chamberlain Manufacturing
    Corporation
845 Larch Avenue
Elmhurst, IL 60126

Daystar Corporation
(B. Tepper)
41 Second Avenue
Burlington, MA 01803

Energy Systems, Inc.
(Terrence Caster)
634 Crest Drive
El Cajon, CA 92021

General Electric/Space
    Division
(Robert Thorpe)
Box 8555
Philadelphia, PA 19101

Helio-Dynamics, Inc.
518 S. Van Ness Ave.
Los Angeles, CA 90020
(Regional)

Honeywell, Inc.
(Paul Kopecay)
2600 Ridgeway Parkway
Minneapolis, MN 55413

Ilse Engineering
(John F. Ilse)
7177 Arrowhead Road
Duluth, MN 55811

J & R Simmons Construction
    Company
2185 Sherwood Drive
So. Daytona, FL 32019
(Regional)

Mr. Sun, Inc.
(Robert G. Kincaid)
501 Archdale Drive,
    Suite 260
Charlotte, NC 28210
(Regional)

Northrup, Inc.
(Linc Eldredge)
302 Nichols Drive
Hutchins, TX 75141

Piper Hydro, Inc.
(James R. Piper)
2895 E La Palma
Anaheim, CA 92806

PPG Industries, Inc.
(Neill M. Barker)
One Gateway Center
Pittsburgh, PA 15143

Revere Copper and Brass, Inc.
(William J. Heidrich)
Solar Energy Dept.
Rome, NY 13440

Reynolds Metals Company
(Chester H. Holtyn)
6601 W. Broad Street
Richmond, VA 23261

Rocky Mountain Sheet Metal
(Don Erickson)
5010 Cook Street
Denver, CO 80216
(Regional)

Skytherm Processes
   Engineering
(Harold R. Hay)
2424 Wilshire Boulevard
Los Angeles, CA 90057

Solar Corporation of America
(J. Edward Taylor)
P.O. Box 399
Warrenton, VA 22186

Solar Systems, Inc.
(Jack Decker)
1802 Dennis Drive
Tyler, TX 75701

Solergy, Inc.
(Ronald H. Smith)
70 Zoe Street
San Francisco, CA 94107

Steelcraft Corporation
(Gary Ford)
Box 12408
Memphis, TN 38112

Sun Harvester Corporation
(Travis Price)
729 7th Avenue
New York, NY 10019
(Regional)

Sun Systems, Inc.
(Dr. Y. B. Safdari)
P.O. Box 155
Eureka, IL 61530
(Regional)

Sunearth, Inc.
(Howard Katz)
Progress Drive
Montgomeryville, PA 18936

Sunsav, Inc.
(Peter H. Ottmar)
250 Canal Street
Lawrence, MA 01840

Sunsource, Inc.
(David L. Collins)
1291 S. Brass Lantern Drive
La Habra, CA 90631

Sunstream (Grumman Corp.)
(Art Barry)
Plant 25
Bethpage, NY

Sunwater Company
(Stewart Williams)
1112 Pioneer Way
El Cajon, CA 92020

Sunworks, Division
   of Enthone, Inc.
(F. C. Perry)
Box 1004
New Haven, CT 06508

Thomason Solar Homes, Inc.
(Harry Thomason)
6802 Walker Mill Rd., S.E.
Washington, DC 20027

Western Energy
(Norman Rees)
459 Forest Ave.
Palo Alto, CA 94302
(Regional)

Solar Collectors: Domestic Water Heating or Pool Heating Only

Burke Rubber Company
(Larry R. Schader)
2250 South 10th Street
San Jose, CA 95112

D. W. Browning Contracting
   Company
(Ike Johnston)
475 Carswell Avenue
Holly Hill, FL 32017
(Regional)

Ecotope Group
(Ken Smith)
Box 618
Snohomish, WA 98230
(Regional)

El Camino Solar Systems
(Terence C. Honikman)
5511 Ekwill St., Suite C
Santa Barbara, CA 93111
(Regional)

Fafco, Inc.
(F. Ford)
138 Jefferson Drive
Menlo Park, CA 94025

Falbel Energy Systems, Inc.
472 Westover Road
Stamford, CT 06902
(Regional)

General Energy Devices, Inc.
(Ian Morgan)
2991 West Bay Drive
Largo, FL 33540

Hitachi American Ltd.
(Toichi Hamajima)
437 Madison Avenue
New York, NY 10022
(Regional)

International Environment
   Corporation
(R.D. Rothschild)
129 Halstead Avenue
Mamaroneck, NY 10543

Largo Solar Systems
(Ron Hannivig)
2525 Key Largo Lane
Fort Lauderdale, FL 33312

Miller Associates
(Roy Everhigham)
156 NW 73rd Street
Miami, FL

OEM Products, Inc.
(D. W. Barlow, Sr.)
220 W. Brandon Boulevard
Brandon, FL 33511

Fred Rice Productions
(Fred Rice)
6313 Peach Avenue
Van Nuys, CA 91411

Sol-Aire
(R. Bruce Springer)
46 Las Cascadas
Orinda, CA 94563
(Regional)

Solar Development, Inc.
(D. Kazimir)
4180 Westroads Dr.
West Palm Beach, FL 33407
(Regional)

Solar Dynamics, Inc.
(E. L. Chester)
4527 E. 11th Ave.
Hialeah, FL 33013
(Regional)

Solar Systems Sales
(George Walters)
180 Country Club Drive
Novato, CA 94947
(Regional)

The Solaray Corporation
(Lawrence M. Judd)
2414 Makiki Heights Drive
Honolulu, HI 96822

Soltex Corporation
(A. E. Cunningham)
Box 55703
Houston, TX 77055
(Regional)

Systems Technology, Inc.
(William S. Cronk)
Box 337
Shalimar, FL 32579
(Regional)

Wallace Co.
Box 511
Gainesville, GA 30501
(Regional)

Wilson Solar Kinetics Corporation
(James A. Pohlman)
Box 17308
West Hartford, CT 06117
(Regional)

2. INSULATING WINDOW DEVICES

(As noted, some of these companies have expressed
interest in marketing insulating window devices,
but are not in production.)

Appropriate Technology Corporation, Box 121,
Townshend, VT 05353
Thermal Curtain, a fabric-lined polyester-filled
curtain, with velcro strips at edges to reduce air
infiltration (under development).

Ark-tic-Seal Systems, Inc., Box 428, Butler, WI
53007
Three roller shades in one valance for control
of heat loss and heat gain; reflective outer shade,
transparent middle shade, absorbent inner shade
to be operated in any combination (custom order
only for large windows—8 ft. x 8 ft. or larger).

The Insulating Shade Company, RFD 1,
Box 689, Durham, CT 06422
Holds patent for roll shade which expands when
in open position to create insulating air space,
installed in normal roll shade hardware (not in
production).

Zomeworks, Box 712, Albuquerque, NM 87103
Plans, specifications, components and use rights
of **Beadwall**; supplies complete **Skylid** system
(custom order).

3. PLANS, LITERATURE ON SYSTEM DESIGN AND/OR LICENSE OR USE RIGHTS

Skytherm Processes and Engineering (See listing under liquid systems)

Thomason Solar Homes, Inc. (See listing under
liquid systems)

Zomeworks: Drumwall, Beadwall, Skylid, Backyard air collector/storage design (see listing
under insulating window devices).

235

4. TOTAL BUILDING PACKAGES (HOUSE AND SOLAR EQUIPMENT)

Acorn Structures, Inc., John Bemis, Box 250, Concord, MA 01742

American Timber Homes, Inc., John Walbridge, Escanaba, MI 49829

5. LITERATURE AND/OR COMPONENTS FOR DO-IT-YOURSELF INSTALLATION

Brace Research Institute, McGill University, Ste. Anne de Bellevue, Montreal, Canada
Publications list available on self-help alternate technologies. Instruction booklet on do-it-yourself liquid collector construction, $1.25.

DIY-Sol Heating Systems, F. Rapp, Box 614, Marlboro, MA 01752
Components and manual on "do-it-yourself" air-type collector.

Edmund Scientific, 100 Edscorp Building, Barrington, NJ 08007
Mail order catalog, $.75, includes some solar energy components.

J. Don Field, 4601-A Renfro Blvd. NW, Roanoke, VA 24017.
Information packet available on site-constructed water-trickling collector construction, $6.00.

Garden Way Publishing, Charlotte, VT 05445
Plan for do-it-yourself "Solar Room," $9.95

Ron Hannivig, 2525 Key Largo Lane, Fort Lauderdale, FL 33312
Information available on site fabricated rooftop collector and storage system (thermosyphon) for domestic water heating.

Ken Harrington, 769 22nd St., Oakland, CA 94612
Data packet on site fabricated liquid collector, $5.00

Kalwall Corporation/Solar Components Division, Scott Keller, Box 237, Manchester, NH 03105
Collector covers, transparent storage containers, other components.

Minnesota Mining and Mfg. Co., D. S. Witnah, Box 33331, Stop 62, St. Paul, MN 55133
Black metal paint, "NEXTEL" (non-selective) for absorbers.

New England Solar Energy Association, Box 121, Townsend, VT 05353
Booklet "Build Your Own Solar Water Heater," $3.50.

Roll-Bond Products, Olin Brass, J. I. Barton, East Alton, IL 62024
Collector absorber plates.

John R. Snell, Route 1, Getna, NB 68028
Information on site fabricated backyard air collector; rock storage with water tank within.

J & R Simmons Construction Co., John Simmons, 2185 Sherwood Drive, South Daytona, FL 32019
Liquid collector shipped in parts for "do-it-yourself" assembly.

Solar Energy Digest, Solar Equipment Division, Box 17776, San Diego, CA 92117
Do-it-yourself plans for Solarsan Solar Water Heater.

Solar Sun Still Inc., Setauket, NY 11733 (Chad Rasemann)
Coating for plastic or glass to prevent condensation and dripping.

Solar Usage Now, 450 E. Tiffin St., Box 306, Bascom, OH 44809
Dealer in solar energy components (collectors, heat exchangers, sensors, controls). Catalog, $1.00.

SOLAR DESIGN CALCULATIONS

This appendix describes calculation methods by which the performance and cost of solar heating designs can be compared. Because performance is so directly related to local climate conditions and the specific type of solar collector used, such calculations are essential in order to make judgments about each design. The methods are based on month-by-month averages of climate and collector performance data, and the calculations can be done "longhand," with an inexpensive calculator making the arithmetic tasks quite simple.

Computer calculations of a heating system's hourly performance often are used to design large buildings, but the longhand methods of monthly averages given here are sufficient for house design.

These methods, however, are not intended to replace the more complex and detailed calculations that are required to determine the specific size of equipment in a solar heating system. Complete calculation methods (for professional architects and engineers) are detailed in the following references:

Reference 1: **ASHRAE Handbook of Fundamentals,** 1972, and **Handbook of Applications,** 1974. ASHRAE, 345 East 47th St., New York, NY 10017

Reference 2: **Criteria for the Design of Solar Heated Buildings,** by E. M. Barber, Jr. and Donald Watson. Sunworks Publications, Guilford, CT. 1975.

Reference 3: **Climatic Atlas of the United States,** U.S. Department of Commerce. U.S. Government Printing Office. Washington, D.C.

Note: These calculations are given for United States house sites only. Similar calculations can be made with appropriate data for sites in other locations, based on local climatic conditions.

237

Any calculation of a building's heat requirement has to be considered as an approximate working estimate only. Even if all climate conditions were constant—which they obviously are not—there is too great a variation in the heating energy used by individual homeowners, because of their own house-use patterns, to make anything but approximate estimates.

Even with computer methods, there are assumptions made that account for wide variations between the calculated heating needs of a building and its actual performance.

A study of seven commonly used computer programs for building energy loads published by the Better Heating-Cooling Council, shows that as much as a 40 percent variation in calculated results is possible, depending upon the method and assumptions used.

In addition, there is a great variation in energy used in homes, depending upon the living patterns of the occupants. In a detailed documentation of houses in use in Twin Rivers, New Jersey, a Princeton research team reported variations of more than 30 percent in consumed energy between different families in identical housing units.

And just because a certain percentage of insulation is added to a building does not guarantee that the owners will see a comparable reduction in the heating requirement. In energy-consumption studies of houses in England that included some with greatly increased insulation, only 50 percent of the house occupants realized an energy savings. The other 50 percent maintained higher temperatures in the dwellings, well above the 68° F. that was used in calculating possible energy savings.

Finally, while average climate statistics are used in the calculations, often there is as much as a 20 percent variation in the weather from year to year.

These points should be kept in mind in making solar calculations. While the calculation methods are useful and indeed necessary to compare different design decisions, they should not be used in any way that might misrepresent their limitations.

The methods given below, however, can be used to make informed judgments about various design alternatives in terms of heating efficiency and heating cost reductions. By using the same method, the assumptions apply equally to any alternatives that are compared.

The calculations and tables can be used for any solar installation in the United States. In addition, blank forms are included at the end of this appendix for easy tabulation of the calculations illustrated here.

There are four steps involved in solar design calculation, each of which is discussed in separate sections of this appendix.

1. **Heating energy requirement:** Determine the monthly heating energy required for space heating and domestic water heating.

2. **Solar contribution:** Determine the monthly heat gain contribution from solar collectors and from windows.

3. **Auxiliary fuel requirement:** By subtracting the monthly solar contribution from the heating energy required, determine the monthly auxiliary fuel requirement.

4. **Life cycle costing:** Based on current and projected costs of auxiliary fuel, determine the annual fuel savings made possible by the solar contribution.

II.1
House-Heating
Energy Requirement

Solar heating can be used for space heating, for domestic water heating, or both. Because two different types of auxiliary fuel might be used, one for space heating, the other for domestic water, the calculations for each are done separately. The combined fuel saving can then be tabulated together in the life-cycle cost analysis (Section II.4, below).

SPACE HEATING REQUIREMENT

A detailed estimate of a house heating requirement involves an extended series of heat-loss calculations for each outside surface, including roof, walls, windows and floors. Such a procedure, used by professional heating engineers, is necessary to evaluate the comparative heat-loss reduction achieved by

Table II.1. *Graphic Method for Determining Design Heat Loss. The method allows one to easily determine the DHL for a house under steady-state heat flow conditions to approximate the energy required to heat a house over some period of time using the degree day concept.*

The graphs show the DHL in Btu/hr, given some fixed temperature difference (dT), between inside and outside. The DHL/dT is shown as a function of the aspect ratio of the house under a variety of conditions. Curves are shown for two different "U" values for glass, one set using 1.13 (Btu/hr/ft^2 degrees F.) for single glazing (dotted lines) and the other 0.61 for double glazing (solid lines).

II.1A. *1200-sq. ft. two-story building, flat roof assumed.*

increased wall or roof insulation, and is detailed in Reference 1.

A shortcut, given in Reference 2, eliminates detailed heat-loss calculations. Instead graphs are used for determining the design heat loss of a building, followed by the calculation of the heat load, based on the design heat loss and local climate data.

Four characteristics of a building largely determine its heat loss:

1. the shape of the building

2. the amount of glass area

3. the amount of insulation used in the building walls and roof

4. the infiltration of outside air through opening doors and other portions of the building structure

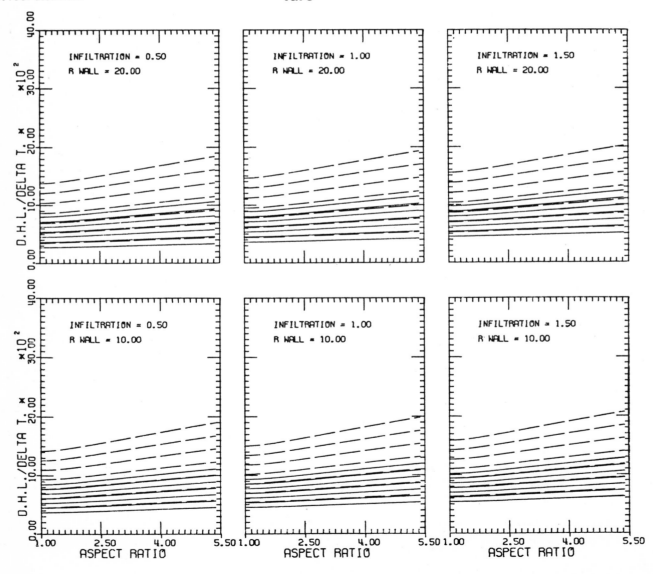

The graphs shown in Table II.1 can be used to approximate the hourly Design Heat Loss of a particular house, based on the size and wall characteristics. This in turn is used to calculate the annual space heating requirement.

The infiltration rate of a poorly insulated house is about 1.50; of standard but good construction about 1.00; and of an extremely well-insulated house about 0.50. The R value of standard wall construction can be taken to average 10.00; of a well-insulated house 20.00. Each combination of these factors is represented by a different graph.

Based on the conditions that apply to a particular house and its square footage, then, the appropriate graph is selected from those shown in Table II.1.

The horizontal axis of the graphs represents the Aspect Ratio of the house. The aspect ratio is the ratio of the house's length and width. Thus a house

Constants for each set of curves were the resistance of the opaque walls and the infiltration of outside air expressed in air changes per hour. Curves are shown representing the DHL for 10, 20, 30, 40, 50, 60, and 70% glass area. The glass area is expressed as a percentage of the total wall area, with 10% glass having the smallest DHL/dT. Thus, the percentage of glass increases directly as one moves from the bottom of each graph to the top. Losses to a slab on grade or to a basement were ignored. Conduction losses through doors were also ignored. The resistance of the roof was taken to be 1.5 x R value of opaque walls. Floor-to-floor height was assumed to be 8 feet. (Reference 2)

II.1B. *2000-sq. ft. two-story building, flat roof assumed.*

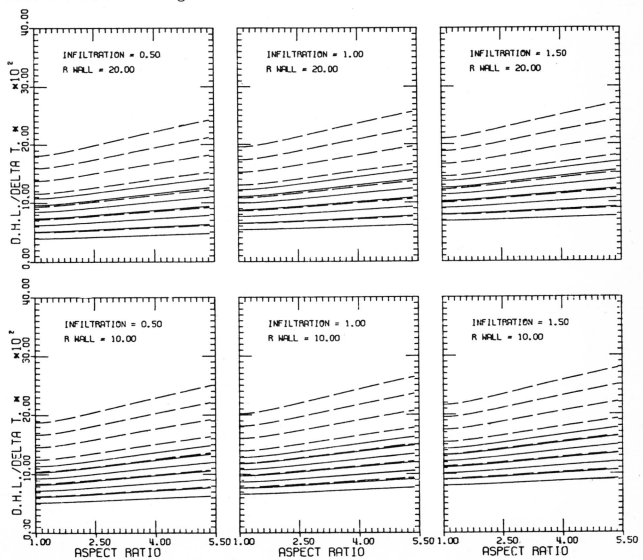

with equal sides would have an aspect ratio of 1; a rectangular plan twice as long as the width would have an aspect ratio of 2/1 or 2, and so forth.

The lines within the graphs are drawn for various percentages of window area to floor area, with insulated glass shown in solid lines and uninsulated single glass in broken lines.

With these determinants, the Design Heat Loss factor required can be read from the vertical axis of the graphs. Thus, for a 1200-square-foot house with an aspect ratio of 1.5 and 20 percent insulated-glass area, infiltration = 1.00 and R wall = 20.00, one can read on the vertical axis the factor for DHL/Delta T = 8.5×10^2. This factor represents in Btus the hourly total Design Heat Loss of the house, divided by Delta T (inside temperature minus the outside temperature).

To determine the monthly heating energy requirement in Btus per month (Qr), the DHL/Delta T factor is multiplied by 24 (hours per day) times a monthly Degree Day factor. The Degree Day factor for major U.S. cities is given in Table II.2. The heating degree days are the number of degrees the daily average temperature is below 65° F. in a particular location. The degree day factor was developed for estimating heating requirements and is used by fuel suppliers for estimating variations in local fuel requirements throughout the year.

In Form 1.1 shown on p. 246, the calculations of the Space Heating Requirement of the house in Denver (used in Chapter 7) are given as an example.

DOMESTIC HOT WATER REQUIREMENT

The monthly energy requirement in Btus for domestic hot water (Qr) is given by the calculation:

$$Qr \text{ (Btus/month)} = G \times 8.33 \times dT \times DM$$

where:

G   = Daily household hot water requirement in gallons

8.33 = the Btu capacity of one gallon of water for each degree Fahrenheit of temperature

dT   = The temperature difference between the hot water supply and the cold water inlet to the system

DM = the number of days per month

STATE AND STATION	JULY	AUG.	SEP.	OCT.	NOV.	DEC.	JAN.	FEB.	MAR.	APR.	MAY	JUNE	ANNUAL
ALA. BIRMINGHAM	0	0	6	93	363	555	592	462	363	108	9	0	2551
HUNTSVILLE	0	0	12	127	426	663	694	557	434	138	19	0	3070
MOBILE	0	0	0	22	213	357	415	300	211	42	0	0	1560
MONTGOMERY	0	0	0	68	330	527	543	417	316	90	0	0	2291
ALASKA ANCHORAGE	245	291	516	930	1284	1572	1631	1316	1293	879	592	315	10864
ANNETTE	242	208	327	567	738	899	949	837	843	648	490	321	7069
BARROW	803	840	1035	1500	1971	2362	2517	2332	2468	1944	1445	957	20174
BARTER IS.	735	775	987	1482	1944	2337	2536	2369	2477	1923	1373	924	19862
BETHEL	319	394	612	1042	1434	1866	1903	1590	1655	1173	806	402	13196
COLD BAY	474	425	525	772	918	1122	1153	1036	1122	951	791	591	9880
CORDOVA	366	391	522	781	1017	1221	1299	1086	1113	864	660	444	9764
FAIRBANKS	171	332	642	1203	1833	2254	2359	1901	1739	1068	555	222	14279
JUNEAU	301	338	483	725	921	1135	1237	1070	1073	810	601	381	9075
KING SALMON	313	322	513	908	1290	1606	1600	1333	1411	966	673	408	11343
KOTZEBUE	381	446	723	1249	1728	2127	2192	1932	2080	1554	1057	636	16105
MCGRATH	208	338	633	1184	1791	2232	2294	1817	1758	1122	636	258	14283
NOME	481	496	693	1094	1455	1820	1879	1666	1770	1314	930	573	14171
SAINT PAUL	605	539	612	862	963	1197	1228	1168	1265	1098	936	726	11199
SHEMYA	577	475	501	784	876	1042	1045	958	1011	885	837	696	9687
YAKUTAT	338	347	474	716	936	1144	1169	1019	1042	840	632	435	9092
ARIZ. FLAGSTAFF	46	68	201	558	867	1073	1169	991	911	651	437	180	7152
PHOENIX	0	0	0	22	234	415	474	328	217	75	0	0	1765
PRESCOTT	0	0	27	245	579	797	865	711	605	360	158	15	4362
TUCSON	0	0	0	25	231	406	471	344	242	75	6	0	1800
WINSLOW	0	0	6	245	711	1008	1054	770	601	291	96	0	4782
YUMA	0	0	0	0	148	319	363	228	130	29	0	0	1217
ARK. FORT SMITH	0	0	12	127	450	704	781	596	456	144	22	0	3292
LITTLE ROCK	0	0	9	127	465	716	756	577	434	126	9	0	3219
TEXARKANA	0	0	0	78	345	561	626	468	350	105	0	0	2533
CALIF. BAKERSFIELD	0	0	0	37	282	502	546	364	267	105	19	0	2122
BISHOP	0	0	42	248	576	797	874	666	539	306	143	36	4227
BLUE CANYON	34	50	120	347	579	766	865	781	791	582	397	195	5507
BURBANK	0	0	6	43	177	301	366	277	239	138	81	18	1646
EUREKA	270	257	258	329	414	499	546	470	505	438	372	285	4643
FRESNO	0	0	0	78	339	558	586	406	319	150	56	0	2492
LONG BEACH	0	0	12	40	156	288	375	297	267	168	90	18	1711
LOS ANGELES	28	22	42	78	180	291	372	302	288	219	158	81	2061
MT. SHASTA	25	34	123	406	696	902	983	784	738	525	347	159	5722
OAKLAND	53	50	45	127	309	481	527	400	353	255	180	90	2870
POINT ARGUELLO	202	186	162	205	291	400	474	392	403	339	298	243	3595
RED BLUFF	0	0	0	53	318	555	605	428	341	168	47	0	2515
SACRAMENTO	0	0	12	81	363	577	614	442	360	216	102	6	2773
SANDBERG	0	0	30	202	480	691	778	661	620	426	264	57	4209
SAN DIEGO	6	0	15	37	123	251	313	249	202	123	84	36	1439
SAN FRANCISCO	81	78	60	143	306	462	508	395	363	279	214	126	3015
SANTA CATALINA	16	0	9	50	165	279	353	308	326	249	192	105	2052
SANTA MARIA	99	93	96	146	270	391	459	370	363	282	233	165	2967
COLO. ALAMOSA	65	99	279	639	1065	1420	1476	1162	1020	696	440	168	8529
COLORADO SPRINGS	9	25	132	456	825	1032	1128	938	893	582	319	84	6423
DENVER	6	9	117	428	819	1035	1132	938	887	558	288	66	6283
GRAND JUNCTION	0	0	30	313	786	1113	1209	907	729	387	146	21	5641
PUEBLO	0	0	54	326	750	986	1085	871	772	429	174	15	5462
CONN. BRIDGEPORT	0	0	66	307	615	986	1079	966	853	510	208	27	5617
HARDFORT	0	6	99	372	711	1119	1209	1061	899	495	177	24	6172
NEW HAVEN	0	12	87	347	648	1011	1097	991	871	543	245	45	5897
DEL. WILMINGTON	0	0	51	270	588	927	980	874	735	387	112	6	4930
FLA. APALACHICOLA	0	0	0	16	153	319	347	260	180	33	0	0	1308
DAYTONA BEACH	0	0	0	0	75	211	248	190	140	15	0	0	879
FORT MYERS	0	0	0	0	24	109	146	101	62	0	0	0	442
JACKSONVILLE	0	0	0	12	144	310	332	246	174	21	0	0	1239
KEY WEST	0	0	0	0	0	28	40	31	9	0	0	0	108
LAKELAND	0	0	0	0	57	164	195	146	99	0	0	0	661
MIAMI BEACH	0	0	0	0	0	40	56	36	9	0	0	0	141
ORLANDO	0	0	0	0	72	198	220	165	105	6	0	0	766
PENSACOLA	0	0	0	19	195	353	400	277	183	36	0	0	1463
TALLAHASSEE	0	0	0	28	198	360	375	286	202	36	0	0	1485
TAMPA	0	0	0	0	60	171	202	148	102	0	0	0	683
WEST PALM BEACH	0	0	0	0	6	65	87	64	31	0	0	0	253
GA. ATHENS	0	0	12	115	405	632	642	529	431	141	22	0	2929
ATLANTA	0	0	18	127	414	626	639	529	437	168	25	0	2983
AUGUSTA	0	0	0	78	333	552	549	445	350	90	0	0	2397
COLUMBUS	0	0	0	87	333	543	552	434	338	96	0	0	2383
MACON	0	0	0	71	297	502	505	403	295	63	0	0	2136
ROME	0	0	24	161	474	701	710	577	468	177	34	0	3326
SAVANNAH	0	0	0	47	246	437	437	353	254	45	0	0	1819
THOMASVILLE	0	0	0	25	198	366	394	305	208	33	0	0	1529
IDAHO BOISE	0	0	132	415	792	1017	1113	854	722	438	245	81	5809
IDAHO FALLS 46W	16	34	270	623	1056	1370	1538	1249	1085	651	391	192	8475
IDAHO FALLS 42NW	16	40	282	648	1107	1432	1600	1291	1107	657	388	192	8760
LEWISTON	0	0	123	403	756	933	1063	815	694	426	239	90	5542
POCATELLO	0	0	172	493	900	1166	1324	1058	905	555	319	141	7033
ILL. CAIRO	0	0	36	164	513	791	856	680	539	195	47	0	3821
CHICAGO	0	0	81	326	753	1113	1209	1044	890	480	211	48	6155
MOLINE	0	9	99	335	774	1181	1314	1100	918	450	189	39	6408
PEORIA	0	6	87	326	759	1113	1218	1025	849	426	183	33	6025
ROCKFORD	6	9	114	400	837	1221	1333	1137	961	516	236	60	6830
SPRINGFIELD	0	0	72	291	696	1023	1135	935	769	354	136	18	5429
IND. EVANSVILLE	0	0	66	220	606	896	955	767	620	237	68	0	4435
FORT WAYNE	0	9	105	378	783	1135	1178	1028	890	471	189	39	6205
INDIANAPOLIS	0	0	90	316	723	1051	1113	949	809	432	177	39	5699
SOUTH BEND	0	6	111	372	777	1125	1221	1070	933	525	239	60	6439
IOWA Burlington	0	0	93	322	768	1135	1259	1042	859	426	177	33	6114
DES MOINES	0	9	99	363	837	1231	1398	1165	967	489	211	39	6808
DUBUQUE	12	31	156	450	906	1287	1420	1204	1026	546	260	78	7376
SIOUX CITY	0	9	108	369	867	1240	1435	1198	989	483	214	39	6951
WATERLOO	12	19	138	428	909	1296	1460	1221	1023	531	229	54	7320

Table II.2. *Monthly total heating degree days (base 65 degrees F.) (Reference 3).*

243

Table II.2.
(Continued)

STATE AND STATION	JULY	AUG.	SEP.	OCT.	NOV.	DEC.	JAN.	FEB.	MAR.	APR.	MAY	JUNE	ANNUAL
KANS. CONCORDIA	0	0	57	276	705	1023	1163	935	781	372	149	18	5479
DODGE CITY	0	0	33	251	666	939	1051	840	719	354	124	9	4986
GOODLAND	0	6	81	381	810	1073	1166	955	884	507	236	42	6141
TOPEKA	0	0	57	270	672	980	1122	893	722	330	124	12	5182
WICHITA	0	0	33	229	618	905	1023	804	645	270	87	6	4620
KY. COVINGTON	0	0	75	291	669	983	1035	893	756	390	149	24	5265
LEXINGTON	0	0	54	239	609	902	946	818	685	325	105	0	4683
LOUISVILLE	0	0	54	248	609	890	930	818	682	315	105	9	4660
LA. ALEXANDRIA	0	0	0	56	273	431	471	361	260	69	0	0	1921
BATON ROUGE	0	0	0	31	216	369	409	294	208	33	0	0	1560
BURRWOOD	0	0	0	0	96	214	298	218	171	27	0	0	1024
LAKE CHARLES	0	0	0	19	210	341	381	274	195	39	0	0	1459
NEW ORLEANS	0	0	0	19	192	322	363	258	192	39	0	0	1385
SHREVEPORT	0	0	0	47	297	477	552	426	304	81	0	0	2184
MAINE CARIBOU	78	115	336	682	1044	1535	1690	1470	1308	858	468	183	9767
PORTLAND	12	53	195	508	807	1215	1339	1182	1042	675	372	111	7511
MD. BALTIMORE	0	0	48	264	585	905	936	820	679	327	90	0	4654
FREDERICK	0	0	66	307	624	955	995	876	741	384	127	12	5087
MASS. BLUE HILL OBSY	0	22	108	381	690	1085	1178	1053	936	579	267	69	6368
BOSTON	0	9	60	316	603	983	1088	972	846	513	208	36	5634
NANTUCKET	12	22	93	332	573	896	992	941	896	621	384	129	5891
PITTSFIELD	25	59	219	524	831	1231	1339	1196	1063	660	326	105	7578
WORCESTER	6	34	147	450	774	1172	1271	1123	998	612	304	78	6969
MICH. ALPENA	68	105	273	580	912	1268	1404	1299	1218	777	446	156	8506
DETROIT (CITY)	0	0	87	360	738	1088	1181	1058	936	522	220	42	6232
ESCANABA	59	87	243	539	924	1293	1445	1296	1203	777	456	159	8481
FLINT	16	40	159	465	843	1212	1330	1198	1066	639	319	90	7377
GRAND RAPIDS	9	28	135	434	804	1147	1259	1134	1011	579	279	75	6894
LANSING	6	22	138	431	813	1163	1262	1142	1011	579	273	69	6909
MARQUETTE	59	81	240	527	936	1268	1411	1268	1187	771	468	177	8393
MUSKEGON	12	28	120	400	762	1088	1209	1100	995	594	310	78	6696
SAULT STE. MARIE	96	105	279	580	951	1367	1525	1380	1277	810	477	201	9048
MINN. DULUTH	71	109	330	632	1131	1581	1745	1518	1355	840	490	198	10000
INTERNATIONAL FALLS	71	112	363	701	1236	1724	1919	1621	1414	828	443	174	10606
MINNEAPOLIS	22	31	189	505	1014	1454	1631	1380	1166	621	288	81	8382
ROCHESTER	25	34	186	474	1005	1438	1593	1366	1150	630	301	93	8295
SAINT CLOUD	28	47	225	549	1065	1500	1702	1445	1221	666	326	105	8879
MISS. JACKSON	0	0	0	65	315	502	546	414	310	87	0	0	2239
MERIDIAN	0	0	0	81	339	518	543	417	310	81	0	0	2289
VICKSBURG	0	0	0	53	279	462	512	384	282	69	0	0	2041
MO. COLUMBIA	0	0	54	251	651	967	1076	874	716	324	121	12	5046
KANSAS	0	0	39	220	612	905	1032	818	682	294	109	0	4711
ST. JOSEPH	0	6	60	285	708	1039	1172	949	769	348	133	15	5484
ST. LOUIS	0	0	60	251	627	936	1026	848	704	312	121	15	4900
SPRINGFIELD	0	0	45	223	600	877	973	781	660	291	105	6	4561
MONT. BILLINGS	6	15	186	487	897	1135	1296	1100	970	570	285	102	7049
GLASGOW	31	47	270	608	1104	1466	1711	1439	1187	648	335	150	8996
GREAT FALLS	28	53	258	543	921	1169	1349	1154	1063	642	384	186	7750
HAVRE	28	53	306	595	1065	1367	1584	1364	1181	657	338	162	8700
HELENA	31	59	294	601	1002	1265	1438	1170	1042	651	381	195	8129
KALISPELL	50	99	321	654	1020	1240	1401	1134	1029	639	397	207	8191
MILES CITY	6	6	174	502	972	1296	1504	1252	1057	579	276	99	7723
MISSOULA	34	74	303	651	1035	1287	1420	1120	970	621	391	219	8125
NEBR. GRAND ISLAND	0	6	108	381	834	1172	1314	1089	908	462	211	45	6530
LINCOLN	0	6	75	301	726	1066	1237	1016	834	402	171	30	5864
NORFOLK	9	0	111	397	873	1234	1414	1179	983	498	233	48	6979
NORTH PLATTE	0	6	123	440	885	1166	1271	1039	930	519	248	57	6684
OMAHA	0	12	105	357	828	1175	1355	1126	939	465	208	42	6612
SCOTTSBLUFF	0	0	138	459	876	1128	1231	1008	921	552	285	75	6673
VALENTINE	9	12	165	493	942	1237	1395	1176	1045	579	288	84	7425
NEV. ELKO	9	34	225	561	924	1197	1314	1036	911	621	409	192	7433
ELY	28	43	234	592	939	1184	1308	1075	977	672	456	225	7733
LAS VEGAS	0	0	0	78	387	617	688	487	335	111	6	0	2709
RENO	43	87	204	490	801	1026	1073	823	729	510	357	189	6332
WINNEMUCCA	0	34	210	536	876	1091	1172	916	837	573	363	153	6761
N. H. CONCORD	6	50	177	505	822	1240	1358	1184	1032	636	298	75	7383
MT. WASH. OBSY.	493	536	720	1057	1341	1742	1820	1663	1652	1260	930	603	13817
N. J. ATLANTIC CITY	0	0	39	251	549	880	936	848	741	420	133	15	4812
NEWARK	0	0	30	248	573	921	983	876	729	381	118	0	4859
TRENTON	0	0	57	264	576	924	989	885	753	399	121	12	4980
N. MEX. ALBUQUERQUE	0	0	12	229	642	868	930	703	595	288	81	0	4348
CLAYTON	0	6	66	310	699	899	986	812	747	429	183	21	5158
RATON	9	28	126	431	825	1048	1116	904	834	543	301	63	6228
ROSWELL	0	0	18	202	573	806	840	641	481	201	31	0	3793
SILVER CITY	0	0	6	183	525	729	791	605	518	261	87	0	3705
N. Y. ALBANY	0	19	138	440	777	1194	1311	1156	992	564	239	45	6875
BINGHAMTON (AP)	22	65	201	471	810	1184	1277	1154	1045	645	313	99	7286
BINGHAMTON (PO)	0	28	141	406	732	1107	1190	1081	949	543	229	45	6451
BUFFALO	19	37	141	440	777	1156	1256	1145	1039	645	329	78	7062
CENTRAL PARK	0	0	30	233	540	902	986	885	760	408	118	9	4871
J. F. KENNEDY INTL.	0	0	36	248	564	933	1029	935	815	480	167	12	5219
LAGUARDIA	0	0	27	223	528	887	973	879	750	414	124	6	4811
ROCHESTER	9	31	126	415	747	1125	1234	1123	1014	597	279	48	6748
SCHENECTADY	0	22	123	422	756	1159	1283	1131	970	543	211	30	6650
SYRACUSE	6	28	132	415	744	1153	1271	1140	1004	570	248	45	6756
N.C. ASHEVILLE	0	0	48	245	555	775	784	683	592	273	87	0	4042
CAPE HATTERAS	0	0	0	78	273	521	580	518	440	177	25	0	2612
CHARLOTTE	0	0	6	124	438	691	691	582	481	156	22	0	3191
GREENSBORO	0	0	33	192	513	778	784	672	552	234	47	0	3805
RALEIGH	0	0	21	164	450	716	725	616	487	180	34	0	3393
WILMINGTON	0	0	0	74	291	521	546	462	357	96	0	0	2347
WINSTON SALEM	0	0	21	171	483	747	753	652	524	207	37	0	3595
N. DAK. BISMARCK	34	28	222	577	1083	1463	1708	1442	1203	645	329	117	8851
DEVILS LAKE	40	53	273	642	1191	1634	1872	1579	1345	753	331	138	9901
FARGO	28	37	219	574	1107	1569	1789	1520	1262	690	332	99	9226
WILLISTON	31	43	261	601	1122	1513	1758	1473	1262	681	357	141	9243

STATE AND STATION	JULY	AUG.	SEP.	OCT.	NOV.	DEC.	JAN.	FEB.	MAR.	APR.	MAY	JUNE	ANNUAL
OHIO AKRON	0	9	96	381	726	1070	1138	1016	871	489	202	39	6037
CINCINNATI	0	0	54	248	612	921	970	837	701	336	118	9	4806
CLEVELAND	9	25	105	384	738	1088	1159	1047	918	552	260	66	6351
COLUMBUS	0	6	84	347	714	1039	1088	949	809	426	171	27	5660
DAYTON	0	6	78	310	696	1045	1097	955	809	429	167	30	5622
MANSFIELD	9	22	114	397	768	1110	1169	1042	924	543	245	60	6403
SANDUSKY	0	6	66	313	684	1032	1107	991	868	495	198	36	5796
TOLEDO	0	16	117	406	792	1138	1200	1056	924	543	242	60	6494
YOUNGSTOWN	6	19	120	412	771	1104	1169	1047	921	540	248	60	6417
OKLA. OKLAHOMA CITY	0	0	15	164	498	766	868	664	527	189	34	0	3725
TULSA	0	0	18	158	522	787	893	683	539	213	47	0	3860
OREG. ASTORIA	146	130	210	375	561	679	753	622	636	480	363	231	5186
BURNS	12	37	210	515	867	1113	1246	988	856	570	366	177	6957
EUGENE	34	34	129	366	585	719	803	627	589	426	279	135	4726
MEACHAM	84	124	288	580	918	1091	1209	1005	983	726	527	339	7874
MEDFORD	0	0	78	372	678	871	918	697	642	432	242	78	5008
PENDLETON	0	0	111	350	711	884	1017	773	617	396	205	63	5127
PORTLAND	25	28	114	335	597	735	825	644	589	396	245	105	4635
ROSEBURG	22	16	105	329	567	713	766	608	570	405	267	123	4491
SALEM	37	31	111	338	594	729	822	647	611	417	273	144	4754
SEXTON SUMMIT	81	81	171	443	666	874	958	809	818	609	465	279	6254
PA. ALLENTOWN	0	0	90	353	693	1045	1116	1002	849	471	167	24	5810
ERIE	0	25	102	391	714	1063	1169	1081	973	585	288	60	6451
HARRISBURG	0	0	63	298	648	992	1045	907	766	396	124	12	5251
PHILADELPHIA	0	0	60	291	621	964	1014	890	744	390	115	12	5101
PITTSBURGH	0	9	105	375	726	1063	1119	1002	874	480	195	39	5987
READING	0	0	54	257	597	939	1001	885	735	372	105	0	4945
SCRANTON	0	19	132	434	762	1104	1156	1028	893	498	195	33	6254
WILLIAMSPORT	0	9	111	375	717	1073	1122	1002	856	468	177	24	5934
R. I. BLOCK IS.	0	16	78	307	594	902	1020	955	877	612	344	99	5804
PROVIDENCE	0	16	96	372	660	1023	1110	988	868	534	236	51	5954
S. C. CHARLESTON	0	0	0	59	282	471	487	389	291	54	0	0	2033
COLUMBIA	0	0	0	84	345	577	570	470	357	81	0	0	2484
FLORENCE	0	0	0	78	315	552	552	459	347	84	0	0	2387
GREENVILLE	0	0	0	112	387	636	648	535	434	120	12	0	2884
SPARTANBURG	0	0	15	130	417	667	663	560	453	144	25	0	3074
S. DAK. HURON	9	12	165	508	1014	1432	1628	1355	1125	600	288	87	8223
RAPID CITY	22	12	165	481	897	1172	1333	1145	1051	615	326	126	7345
SIOUX FALLS	19	25	168	462	972	1361	1544	1285	1082	573	270	78	7839
TENN. BRISTOL	0	0	51	236	573	828	828	700	598	261	68	0	4143
CHATTANOOGA	0	0	18	143	468	698	722	577	453	150	25	0	3254
KNOXVILLE	0	0	30	171	489	725	732	613	493	198	43	0	3494
MEMPHIS	0	0	18	130	447	698	729	585	456	147	22	0	3232
NASHVILLE	0	0	30	158	495	732	778	644	512	189	40	0	3578
OAK RIDGE (CO)	0	0	39	192	531	772	778	669	552	228	56	0	3817
TEX. ABILENE	0	0	0	99	366	586	642	470	347	114	0	0	2624
AMARILLO	0	0	18	205	570	797	877	664	546	252	56	0	3985
AUSTIN	0	0	0	31	225	388	468	325	223	51	0	0	1711
BROWNSVILLE	0	0	0	0	66	149	205	106	74	0	0	0	600
CORPUS CHRISTI	0	0	0	0	120	220	291	174	109	0	0	0	914
DALLAS	0	0	0	62	321	524	601	440	319	90	6	0	2363
EL PASO	0	0	0	84	414	648	685	445	319	105	0	0	2700
FORT WORTH	0	0	0	65	324	536	614	448	319	99	0	0	2405
GALVESTON	0	0	0	0	138	270	350	258	189	30	0	0	1235
HOUSTON	0	0	0	6	183	307	384	288	192	36	0	0	1396
LAREDO	0	0	0	0	105	217	267	134	74	0	0	0	797
LUBBOCK	0	0	18	174	513	744	800	613	484	201	31	0	3578
MIDLAND	0	0	0	87	381	592	651	468	322	90	0	0	2591
PORT ARTHUR	0	0	0	22	207	329	384	274	192	39	0	0	1447
SAN ANGELO	0	0	0	68	318	536	567	412	288	66	0	0	2255
SAN ANTONIO	0	0	0	31	207	363	428	286	195	39	0	0	1549
VICTORIA	0	0	0	6	150	270	344	230	152	21	0	0	1173
WACO	0	0	0	43	270	456	536	389	270	66	0	0	2030
WICHITA FALLS	0	0	0	99	381	632	698	518	378	120	6	0	2832
UTAH MILFORD	0	0	99	443	867	1141	1252	988	822	519	279	87	6497
SALT LAKE CITY	0	0	81	419	849	1082	1172	910	763	459	233	84	6052
WENDOVER	0	0	48	372	822	1091	1178	902	729	408	177	51	5778
VT. BURLINGTON	28	65	207	539	891	1349	1513	1333	1187	714	353	90	8269
VA. CAPE HENRY	0	0	0	112	360	645	694	633	536	246	53	0	3279
LYNCHBURG	0	0	51	223	540	822	849	731	605	267	78	0	4166
NORFOLK	0	0	0	136	408	698	738	655	533	216	37	0	3421
RICHMOND	0	0	36	214	495	784	815	703	546	219	53	0	3865
ROANOKE	0	0	51	229	549	825	834	722	614	261	65	0	4150
WASH. NAT'L. AP.	0	0	33	217	519	834	871	762	626	288	74	0	4224
WASH. OLYMPIA	68	71	198	422	636	753	834	675	645	450	307	177	5236
SEATTLE	50	47	129	329	543	657	738	599	577	396	242	117	4424
SEATTLE BOEING	34	40	147	384	624	763	831	655	608	411	242	99	4838
SEATTLE TACOMA	56	62	162	391	633	750	828	678	657	474	295	159	5145
SPOKANE	9	25	168	493	879	1082	1231	980	834	531	288	135	6655
STAMPEDE PASS	273	291	393	701	1008	1178	1287	1075	1085	855	654	483	9283
TATOOSH IS.	295	279	306	406	534	639	713	613	645	525	431	333	5719
WALLA WALLA	0	0	87	310	681	843	986	745	589	342	177	45	4805
YAKIMA	0	12	144	450	828	1039	1163	868	713	435	220	69	5941
W. VA. CHARLESTON	0	0	63	254	591	865	880	770	648	300	96	9	4476
ELKINS	9	25	135	400	729	992	1008	896	791	444	198	48	5675
HUNTINGTON	0	0	63	257	585	856	880	764	636	294	99	12	4446
PARKERSBURG	0	0	60	264	606	905	942	826	691	339	115	6	4754
WIS. GREEN BAY	28	50	174	484	924	1333	1494	1313	1141	654	335	99	8029
LA CROSSE	12	19	153	437	924	1339	1504	1277	1070	540	245	69	7589
MADISON	25	40	174	474	930	1330	1473	1274	1113	618	310	102	7863
MILWAUKEE	43	47	174	471	876	1252	1376	1193	1054	642	372	135	7635
WYO. CASPER	6	16	192	524	942	1169	1290	1084	1020	657	381	129	7410
CHEYENNE	19	31	210	543	924	1101	1228	1056	1011	672	381	102	7278
LANDER	6	19	204	555	1020	1299	1417	1145	1017	654	381	153	7870
SHERIAN	25	31	219	539	948	1200	1355	1154	1054	642	366	150	7683

	DHL/Delta T X 24	X	DDM	=	Qr Btus/mo.
JANUARY	$5.5 \times 10^2 \times 24 = 13,200$	X	1004	=	13.25×10^6
FEBRUARY	''	X	851	=	11.23
MARCH	''	X	800	=	10.56
APRIL	''	X	492	=	6.49
MAY	''	X	254	=	3.35
JUNE	''	X	48	=	.63
JULY	''	X	0	=	0
AUGUST	''	X	0	=	0
SEPTEMBER	''	X	90	=	1.18
OCTOBER	''	X	366	=	4.83
NOVEMBER	''	X	714	=	9.42
DECEMBER	''	X	905	=	11.94

TOTAL Qr = 72.88×10^6
Btus/yr.

© Donald Watson

Qr = heating energy required

DHL/Delta T = design heat loss divided by design temperature differential $(t_i - t_o)$ in Btus/° F./hour. (Table II.1)

DDM = monthly degree days (Table II.2)   *Denver City*

Form 1.1. Heating Energy Requirement, completed for the Denver example, Chapter 7. The DHL/Delta T factor is estimated from the Table II.1 graph for a 1200 S.F. building, infiltration = 1.00, R wall = 20.00. The aspect ratio is 1.5, the window area = 20%, with insulated glass. Thus the second solid line curve from the bottom at the 1.5 point on the horizontal axis reads 5.5×10^2 on the vertical axis, or a DHL/Delta T factor of 550.

This factor represents in Btus/° F/hour the Design Heat Loss divided by the difference between the inside temperature (say 68° F.) and the outside design temperature (3° F. for Denver). Thus, while a calculation of the Design Heat Loss (DHL) alone is not required for our calculations here, it can be estimated from the Table II.1 graphs: For the Denver house, the DHL = 550 multiplied by (68 − 3) = 35,750 Btus/hr.

Once the DHL/Delta T factor is determined, it is multiplied by 24 (hours per day) and the monthly Degree Day factors from Table II.2, the total being the monthly heating requirement of the house.

G (Daily Hot Water Requirement). The amount of hot water consumed by different households varies considerably, depending on the relative use of dishwasher, clothes washer, showers and baths. Detailed studies of domestic hot water consumption in the United States and Canada put the average daily consumption of hot water between 10 and 20 gallons per person, the latter figure including the hot water demand of an automatic clothes washer.

dT (Temperature Differential). The contribution of solar collectors to domestic water needs will vary according to local climate characteristics, including the temperature of the cold water supply either from the city water main or from ground water sources. For estimate purposes, the inlet temperature can be assumed to be equal to the average monthly air temperature (given in Reference 3). The temperature of the water supplied to household fixtures is usually set by a control or mixing valve at 120° F., since above this the hot water may cause scalding.

Thus, if one assumes a temperature differential of 120° F. – 50° F. = 70° F., the hot water heating energy requirement for a family of four would be:

$$Qr \text{ (Btus/month)} = 4 \text{ people} \times 20 \text{ gallons/person} \times$$
$$8.33/\text{gal}/° \text{ F.} \times 70° \text{ F.} \times 30 \text{ days}$$
$$= 1.4 \times 10^6 \text{ Btus/month}$$

In the calculation of solar contribution and auxiliary fuel requirement to be detailed in following sections, the monthly domestic water heating requirement can be calculated each month based on local variations in ground water temperature or assumed to be constant throughout the year.

II.2 Solar Heating Contribution

The Solar Heat Gain from windows and from collectors can each be calculated, as appropriate to the heating system under consideration.

The effectiveness of the Solar Heat Gain from windows and collectors must be estimated in relation to the total heating system design that is used. Without heat storage, only a sunny daytime solar contri-

247

bution can be assumed. The calculations related to windows, collectors and storage are discussed separately in this section.

WINDOW HEAT GAIN

The amount of solar radiation that strikes a window depends upon:

1. the latitude of the building (the position of the sun and the hours of sunlight vary at each latitude)

2. the orientation of the window with respect to true south

3. the amount of reflection of solar radiation on the window from adjacent ground and buildings

4. the percentage of actual clear sunny hours (which varies in each location but can be estimated from average cloud-cover statistics)

5. the amount of shading of the glass from nearby trees and other obstructions, including window overhangs

The amount of actual solar heat that then is usefully transmitted through the glass and is available to reduce the house-heat requirements depends upon:

6. the type of window glass used and the shading effect of any curtains on the interior

7. the reflection losses off the glass—which depends on the direction or the angle of solar incidence

8. the efficiency of the house design and heating system itself in taking advantage of solar heat gain from windows

Window Heat Gain and its effective heating energy contribution (Qw) can be calculated as follows:

$$Qw/month = WHG \times PA \times DM \times WA \times SC \times SE$$

248

where:

WHG = the heat gained daily in Btus per square foot of window

PA = the percent of actual sunshine

DM = the number of days per month

WA = the square foot area of the unshaded portion of the window

SC = the shading coefficient of the glass itself (plus inside curtains, if used)

SE = the efficiency of utilization of the window heat gain assumed for the particular design

WHG (window heat gain). The daily window heat gain through a vertical south-facing glass window is given below in Table II.3. The values are shown for each month of the year and represent the Btu/SF/day heat gain through south-facing glass at major northern latitudes.

The values given in Table II.3 assume a sea level altitude. In actuality, locations along the same latitude will vary a great deal in altitude and resulting sky clearness, which is also affected by local pollution. Figure II.3A indicates factors for sky clearness by which the Table II.3 values can be adjusted, if appropriate to the location.

Ground reflectance gains of 20 percent are assumed in the chart values. Reflectors positioned

Table II.3. *Window heat gain (in Btus/ SF per day) of south-facing vertical glass— DS (1/8 inch) sheet glass, ground reflectance of 0.20; values derived by graphical interpolation of data from ASHRAE Window Heat Gain Tables.(References 1 and 2) include window heat gain values for all major orientations. (Source: Hill and Harrigan, Consulting Engineers)*

LAT	32°	34°	36°	38°	40°	42°	44°	46°	48°
JAN	1670	1670	1660	1640	1630	1600	1570	1510	1410
FEB	1560	1580	1610	1620	1630	1640	1640	1630	1610
MAR	1180	1230	1280	1330	1380	1430	1470	1510	1530
APR	720	780	850	920	980	1040	1100	1160	1210
MAY	500	540	590	650	710	770	830	900	970
JUN	440	470	520	560	620	670	730	800	870
JUL	490	530	580	630	690	750	810	880	940
AUG	700	760	820	880	940	1000	1060	1120	1170
SEP	1150	1200	1250	1300	1340	1380	1420	1440	1470
OCT	1500	1530	1550	1560	1570	1580	1570	1560	1540
NOV	1640	1640	1630	1620	1600	1570	1530	1480	1380
DEC	1690	1670	1630	1600	1560	1510	1450	1370	1250

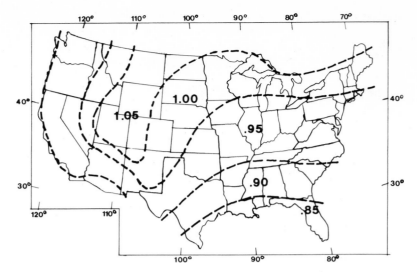

to reflect winter sun on the full height of the window could increase the window heat gain values by as much as 50 percent more.

PA (percent actual). Statistics on the percentage of possible sunshine are maintained by local weather stations throughout the United States. The month-by-month averages for major cities in the United States are shown in Table II.4. For locations not shown, local airports that keep weather data, or state or federal agencies that maintain meterological records, can supply similar statistics. (These percentages represent the average duration of sunshine compared to one hundred percent clear-day sunshine. The effect of diffuse radiation from cloudy skies is neglected.)

WA (window area). The window area is the square foot size of the actual glass that is exposed to the sun. The effect of shadows from obstructions such as trees and nearby building shapes, including window overhangs, should be considered on a month-by-month basis. For example, a one-foot overhang above a window may shade 10 percent of the glass area in December, 15 percent in November and January, and so on.

Table II.5 gives the angles of solar altitude and azimuth, from which one can estimate the amount of shading caused by obstructions in front of windows. The same angles also can be used to determine the size of overhangs desired to block the sun from a window during the summer months and to admit the sun during the heating season.

250

MEAN PERCENTAGE OF POSSIBLE SUNSHINE FOR SELECTED LOCATIONS

STATE AND STATION	YEARS	JAN.	FEB.	MAR.	APR.	MAY	JUNE	JULY	AUG.	SEPT.	OCT.	NOV.	DEC.	ANNUAL
ALA. BIRMINGHAM	56	43	49	56	63	66	67	62	65	66	67	58	44	59
MONTGOMERY	49	51	53	61	69	73	72	66	69	69	71	64	48	64
ALASKA, ANCHORAGE	19	39	46	56	58	50	51	45	39	35	32	33	29	45
FAIRBANKS	20	34	50	61	68	55	53	45	35	31	28	38	29	44
JUNEAU	14	30	32	39	37	34	35	28	30	25	18	21	18	30
NOME	29	44	46	48	53	51	48	32	26	34	35	36	30	41
ARIZ. PHOENIX	64	76	79	83	88	93	94	84	84	89	88	84	77	85
YUMA	52	83	87	91	94	97	98	92	91	93	93	90	83	91
ARK. LITTLE ROCK	66	44	53	57	62	67	72	71	73	71	74	58	47	62
CALIF. EUREKA	49	40	44	50	53	54	56	51	46	52	48	42	39	49
FRESNO	55	46	63	72	83	89	94	97	97	93	87	73	47	78
LOS ANGELES	63	70	69	70	67	68	69	80	81	80	76	79	72	73
RED BLUFF	39	50	60	65	75	79	86	95	94	89	77	64	50	75
SACRAMENTO	48	44	57	67	76	82	90	96	95	92	82	65	44	77
SAN DIEGO	68	68	67	68	66	60	60	67	70	70	70	76	71	68
SAN FRANCISCO	64	53	57	63	69	70	75	68	63	70	70	62	54	66
COLO. DENVER	64	67	67	65	63	61	69	68	68	71	71	67	65	67
GRAND JUNCTION	57	58	62	64	67	71	79	76	72	77	74	67	58	69
CONN. HARTFORD	48	46	55	56	54	57	60	62	60	57	55	46	46	56
D. C. WASHINGTON	66	46	53	56	57	61	64	64	62	62	61	54	47	58
FLA. APALACHICOLA	26	59	62	62	71	77	70	64	63	62	74	66	53	65
JACKSONVILLE	60	58	59	66	71	71	63	62	63	58	58	61	53	62
KEY WEST	45	68	75	78	78	76	70	69	71	65	65	69	66	71
MIAMI BEACH	48	66	72	73	73	68	62	65	67	62	62	65	65	67
TAMPA	63	63	67	71	74	75	66	61	64	64	67	67	61	68
GA. ATLANTA	65	48	53	57	65	68	68	62	63	65	67	60	47	60
HAWAII. HILO	9	48	42	41	34	31	41	44	38	42	41	34	36	39
HONOLULU	53	62	64	60	62	64	66	67	70	70	68	63	60	65
LIHUE	9	48	48	48	46	51	60	58	59	67	58	51	49	54
IDAHO, BOISE	20	40	48	59	67	68	75	89	86	81	66	46	37	66
POCATELLO	21	37	47	58	64	66	72	82	81	78	66	48	36	64
ILL. CAIRO	30	46	53	59	65	71	77	82	79	75	73	56	46	65
CHICAGO	66	44	49	53	56	63	69	73	70	65	61	47	41	59
SPRINGFIELD	59	47	51	54	58	64	69	76	72	73	64	53	45	60
IND. EVANSVILLE	48	42	49	55	61	67	73	78	76	73	67	52	42	64
FT. WAYNE	48	38	44	51	55	62	69	74	69	64	58	41	38	57
INDIANAPOLIS	63	41	47	49	55	62	68	74	70	68	64	48	39	59
IOWA. DES MOINES	66	56	56	56	59	62	66	75	70	64	64	53	48	62
DUBUQUE	54	48	52	52	58	60	63	73	67	61	55	44	40	57
SIOUX CITY	52	55	58	58	59	63	67	75	72	67	65	53	50	63
KANS. CONCORDIA	52	60	60	62	63	65	73	79	76	72	70	64	58	67
DODGE CITY	70	67	66	68	68	68	74	78	78	76	75	70	67	71
WICHITA	46	61	63	64	64	66	73	80	77	73	69	67	59	69
KY. LOUISVILLE	59	41	47	52	57	64	68	72	69	68	64	51	39	59
LA. NEW ORLEANS	69	49	50	57	63	66	64	58	60	64	70	60	46	59
SHREVEPORT	18	48	54	58	60	69	78	79	80	79	77	65	60	69
MAINE, EASTPORT	58	45	51	52	52	51	53	55	57	54	50	37	40	50
MASS. BOSTON	67	47	56	57	56	59	62	64	63	61	58	48	48	57
MICH. ALPENA	45	29	43	52	56	59	64	70	64	52	44	24	22	51
DETROIT	69	34	42	48	52	58	65	69	66	61	54	35	29	53
GRAND RAPIDS	56	26	37	48	54	60	66	72	67	58	50	31	22	49
MARQUETTE	55	31	40	47	52	53	56	63	57	47	38	24	24	47
S. STE. MARIE	60	28	44	50	54	54	59	63	58	45	36	21	22	47
MINN. DULUTH	49	47	55	60	58	58	60	68	63	53	47	36	40	55
MINNEAPOLIS	45	49	54	55	57	60	64	72	69	60	54	40	40	56
MISS. VICKSBURG	66	46	50	57	64	69	73	69	72	74	71	60	45	64
MO. KANSAS CITY	69	55	57	59	60	64	70	76	73	70	67	59	52	65
ST. LOUIS	68	48	49	56	59	64	68	72	68	67	65	54	44	61
SPRINGFIELD	45	48	54	57	60	63	69	77	72	71	65	58	48	63
MONT. HAVRE	55	49	58	61	63	63	65	78	75	64	57	48	46	62
HELENA	65	46	55	58	60	59	63	77	74	63	57	48	43	60
KALISPELL	50	28	40	49	57	58	60	77	73	61	50	28	20	53
NEBR. LINCOLN	55	57	59	60	60	63	69	76	71	67	66	59	55	64
NORTH PLATTE	53	63	63	64	62	64	72	78	74	72	70	62	58	68
NEV. ELY	21	61	64	68	65	67	79	79	81	81	73	67	62	72
LAS VEGAS	19	74	77	78	81	85	91	84	86	92	84	83	75	82
RENO	51	59	64	69	75	77	82	90	89	86	76	68	56	76
WINNEMUCCA	53	52	60	64	70	76	83	90	90	86	75	62	53	74
N. H. CONCORD	44	48	53	55	53	51	56	57	58	55	50	43	43	52
N. J. ATLANTIC CITY	62	51	57	58	59	62	65	67	66	65	54	58	52	60

MEAN PERCENTAGE OF POSSIBLE SUNSHINE FOR SELECTED LOCATIONS

STATE AND STATION	YEARS	JAN.	FEB.	MAR.	APR.	MAY	JUNE	JULY	AUG.	SEPT.	OCT.	NOV.	DEC.	ANNUAL
N. MEX. ALBUQUERQUE	28	70	72	72	76	79	84	76	75	81	80	79	70	76
ROSWELL	47	69	72	75	77	76	80	76	75	74	74	74	69	74
N. Y. ALBANY	63	43	51	53	53	57	62	63	61	58	54	39	38	53
BINGHAMTON	63	31	39	41	44	50	56	54	51	47	43	29	26	44
BUFFALO	49	32	41	49	51	59	67	70	67	60	51	31	28	53
CANTON	43	37	47	50	48	54	61	63	61	54	45	30	31	49
NEW YORK	83	49	56	57	59	62	65	66	64	64	61	53	50	59
SYRACUSE	49	31	38	45	50	58	64	67	63	56	47	29	26	50
N. C. ASHEVILLE	57	48	53	56	61	64	63	59	59	62	64	59	48	58
RALEIGH	61	50	56	59	64	67	65	62	62	63	64	62	52	61
N. DAK. BISMARCK	65	52	58	56	57	58	61	73	69	62	59	49	48	59
DEVILS LAKE	55	53	60	59	60	59	62	71	67	59	56	44	45	58
FARGO	39	47	55	56	58	62	63	73	69	60	57	39	46	59
WILLISTON	43	51	59	60	63	66	66	78	75	65	60	48	48	63
OHIO, CINCINNATI	44	41	46	52	56	62	69	72	68	68	60	46	39	57
CLEVELAND	65	29	36	45	52	61	67	71	68	62	54	32	25	50
COLUMBUS	65	36	44	49	54	63	68	71	68	66	60	44	35	55
OKLA, OKLAHOMA CITY	62	57	60	63	64	65	74	78	78	74	68	64	57	68
OREG. BAKER	46	41	49	56	61	63	67	83	81	74	62	46	37	60
PORTLAND	69	27	34	41	49	52	55	70	65	55	42	28	23	48
ROSEBURG	29	24	32	40	51	57	59	79	77	68	42	28	18	51
PA. HARRISBURG	60	43	52	55	57	61	65	68	63	62	58	47	43	57
PHILADELPHIA	66	45	56	57	58	61	62	64	61	62	61	53	49	57
PITTSBURGH	63	32	39	45	50	57	62	64	61	62	54	39	30	51
R. I. BLOCK ISLAND	48	45	54	47	56	58	60	62	62	60	59	50	44	56
S. C. CHARLESTON	61	58	60	65	72	73	70	66	66	67	68	68	57	66
COLUMBIA	55	53	57	62	68	69	68	63	65	64	68	64	51	63
S. DAK. HURON	62	55	62	60	62	65	68	76	72	66	61	52	49	63
RAPID CITY	53	58	62	63	62	61	66	73	73	69	66	58	54	64
TENN. KNOXVILLE	62	42	49	53	59	64	66	64	59	64	64	53	41	57
MEMPHIS	55	44	51	57	64	68	74	73	74	70	69	58	45	64
NASHVILLEE	63	42	47	54	60	65	69	69	68	69	65	55	42	59
TEX. ABILENE	14	64	68	73	66	73	86	83	85	73	71	72	66	73
AMARILLO	54	71	71	75	75	75	82	81	81	79	76	76	70	76
AUSTIN	33	46	50	57	60	62	72	76	79	70	70	57	49	63
BROWNSVILLE	37	44	49	51	57	65	73	78	78	67	70	54	44	61
DEL RIO	36	53	55	61	63	60	66	75	80	69	66	58	52	63
EL PASO	53	74	77	81	85	87	87	78	78	80	82	80	73	80
FT. WORTH	33	56	57	65	66	67	75	78	78	74	70	63	58	68
GALVESTON	66	50	50	55	61	69	76	72	71	70	74	62	49	63
SAN ANTONIO	57	48	51	56	58	60	69	74	75	69	67	55	49	62
UTAH, SALT LAKE CITY	22	48	53	61	68	73	78	82	82	84	73	56	49	69
VT. BURLINGTON	54	34	43	48	47	53	59	62	59	51	43	25	24	46
VA. NORFOLK	60	50	57	60	63	67	66	66	66	63	64	60	51	62
RICHMOND	56	49	55	59	63	67	66	65	62	63	64	58	50	61
WASH. NORTH HEAD	44	28	37	42	48	48	48	50	46	48	41	31	27	41
SEATTLE	26	27	34	42	48	53	48	62	56	53	36	28	24	45
SPOKANE	62	26	41	53	63	64	68	82	79	68	53	28	22	58
TATOOSH ISLAND	49	26	36	39	45	47	46	48	44	47	38	26	23	40
WALLA WALLA	44	24	35	51	63	67	72	86	84	72	59	33	20	60
YAKIMA	18	34	49	62	70	72	74	86	86	74	61	38	29	65
W. VA. ELKINS	55	33	37	42	47	55	55	56	53	55	51	41	33	48
PARKERSBURG	62	30	36	42	49	56	60	63	60	60	53	37	29	48
WIS. GREEN BAY	57	44	51	55	56	58	64	70	65	58	52	40	40	55
MADISON	59	44	49	52	53	58	64	70	66	60	56	41	38	56
MILWAUKEE	59	44	48	53	56	60	65	73	67	62	56	44	39	57
WYO. CHEYENNE	63	65	66	64	61	59	68	70	68	69	69	65	63	66
LANDER	57	66	70	71	66	65	74	76	75	72	67	61	62	69
SHERIDAN	52	56	61	62	61	61	67	76	74	67	60	53	52	64
YELLOWSTONE PARK	35	39	51	55	57	56	63	73	71	65	57	45	38	56
P. R. SAN JUAN	57	64	69	71	66	59	62	65	67	61	63	63	65	65

Table II.4. *Monthly average percent of possible sunshine in major U. S. locations. (References 1 and 2)*

SC (shading coefficient). The shading coefficient of the window depends on the specific type of glass that is used and the effect of inside curtains, if any are used. The shading coefficient for the 1/8-inch clear glass values shown in the Table II.3 is equal to 1, so that there is no loss of heat gain due to shading from the glass itself. If the glass is likely to remain dirty, or if insect screening is installed, then this figure should be reduced. Typical shading coefficients of various glass and curtain types are given in Table II.6.

Table II.5. *Solar position — hourly and monthly — for major latitudes. (References 1 and 2).*

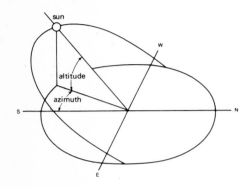

Date	Solar Time A.M.	Solar Time P.M.	Solar Position Alt.	Azimuth	Direct Normal Irradiation, Btuh/sq ft
Jan 21	7	5	4.8	65.6	70
	8	4	16.9	58.3	239
	9	3	27.9	48.8	287
	10	2	37.2	36.1	308
	11	1	43.6	19.6	317
	12	12	46.0	0.0	320
Feb 21	7	5	9.0	73.9	153
	8	4	21.9	66.4	261
	9	3	33.9	56.8	297
	10	2	44.5	43.5	313
	11	1	52.2	24.5	321
	12	12	55.2	0.0	323
Mar 21	7	5	13.7	83.8	194
	8	4	27.2	76.8	267
	9	3	40.2	67.9	295
	10	2	52.3	54.8	308
	11	1	61.9	33.4	315
	12	12	66.0	0.0	317
Apr 21	6	6	4.7	100.6	40
	7	5	18.3	94.9	203
	8	4	32.0	89.0	257
	9	3	45.6	81.9	281
	10	2	59.0	71.8	293
	11	1	71.1	51.6	298
	12	12	77.6	0.0	300
May 21	6	6	8.0	108.4	85
	7	5	21.2	103.2	203
	8	4	34.6	98.5	248
	9	3	48.3	93.6	269
	10	2	62.0	87.7	280
	11	1	75.5	76.9	286
	12	12	86.0	0.0	287
June 21	6	6	9.3	111.6	97
	7	5	22.3	106.8	200
	8	4	35.5	102.6	242
	9	3	49.0	98.7	262
	10	2	62.6	95.0	273
	11	1	76.3	90.7	279
	12	12	89.5	0.0	280
July 21	6	6	8.2	109.0	81
	7	5	21.4	103.8	195
	8	4	34.8	99.2	239
	9	3	48.4	94.5	261
	10	2	62.1	89.0	272
	11	1	75.7	79.2	278
	12	12	86.6	0.0	279
Aug 21	6	6	5.0	101.3	34
	7	5	18.5	95.6	186
	8	4	32.2	89.7	240
	9	3	45.9	82.9	265
	10	2	59.3	73.0	277
	11	1	71.6	53.2	283
	12	12	78.3	0.0	285
Sept 21	7	5	13.7	83.8	172
	8	4	27.2	76.8	248
	9	3	40.2	67.9	277
	10	2	52.3	54.8	292
	11	1	61.9	33.4	298
	12	12	66.0	0.0	301
Oct 21	7	5	9.1	74.1	137
	8	4	22.0	66.7	246
	9	3	34.1	57.1	284
	10	2	44.7	43.8	300
	11	1	52.5	24.7	308
	12	12	55.5	0.0	311
Nov 21	7	5	4.9	65.8	66
	8	4	17.0	58.4	232
	9	3	28.0	48.9	281
	10	2	37.3	36.3	302
	11	1	43.8	19.7	311
	12	12	46.2	0.0	314
Dec 21	7	5	3.2	62.6	29
	8	4	14.9	55.3	225
	9	3	25.5	46.0	281
	10	2	34.3	33.7	304
	11	1	40.4	18.2	314
	12	12	42.6	0.0	317

Latitude N. 24°

252

SE (system efficiency). Not all of the solar heat gain through windows can be considered as a direct contribution to the heat requirements of a building. Typically, window heat gain will overheat the area next to the glass, leaving the rest of the

Date	Solar Time A.M.	Solar Time P.M.	Alt.	Azimuth	Direct Normal Irradiation, Btuh/sq ft
Jan 21	7	5	1.4	65.2	1
	8	4	12.5	56.5	202
	9	3	22.5	46.0	269
	10	2	30.6	33.1	295
	11	1	36.1	17.5	306
	12	12	38.0	0.0	309
Feb 21	7	5	6.7	72.8	111
	8	4	18.5	63.8	244
	9	3	29.3	52.8	287
	10	2	38.5	38.9	305
	11	1	44.9	21.0	314
	12	12	47.2	0.0	316
Mar 21	7	5	12.7	81.9	184
	8	4	25.1	73.0	260
	9	3	36.8	62.1	289
	10	2	47.3	47.5	304
	11	1	55.0	26.8	310
	12	12	58.0	0.0	312
Apr 21	6	6	6.1	99.9	66
	7	5	18.8	92.2	206
	8	4	31.5	84.0	256
	9	3	43.9	74.2	278
	10	2	55.7	60.3	290
	11	1	65.4	37.5	296
	12	12	69.6	0.0	298
May 21	6	6	10.4	107.2	118
	7	5	22.8	100.1	211
	8	4	35.4	92.9	249
	9	3	48.1	84.7	269
	10	2	60.6	73.3	279
	11	1	72.0	51.9	285
	12	12	78.0	0.0	286
June 21	6	6	12.2	110.2	130
	7	5	24.3	103.4	209
	8	4	36.9	96.8	244
	9	3	49.6	89.4	263
	10	2	62.2	79.7	273
	11	1	74.2	60.9	278
	12	12	81.5	0.0	280
July 21	6	6	10.7	107.7	113
	7	5	23.1	100.6	203
	8	4	35.7	93.6	241
	9	3	48.4	85.5	261
	10	2	60.9	74.3	271
	11	1	72.4	53.3	277
	12	12	78.6	0.0	278
Aug 21	6	6	6.5	100.5	59
	7	5	19.1	92.8	189
	8	4	31.8	84.7	239
	9	3	44.3	75.0	263
	10	2	56.1	61.3	275
	11	1	66.0	38.4	281
	12	12	70.3	0.0	283
Sep 21	7	5	12.7	81.9	163
	8	4	25.1	73.0	240
	9	3	36.8	62.1	272
	10	2	47.3	47.5	287
	11	1	55.0	26.8	294
	12	12	58.0	0.0	296
Oct 21	7	5	6.8	73.1	98
	8	4	18.7	64.0	229
	9	3	29.5	53.0	273
	10	2	38.7	39.1	292
	11	1	45.1	21.1	301
	12	12	47.5	0.0	304
Nov 21	7	5	1.5	65.4	1
	8	4	12.7	56.6	196
	9	3	22.6	46.1	262
	10	2	30.8	33.2	288
	11	1	36.2	17.6	300
	12	12	38.2	0.0	303
Dec 21	8	4	10.3	53.8	176
	9	3	19.8	43.6	257
	10	2	27.6	31.2	287
	11	1	32.7	16.4	300
	12	12	34.6	0.0	304

Latitude N. 32°

Date	Solar Time A.M.	Solar Time P.M.	Alt.	Azimuth	Direct Normal Irradiation, Btuh/sq ft
Jan 21	8	4	8.1	55.3	141
	9	3	16.8	44.0	238
	10	2	23.8	30.9	274
	11	1	28.4	16.0	289
	12	12	30.0	0.0	293
Feb 21	7	5	4.3	72.1	55
	8	4	14.8	61.6	219
	9	3	24.3	49.7	271
	10	2	32.1	35.4	293
	11	1	37.3	18.6	303
	12	12	39.2	0.0	306
Mar 21	7	5	11.4	80.2	171
	8	4	22.5	69.6	250
	9	3	32.8	57.3	281
	10	2	41.6	41.9	297
	11	1	47.7	22.6	304
	12	12	50.0	0.0	306
Apr 21	6	6	7.4	98.9	89
	7	5	18.9	89.5	207
	8	4	30.3	79.3	253
	9	3	41.3	67.2	275
	10	2	51.2	51.4	286
	11	1	58.7	29.2	292
	12	12	61.6	0.0	294
May 21	5	7	1.9	114.7	1
	6	6	12.7	105.6	143
	7	5	24.0	96.6	216
	8	4	35.4	87.2	249
	9	3	46.8	76.0	267
	10	2	57.5	60.9	277
	11	1	66.2	37.1	282
	12	12	70.0	0.0	284
June 21	5	7	4.2	117.3	21
	6	6	14.8	108.4	154
	7	5	26.0	99.7	215
	8	4	37.4	90.7	246
	9	3	48.8	80.2	262
	10	2	59.8	65.8	272
	11	1	69.2	41.9	276
	12	12	73.5	0.0	278
July 21	5	7	2.3	115.2	2
	6	6	13.1	106.1	137
	7	5	24.3	97.2	208
	8	4	35.8	87.8	241
	9	3	47.2	76.7	259
	10	2	57.9	61.7	269
	11	1	66.7	37.9	274
	12	12	70.6	0.0	276
Aug 21	6	6	7.9	99.5	80
	7	5	19.3	90.0	191
	8	4	30.7	79.9	236
	9	3	41.8	67.9	259
	10	2	51.7	52.1	271
	11	1	59.3	29.7	277
	12	12	62.3	0.0	279
Sep 21	7	5	11.4	80.2	149
	8	4	22.5	69.6	230
	9	3	32.8	57.3	263
	10	2	41.6	41.9	279
	11	1	47.7	22.6	287
	12	12	50.0	0.0	290
Oct 21	7	5	4.5	72.3	48
	8	4	15.0	61.9	203
	9	3	24.5	49.8	257
	10	2	32.4	35.6	280
	11	1	37.6	18.7	290
	12	12	39.5	0.0	293
Nov 21	8	4	8.2	55.4	136
	9	3	17.0	44.1	232
	10	2	24.0	31.0	267
	11	1	28.6	16.1	283
	12	12	30.2	0.0	287
Dec 21	8	4	5.5	53.0	88
	9	3	14.0	41.9	217
	10	2	20.7	29.4	261
	11	1	25.0	15.2	279
	12	12	26.6	0.0	284

Latitude N. 40°

space and particularly the north side of a building still calling for heat.

If a thermostat is placed in the cold side of the building, then the window heat gain may make little difference to the operation of the mechanical heat-

Table II.5. *(Continued)*

Date	Solar Time A.M.	Solar Time P.M.	Solar Position Alt.	Solar Position Azimuth	Direct Normal Irradiation, Btuh/sq ft
Jan 21	8	4	3.5	54.6	36
	9	3	11.0	42.6	185
	10	2	16.9	29.4	239
	11	1	20.7	15.1	260
	12	12	22.0	0.0	267
Feb 21	7	5	1.8	71.7	3
	8	4	10.9	60.0	180
	9	3	19.0	47.3	247
	10	2	25.5	33.0	275
	11	1	29.7	17.0	288
	12	12	31.2	0.0	291
Mar 21	7	5	10.0	78.7	152
	8	4	19.5	66.8	235
	9	3	28.2	53.4	270
	10	2	35.4	37.8	287
	11	1	40.3	19.8	295
	12	12	42.0	0.0	297
Apr 21	6	6	8.6	97.8	108
	7	5	18.6	86.7	205
	8	4	28.5	74.9	247
	9	3	37.8	61.2	269
	10	2	45.8	44.6	281
	11	1	51.5	24.0	287
	12	12	53.6	0.0	289
May 21	5	7	5.2	114.3	41
	6	6	14.7	103.7	162
	7	5	24.6	93.0	218
	8	4	34.6	81.6	248
	9	3	44.3	68.3	264
	10	2	53.0	51.3	274
	11	1	59.5	28.6	279
	12	12	62.0	0.0	280
June 21	5	7	7.9	116.5	77
	6	6	17.2	106.2	172
	7	5	27.0	95.8	219
	8	4	37.1	84.6	245
	9	3	46.9	71.6	260
	10	2	55.8	54.8	269
	11	1	62.7	31.2	273
	12	12	65.4	0.0	275
July 21	5	7	5.7	114.7	42
	6	6	15.2	104.1	155
	7	5	25.1	93.5	211
	8	4	35.1	82.1	240
	9	3	44.8	68.8	256
	10	2	53.5	51.9	266
	11	1	60.1	29.0	271
	12	12	62.6	0.0	272
Aug 21	6	6	9.1	98.3	98
	7	5	19.1	87.2	189
	8	4	29.0	75.4	231
	9	3	38.4	61.8	253
	10	2	46.4	45.1	265
	11	1	52.2	24.3	271
	12	12	54.3	0.0	273
Sep 21	7	5	10.0	78.7	131
	8	4	19.5	66.8	215
	9	3	28.2	53.4	251
	10	2	35.4	37.8	269
	11	1	40.3	19.8	277
	12	12	42.0	0.0	280
Oct 21	7	5	2.0	71.9	3
	8	4	11.2	60.2	165
	9	3	19.3	47.4	232
	10	2	25.7	33.1	261
	11	1	30.0	17.1	274
	12	12	31.5	0.0	278
Nov 21	8	4	3.6	54.7	36
	9	3	11.2	42.7	178
	10	2	17.1	29.5	232
	11	1	20.9	15.1	254
	12	12	22.2	0.0	260
Dec 21	9	3	8.0	40.9	140
	10	2	13.6	28.2	214
	11	1	17.3	14.4	242
	12	12	18.6	0.0	250

Latitude N. 48°

Date	Solar Time A.M.	Solar Time P.M.	Solar Position Alt.	Solar Position Azimuth	Direct Normal Irradiation, Btuh/sq ft
Jan 21	9	3	5.0	41.8	77
	10	2	9.9	28.5	170
	11	1	12.9	14.5	206
	12	12	14.0	0.0	216
Feb 21	8	4	6.9	59.0	115
	9	3	13.5	45.6	207
	10	2	18.7	31.2	245
	11	1	22.0	15.9	262
	12	12	23.2	0.0	267
Mar 21	7	5	8.3	77.5	127
	8	4	16.2	64.4	215
	9	3	23.3	50.3	253
	10	2	29.0	34.9	272
	11	1	32.7	17.9	281
	12	12	34.0	0.0	284
Apr 21	5	7	1.4	108.8	0
	6	6	9.6	96.5	122
	7	5	18.0	84.1	201
	8	4	26.1	70.9	240
	9	3	33.6	56.3	261
	10	2	39.9	39.7	273
	11	1	44.1	20.7	279
	12	12	45.6	0.0	280
May 21	4	8	1.2	125.5	0
	5	7	8.5	113.4	92
	6	6	16.5	101.5	175
	7	5	24.8	89.3	219
	8	4	33.1	76.3	244
	9	3	40.9	61.6	259
	10	2	47.6	44.2	268
	11	1	52.3	23.4	273
	12	12	54.0	0.0	275
June 21	4	8	4.2	127.2	21
	5	7	11.4	115.3	121
	6	6	19.3	103.6	185
	7	5	27.6	91.7	221
	8	4	35.9	78.8	243
	9	3	43.8	64.1	256
	10	2	50.7	46.4	264
	11	1	55.6	24.9	268
	12	12	57.4	0.0	270
July 21	4	8	1.7	125.8	0
	5	7	9.0	113.7	91
	6	6	17.0	101.9	169
	7	5	25.3	89.7	212
	8	4	33.6	76.7	236
	9	3	41.4	62.0	251
	10	2	48.2	44.6	260
	11	1	52.9	23.7	265
	12	12	54.6	0.0	267
Aug 21	5	7	2.0	109.2	1
	6	6	10.2	97.0	112
	7	5	18.5	84.5	186
	8	4	26.7	71.3	224
	9	3	34.3	56.7	245
	10	2	40.5	40.0	257
	11	1	44.8	20.9	263
	12	12	46.3	0.0	265
Sep 21	7	5	8.3	77.5	107
	8	4	16.2	64.4	194
	9	3	23.3	50.3	233
	10	2	29.0	34.9	253
	11	1	32.7	17.9	263
	12	12	34.0	0.0	266
Oct 21	8	4	7.1	59.1	103
	9	3	13.8	45.7	192
	10	2	19.0	31.3	230
	11	1	22.3	16.0	247
	12	12	23.5	0.0	252
Nov 21	9	3	5.2	41.9	75
	10	2	10.1	28.5	164
	11	1	13.1	14.5	200
	12	12	14.2	0.0	210
Dec 21	9	3	1.9	40.5	5
	10	2	6.6	27.5	113
	11	1	9.5	13.9	165
	12	12	10.6	0.0	180

Latitude N. 56°

Glass Type	U Value	Shading Coefficient			
			light	drapery	
		no	Venetian		
	Btu/hour/F^2/°F	shade	blinds	light	dark
Clear Glass 1/8"	1.10	1.00	0.55	0.56	0.70
Clear Glass 1/4"	1.10	0.93	0.55	0.56	0.70
Clear Glass 1/2"	1.10	0.88	0.54	0.52	0.66
Grey Glass 1/4"	1.10	0.68	0.52	0.44	0.52
Thermopane 1/8" glass with 1/4" airspace	0.60	0.87	0.51	0.50	0.58

ing system, which would still cycle on to supply heat to the spaces without sun-oriented windows.

In short, window heat gain is effective only if there is provision to use that heat in the design of the mechanical heating system. Thus one must make a judgment about what percentage of the window heat gain can be assumed to be effectively reducing the house heating requirement—based on the "system efficiency" of the design. Although there are no current empirical studies available to establish the system efficiency of window heat gain designs, using the following system efficiency percentages is recommended:

— **Solar-oriented windows in well-insulated houses** — 70%

— **Solar windows with exposed masonry surfaces on the room interior** — 80%

— **Solar windows in open-plan houses** (to permit natural heat flow to the north side or upper portions of the house) — 80%

— **Solar windows with recirculating air fans** (to distribute heat throughout the house) — 90%

— **Solar windows with low-temperature heat storage systems** — 100%

Form 1.2 shown on next page gives the calculations of the Window Heat Gain Contribution of the Denver house example.

Table 11.6. *Shading Coefficient (SC) of various vertical window glass types with and without draperies. The values given in Table 11.3 should be reduced by the above percentages to calculate window heat gain. Extracted from Reference 1 and from Libby-Owens-Ford product literature.*

	WHG	X	PA	X	DM	X	WA	X	SC	=	Qw Btus/mo.
JANUARY	1793	X	.67	X	31	X	150	X	.5	=	2.79×10^6
FEBRUARY	1793	X	.67	X	28	X		X		=	2.52
MARCH	1518	X	.65	X	31	X		X		=	2.29
APRIL	1078	X	.63	X	30	X		X		=	1.53
MAY	781	X	.61	X	31	X		X		=	1.10
JUNE	682	X	.69	X	30	X		X		=	1.06
JULY	759	X	.68	X	31	X		X		=	1.19
AUGUST	1034	X	.68	X	31	X		X		=	1.63
SEPTEMBER	1474	X	.71	X	30	X		X		=	2.35
OCTOBER	1727	X	.71	X	31	X		X		=	2.85
NOVEMBER	1760	X	.67	X	30	X		X		=	2.65
DECEMBER	1716	X	.65	X	31	X		X		=	2.59

TOTAL Qw = 24.55×10^6
                                        Btus/year

© Donald Watson

Qw = heating available thru windows (*before* System Losses)

WHG = clear day heat gain thru vertical glass (Table II.3)
corrected for sky clearness factor of __*1.1*__ (Table II.3A)

PA = percentage of possible sunshine (Table II.4)

DM = days per month

WA = glass area (ft²) = *150 SF*

SC = shading coefficient of window glazing (Table II.6)

Form 1.2. Solar Heat Gain through South Windows, *completed for the Denver example, Alternate E. The Table II.3 values for 40° Latitude are increased by 1.1 to correct for sky clearness in the Denver region. The Percent Actual sunshine values are from Table II.4 for the Denver City location. The shading coefficient of .5 was selected to represent losses due to insulated glass, screens and shading from overhangs. The total window heat gain from this calculation must be further reduced* **according** *to the system efficiency assumed for the particular house design.*

COLLECTOR HEAT GAIN

Just as with a window, the amount of solar radiation that falls upon a collector depends upon latitude, orientation and the percentage of clear sunny hours available.

A solar collector is designed to absorb and transfer heat effectively to the working fluid. In simple terms, its efficiency rating is based on the amount of heat that is recovered from a collector compared to the amount of solar heat that falls on its collector surface.

256

The efficiency of heat collection, while greatly determined by the design of the collector, also can be affected by the rate of flow through the collector, the temperatures maintained in storage (which determine the inlet temperature of liquid or air supplied to the collector) and heat losses, if any, in the collector-to-storage loop.

Efficiency also is a function of the outside air temperature and the minimum usable temperature required from the collector. A collector is therefore most efficient at lower operating temperatures, as seen previously in Figure 4.6.

The monthly heat gain from a collector (Qc) can be estimated by the equation:

$$Qc/month = Ic \times D \times PA \times DM \times CA \times E$$

where:

Ic = Clear Day Value for insolation in Btus per hour available to the collector, if facing due south, as a function of its latitude and angle of tilt

D = the percent reduction of true south values for insolation, according to the deviation of the collector orientation from true south

PA = percent actual sunshine

DM = days per month

CA = net collector area

E = average monthly collection efficiency as a function of insolation, outside air temperature, and minimum usable outlet temperature

Ic (Insolation). The values for the daily amount of solar radiation, or "insolation," that falls upon a south-facing collector under clear-day conditions for northern latitudes and various tilt angles are tabulated in Table II.7. These values also confirm which tilt angles receive the greatest amount of clear-day insolation for each month in each latitude. The table values can also be corrected for sky clearness, if appropriate, as shown in Figure II.3A.

D. Because the values given in Table II.7 show insolation for true south orientations only, collectors facing in directions other than true south must be reduced according to the percentages shown in Table II.8. As can be seen, a deviation up to 10° from true south shows no appreciable reduction in insolation values. As mentioned previously, a bias

Table II.7A to F. *Day-long insolation values (in Btus/SF) on south-facing collector surface at various tilt angles — 0% ground reflectance; 1.0 clearness factor; values derived by graphical interpolation of data from ASHRAE Insolation Tables. (References 1 and 2) (Source: Hill and Harrigan, Consulting Engineers)*

in orientation to the southwest may be desirable due to the higher outside air temperatures in the afternoon depending on design conditions.

PA (percent actual). As described for window heat gain calculation, monthly averages of the percentage of possible sunshine listed in Table II.4 also apply to solar collector heat-gain calculations.

LAT	32°	34°	36°	38°	40°	42°	44°	46°	48°
JAN	1840	1800	1760	1710	1660	1600	1530	1460	1360
FEB	2190	2110	2130	2090	2060	2020	1980	1930	1880
Mar	2380	2350	2340	2320	2310	2280	2260	2230	2210
APR	2440	2440	2430	2420	2410	2400	2380	2370	2360
MAY	2450	2460	2450	2450	2440	2430	2430	2420	2420
JUN	2440	2440	2440	2430	2430	2430	2420	2420	2420
JUL	2440	2440	2430	2420	2410	2400	2400	2400	2390
AUG	2390	2380	2370	2360	2350	2340	2330	2320	2300
SEP	2290	2270	2250	2230	2210	2190	2170	2130	2100
OCT	2100	2070	2040	2000	1960	1920	1880	1830	1770
NOV	1820	1770	1730	1680	1640	1580	1520	1430	1340
DEC	1700	1650	1600	1540	1480	1420	1340	1250	1140

Table II.7A. Collector Tilt Angle = Lat − 10°

LAT	32°	34°	36°	38°	40°	42°	44°	46°	48°
JAN	2010	1970	1920	1870	1810	1750	1680	1590	1480
FEB	2300	2270	2240	2200	2160	2120	2070	2020	1970
MAR	2400	2380	2370	2350	2330	2310	2290	2260	2230
APR	2360	2350	2340	2330	2320	2310	2300	2280	2270
MAY	2280	2280	2270	2260	2260	2250	2240	2240	2230
JUN	2230	2230	2230	2220	2220	2220	2210	2200	2200
JUL	2250	2250	2240	2240	2230	2230	2220	2210	2200
AUG	2300	2290	2280	2270	2260	2250	2230	2220	2200
SEP	2310	2290	2270	2250	2230	2200	2180	2150	2120
OCT	2210	2180	2140	2100	2060	2020	1970	1920	1860
NOV	1980	1940	1890	1840	1780	1720	1650	1560	1450
DEC	1890	1830	1770	1710	1630	1560	1530	1380	1250

Table II.7B. Collector Tilt Angle = Lat + 0°

CA (collector area). The net square foot area of the absorber should be used, not the outside dimensions of the collector. Because of the shading effect from the collector container's trim, the actual absorber area may be only 85 to 90% of the total outside collector dimension. Manufacturer's literature should indicate the net absorber area as well as outside collector dimensions.

LAT	32°	34°	36°	38°	40°	42°	44°	46°	48°
JAN	2070	2020	1970	1920	1860	1790	1730	1630	1520
FEB	2330	2300	2270	2230	2190	2150	2100	2060	2000
MAR	2390	2370	2360	2340	2320	2300	2270	2240	2210
APR	2280	2270	2270	2260	2250	2240	2230	2210	2190
MAY	2180	2180	2180	2170	2160	2140	2120	2080	2030
JUN	2120	2120	2120	2110	2100	2090	2090	2080	2080
JUL	2140	2140	2140	2130	2130	2130	2130	2140	2150
AUG	2220	2220	2210	2200	2180	2160	2130	2090	2030
SEP	2290	2270	2250	2230	2210	2180	2160	2130	2100
OCT	2230	2200	2160	2120	2080	2030	1970	1900	1800
NOV	2030	1990	1940	1890	1830	1770	1700	1600	1480
DEC	1950	1890	1830	1770	1690	1620	1530	1430	1300

Table II.7C. Collector Tilt Angle = Lat + 5°

LAT	32°	34°	36°	38°	40°	42°	44°	46°	48°
JAN	2120	2080	2030	1970	1910	1840	1760	1670	1550
FEB	2350	2320	2280	2240	2200	2160	2120	2070	2020
MAR	2360	2340	2320	2300	2280	2260	2240	2210	2180
APR	2210	2200	2190	2180	2170	2160	2150	2130	2110
MAY	2060	2050	2050	2050	2040	2030	2020	2020	2010
JUN	1990	1990	1980	1980	1970	1970	1960	1960	1950
JUL	2030	2030	2020	2010	2010	2000	1990	1980	1970
AUG	2140	2130	2120	2110	2100	2090	2080	2060	2050
SEP	2260	2240	2220	2200	2180	2160	2140	2100	2070
OCT	2250	2220	2180	2140	2100	2050	2000	1950	1890
NOV	2080	2040	1990	1930	1870	1800	1720	1630	1520
DEC	2020	1960	1890	1820	1740	1650	1560	1450	1330

Table II.7D. Collector Tilt Angle = Lat + 10°

E (collector efficiency). The efficiency of a collector depends upon factors which vary a great deal: the amount of solar radiation available, the outside air temperature, the operating temperatures of the solar heating system and the collector design itself. An accurate estimate of collector efficiency therefore involves complex calculations of these variables.

LAT	32°	34°	36°	38°	40°	42°	44°	46°	48°
JAN	2150	2100	2050	1990	1930	1860	1790	1700	1570
FEB	2340	2310	2280	2240	2200	2170	2120	2070	2020
MAR	2320	2300	2270	2250	2230	2210	2190	2170	2140
APR	2120	2110	2100	2080	2070	2050	2040	2030	2020
MAY	1940	1940	1930	1930	1920	1910	1900	1890	1880
JUN	1850	1850	1840	1840	1830	1820	1820	1810	1800
JUL	1900	1890	1880	1870	1870	1870	1880	1890	1910
AUG	2050	2050	2040	2030	2020	2010	1990	1970	1950
SEP	2220	2200	2180	2160	2140	2120	2090	2060	2030
OCT	2250	2220	2180	2130	2090	2050	2000	1940	1870
NOV	2120	2070	2020	1960	1900	1830	1760	1670	1540
DEC	2060	2000	1930	1860	1780	1700	1610	1500	1330

Table II.7E. Collector Tilt Angle = Lat + 15°

LAT	32°	34°	36°	38°	40°	42°	44°	46°	48°
JAN	2170	2120	2060	2000	1940	1870	1790	1700	1580
FEB	2320	2290	2250	2220	2180	2140	2100	2040	1980
MAR	2250	2230	2210	2190	2170	2140	2120	2090	2070
APR	1990	1980	1980	1970	1960	1950	1930	1920	1900
MAY	1790	1780	1780	1770	1760	1750	1740	1730	1730
JUN	1690	1690	1680	1670	1670	1660	1650	1650	1640
JUL	1750	1750	1740	1730	1730	1720	1720	1700	1690
AUG	1930	1920	1910	1900	1890	1980	1970	1950	1840
SEP	2150	2130	2110	2090	2070	2040	2020	1990	1970
OCT	2230	2200	2160	2110	2070	2030	1970	1920	1870
NOV	2130	2080	2030	1970	1910	1830	1760	1670	1540
DEC	2090	2030	1960	1880	1800	1720	1630	1520	1360

Table II.7F. Collector Tilt Angle = Lat + 20°

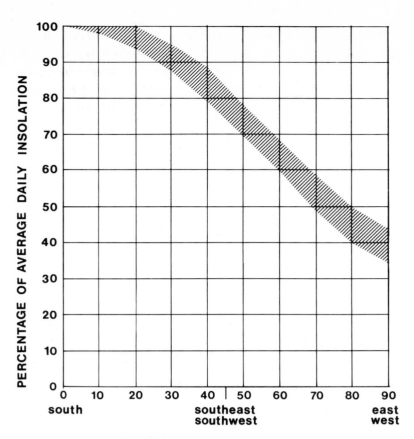

AZIMUTH deviation from true south

Table II.8. *Deviation from True South. Percent reduction of Table II.7 values if collector is off true south (winter months shown). (Reference 2)*

However, for working estimates of the potential heat gain from collectors, a percentage that represents the average collection efficiency either monthly or averaged over the heating season can be used. As shown in Chapter 5 in the documentation of Massachusetts Institute of Technology Solar House IV, the average annual collection efficiency of the collector design that was used equalled 43 percent over the two years that the tests were made. The lowest and highest monthly efficiencies varied from this by only 5 percent. The Massachusetts Institute of Technology collector was a two-glass-cover aluminum collector with black paint. There were some inefficiencies in the frame design which resulted in shading and heat losses. The improvements in collector design since then are represented in collection efficiencies as shown in Table II.9.

The instantaneous efficiency that is normally shown in collector manufacturer's literature should be reduced by 20 percent to account for reduced collection efficiency in relation to day-long radiation.

261

Table II.9. *Instantaneous Efficiency of Various Collector Types. Representative only, based on performance data reported by Beard (1976), Converse (1976) and Wormser (1976). Performance of collectors from different manufacturers varies according to construction details. Updated efficiency data are available from manufacturers.*

1 - *Site-fabricated air-collector in vertical installation*
2 - *Site-fabricated water-trickling collector*
3 - *Air collector — double-glazed with non-selective black*
4 - *Liquid collector — Double-glazed with non-selective black*
5 - *Liquid collector — double-glazed anti-reflective coating on glazing and selective coating on absorber*
6 - *Liquid or air collector — single-glazed with selective coating*
7 - *Liquid collector with internal heat trap*
8 - *Evacuated tube collector*

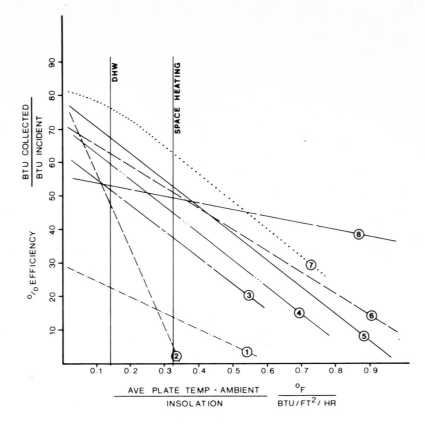

The efficiency of a collector depends upon its average operating temperature above the outside air temperature and the average available solar insolation.
For domestic hot water heating, assume an average operating temperature of 45 degrees above the outside ambient. Thus if local average yearly insolation equals 320 Btu/SF/hr, the collector efficiency should be read at $\dfrac{45}{320}$ = 0.14 *on the horizontal axis. For space heating, assume an average operating temperature of* $90°$ *above the outside ambient. Thus if local average winter insolation equals 280 Btus/SF/hr., the collector efficiency should be read at* $\dfrac{90}{280}$ = 0.32 *on the horizontal axis.*

Efficient system designs may permit lower operating temperatures (50 to 80 degrees F. above outside air temperatures) which are preferred since collection efficiency is thus improved. In the calculation method shown on Form 1.3, the Table II.9 collector efficiency numbers should be reduced by 20% to account for hours when there is insufficient sunshine to justify collection.

   In Form 1.3 opposite, the Denver example house calculation is shown with the Table II.7 values increased by 10 percent to adjust for the relatively high altitude and sky clearness in Denver.
   Some manufacturers provide performance data on the monthly output of their solar collectors that can be compared with these calculation results.
   The estimate of solar collector output given by the calculations does not include possible heat loss in transferring heat from collector to storage to space. To assume maximum system efficiency,

PROJECT: *DENVER ALTERNATE E*
SOLAR HEAT GAIN FROM COLLECTORS (Q_c)

FORM 1.3

	Ic	X	PA	X	DM	X	CA	X	E	=	Qc Btus/mo.
JANUARY	2101	X	.67	X	31	X	223	X	.5	=	4.87 x 10⁶
FEBRUARY	2420	X	.67	X	28	X		X		=	5.06
MARCH	2508	X	.65	X	31	X		X		=	5.63
APRIL	2387	X	.63	X	30	X		X		=	5.03
MAY	2244	X	.61	X	31	X		X		=	4.73
JUNE	2167	X	.69	X	30	X		X		=	5.00
JULY	2211	X	.68	X	31	X		X		=	5.19
AUGUST	2310	X	.68	X	31	X		X		=	5.43
SEPTEMBER	2398	X	.71	X	30	X		X		=	5.69
OCTOBER	2310	X	.71	X	31	X		X		=	5.66
NOVEMBER	2057	X	.67	X	30	X		X		=	4.61
DECEMBER	1914	X	.65	X	31	X		X		=	4.30

TOTAL Qc =

61.2 X 10⁶
Btus/year

© Donald Watson

Q_c = energy available from collectors (*before* System Losses)
I_c = clear day insolation Btus/day/ft.² (Table II.7) collector tilt = <u>*Lat* + 10°</u> = 50°
   clearness factor = <u>1.1</u> (Table II.3A)
   collector orientation = <u>S</u> (If off-True South, see Table II.8)
PA = percentage of possible sunshine (Table II.4)
DM = days per month
CA = net usable collector absorber area **223** SF
E = overall collection efficiency at Delta T of <u>80</u> ° F. (Table II.9) *(.63 x .8 = .5)*

Form 1.3. Solar Heat Gain from Collectors, completed for the Denver example, Alternate E. The Table II.7 values are increased by 1.1. to correct for sky clearness in the Denver region. The Percent Actual sunshine values are the same as used on Form 1.2. As indicated in Table II.9, the instantaneous efficiency of the collector is reduced by 80% to reflect daylong performance relative to available radiation. The total collector heat gain from this calculation must be further reduced if system losses are assumed, according to the specific layout of the solar system in relation to the house design.

the collector, storage, and distribution center should be close to one another, with a minimum number of bends in pipes and ducts. Minimum heat losses can be assumed when the collector and storage elements are part of the house construction and where collector and storage heat transfer is efficiently accomplished.

For designs where such a layout is not practical, the collector heat gain calculation should be reduced by 5 to 10 percent for heat losses within the storage and distribution system.

THERMAL STORAGE: SIZE AND CAPACITY

The volume used for heat storage, whether water or rock, usually is limited as much by building area and construction costs and available container sizes as by solar design factors. However, depending on the local winter sunshine characteristics, it may be desirable to limit the size of storage to only one day carry-over (as in the U.S. southwest) or to attempt a longer term carry-over by increased storage volume.

It is possible to estimate roughly the amount of heat that can be stored in a given volume of water or rock by the following equation:

$$\text{Btus stored/unit volume} = \text{Density} \times \text{Specific Heat} \times dTS$$

where:

dTS (storage temperature differential) is the range of usable temperature that can be stored effectively and recovered from a given heat-storage design. The usable temperature range depends upon the specific system, but for estimating purposes, a maximum storage temperature in northern climates during the winter season can be assumed to be 130° F. and a minimum usable storage temperature 85° F., (assuming large ducts and carefully placed heat supply outlets). Thus for standard solar system design, dTS would be 130° − 85° F. = 45° F.

The average density of water is 62.4 pounds per cubic foot or 8.33 pounds per gallon. The specific heat of water is 1 Btu per pound per degree Fahrenheit.

Thus:

$$\text{Btu stored/gallon} = 8.33 \text{ lb/gal.} \times 1 \times dTS \text{ or}$$
$$8.33 \times dTS$$

The average density of solid rock is 140 pounds per cubic foot. One can assume about 30 percent of the volume of the rock storage is air, so that the average density of the rock storage equals 100 pounds per cubic foot.

The specific heat of rock averages about 0.2 Btus per pound per degree Fahrenheit.

Thus:

$$\text{Btus stored/Ft.}^3 = 100 \text{ lb/ft.}^3 \times 0.2 \text{ Btu/lb/F}^\circ \times dTS \text{ or}$$
$$20 \times dTS$$

These calculations give the heat storage capacity of a unit of water or rock, which can be multiplied by the volume of water or of rock and the assumed storage temperature differential, to determine the heat-storage capacity of a particular design.

For example, a 2500-gallon water storage tank (roughly 12 feet long × 6 feet in diameter), with an assumed dTS = 45°F.:

$$\text{Btus stored} = 2500 \times 8.33 \times 45 = 940,000 \text{ Btus}$$

Carry-over Capacity. The number of hours that the heat stored in a given volume of storage will provide usable heat is its "carry-over" capacity. It depends on the heat requirements of a particular house design as represented by the Design Heat Loss.

For rough estimates, the daily heat requirement in mid-winter can be assumed to be one half of the Design Heat Loss. So that:

$$\text{Carry-over (hours)} = \frac{\text{Btus stored/volume}}{\frac{1}{2} \times \text{DHL (Btus/hr.)}}$$

In a northern climate, a moderately sized, well-insulated house might have a Design Heat Loss of 40,000 Btus hr. So, in the example of the 2500-gallon water storage, the carry-over is:

$$\text{Carry-over (hours)} = \frac{2500 \times 8.33 \times 45}{\frac{1}{2} \times 40,000} = \frac{940,000}{20,000} = 47 \text{ hrs.}$$

The same formula can be used to determine the required volume, given other storage temperature differentials or carry-over requirements. The storage capacity of passive systems can be estimated using the same calculation adjusted to the density and specific heat of the rock storage used and the lower temperature differential associated with passive systems.

Two items of judgment are critical in making estimates for passive storage design to reflect the particular characteristics of the storage installation:

the effective storage temperature range and the efficiency of heat transfer.

If a masonry wall is exposed to the interior of a room, it can give off an effective heating effect when it is as low as 70° F.

If the wall is heated during the day by the super-heated room air (as in the design shown in Figure 3.4), then its temperature may reach as high as 80° F. Thus the dTS could be assumed to be 80° –70° = 10° F.

In the rock storage used in a house or greenhouse heat-recovery system, the temperature of the return air may average 90° F., and can be stored in an underfloor radiant slab where it is effective to as low as 70° F., for a dTS = 90° –70° F. = 20° F.

If the masonry wall is used as a collector as well as a radiant heating wall exposed directly to the interior (as in Figure 3.5), and is insulated at night, then its effective temperature may average 100° F. on the interior surface for a dTS of 100° –70° F. = 30° F.

These temperatures are generalized on the basis of results reported from a few operating examples. In the future, more complete performance characteristics of various passive systems will permit more accurate calculation. But it can be readily seen that the storage volume in passive systems must be increased proportionately to the lower temperature ranges available from window and house-heat recovery systems.

II.3
Auxiliary Fuel
Requirement:

Depending on the solar heating alternative used, the monthly solar heating contribution subtracted from the monthly heating energy requirement gives the monthly requirement for auxiliary fuel (Qaux).

The continuation of the Denver house example calculation is shown in Form 1.4. A separate form can be completed for each alternative considered.

The result is a tabulation of the auxiliary energy required in Btus per month. The total auxiliary energy required annually can then be totaled and converted into equivalent fuel requirements according to the conversion factors shown in Table II.10.

PROJECT: _DENVER ALTERNATE E_
AUXILIARY FUEL REQUIREMENT ($Qaux$)

	Qr	−	Qw^*	+	Qc^*	=	$Qaux$ Btus/mo.
JANUARY	13.25×10^6	−	2.23×10^6	+	4.87×10^6	=	6.15×10^6
FEBRUARY	11.23	−	2.02	+	5.06	=	4.15
MARCH	10.56	−	1.83	+	5.63	=	3.10
APRIL	6.49	−	1.22	+	5.03	=	$.24$
MAY	3.35	−	$.88$	+	4.73	=	—
JUNE	$.63$	−	$.85$	+	5.00	=	—
JULY	0	−	$.95$	+	5.19	=	—
AUGUST	0	−	1.30	+	5.43	=	—
SEPTEMBER	1.18	−	1.88	+	5.69	=	—
OCTOBER	4.83	−	2.28	+	5.66	=	—
NOVEMBER	9.42	−	2.12	+	4.61	=	2.69
DECEMBER	11.94	−	2.07	+	4.30	=	5.57

TOTAL $Qaux$ = 21.9×10^6
Btus/year

Qr = heating energy required
Qw^* = energy available from windows. Assume __80__ % System efficiency   _(Form 1.2 × .8)_
Qc^* = energy available from collectors. Assume __0__ % System losses   _(Form 1.3)_

* The totals from Forms 1.2 and 1.3 must be adjusted to reflect assumed System efficiency and losses.

% Solar Capacity = $\dfrac{Qr - Qaux}{Qr}$ = $\dfrac{72.88 - 21.9}{72.88}$ = $\dfrac{50.98}{72.88}$ = 69%

© Donald Watson

Form 1.4. Auxiliary Fuel Requirement, completed for the Denver example, Alternate E. Qr is taken from Form 1.1. Qw* represents an 80% reduction of the Form 1.2 calculations to account for the system efficiency of the window heat recovery used in the Alternate E design.

0% collector system losses are assumed due to the fact that the entire shortage and distribution system are within the house design and are efficiently arranged. The auxiliary fuel requirement must be tabulated on a monthly basis.

Fuel Source	Fuel Content	% Burning Efficiency	Conversion Factor (fuel content x % burning efficiency)	Representative Local Cost	Representative Cost/Million Btus (local fuel cost x 10^6 Btus ÷ conversion factor)
1 gallon #2 oil	140,000 Btus/gallon	80[1]	112,000 Btus/gallon	$0.42/gallon	$3.75/$10^6$ Btus
1 gallon #2 oil	140,000 Btus/gallon	70[2]	98,000 Btus/gallon	$0.42/gallon	4.29
1 cubic foot natural gas	1,000 Btus/cubic foot	80[1]	800 Btus/cubic foot	$0.0037/cubic foot	4.63
1 cubic foot natural gas	1,000 Btus/cubic foot	70[2]	700 Btus/cubic foot	$0.0037/cubic foot	5.29
1 therm LP gas	9,300 Btus/therm	80[1]	7,440 Btus/therm	$0.06/therm	8.02
1 therm LP gas	9,300 Btus/therm	70[2]	6,510 Btus/therm	$0.06/therm	9.22
1 kWh electric heat	3,413 Btus/kWh	95[3]	3,242 Btus/kWh	$0.045/kWh	13.88
1 kWh electric heat	3,413 Btus/kWh	80[2]	2,730 Btus/kWh	$0.045/kWh	16.48
1 cord Hickory	35,300,000 Btus/cord	70[4]	24,710,000 Btus/cord	$80/cord[5]	3.24
1 cord red oak	30,400,000 Btus/cord	70[4]	21,280,000 Btus/cord	$70/cord	3.30
1 cord ash	28,300,000 Btus/cord	70[4]	19,810,000 Btus/cord	$60/cord	3.03
1 cord red maple	26,300,000 Btus/cord	70[4]	18,410,000 Btus/cord	$60/cord	3.30

Table II.10. *The Equivalent Fuel Content and Cost of Various Conventional Heating Fuel Sources. Cost per million Btus can be recalculated using local fuel costs by the formulas shown in the table heading.*

(1) high-efficiency furnace
(2) standard furnace, regularly maintained
(3) baseboard or fan units
(4) wood-burning furnace, regularly maintained; wood less than 12% moisture
(5) disregards labor required for loading

The annual fuel savings at present fuel costs can also be estimated by calculating from Form 1.4 the solar energy actually used per month (Qr–Qaux) and converting it to equivalent fuel dollars.

It will be seen that the fuel chosen for cost comparison will greatly influence the relative economic attractiveness of a solar installation. For realistic comparison, the most competitive local fuel rate should be used.

Reference 2 gives a method of estimating the energy requirement and potential solar contribution of solar installations on existing houses, based on fuel conversion factors and actual fuel bill records.

After estimating the annual fuel-cost savings in current fuel dollars (as discussed in the previous section), the accumulated fuel savings over a given period of years can be calculated, with an annual rate of fuel-cost escalation that must be selected according to one's own best judgment.

As shown in the example in Chapter 7, it is both easy and reasonable to calculate the accumulated fuel savings for the same number of years as the mortgage period over which the solar installation is financed. While the average length of home mortgage periods is currently extending beyond 20 years, the examples in this book are considered as 20 year investments. As previously mentioned, fuel cost rises in the range of 8 to 10 percent per annum over this period are generally accepted as a projected fuel escalation rate for life-cycle cost estimates.

Table II.11 shows the value of a dollar in fuel savings over 20 years at various rates of fuel escalation (from 2 to 16 percent per annum). Thus, a fuel-cost savings of $300 in present fuel costs over a 20-year period at a 10 percent annual fuel-cost increase = $300 × 61.99 = $18,597. Divided by the total number of months in the 20-year period, this represents an average monthly fuel cost savings of $18,597 ÷ 240, or $77.49.

From the total fuel savings, one must subtract the added investment in the building construction due to the solar installation cost-differential, including financing charges. (The solar cost-differential is equal to the installed cost of the solar heating system minus the installed cost of a conventional heating system.)

The interest rate chart (Table II.12) shows the total 20-year cost of a dollar borrowed at various rates of interest and repaid monthly, with multiples given for both the monthly and yearly costs of each dollar of principal borrowed, plus interest. Thus, if the solar installation that saves $300 per year at current fuel costs is estimated to require $5000 over and above the conventional heating system, the

Table II.11. *Long-term value of one dollar in current fuel cost savings at various rates of annual fuel cost increase.*

Example: A dollar saved in current fuel costs at 10% fuel cost increase = $61.99 over a twenty-year period, or an average of $3.10 per year. A solar heating installation that saves $300 per year in current fuel costs will thus realize a total savings of $300 x $3.10 x 20 years = $18,600, or $930 as a twenty-year annual average saving. The added installation cost of the solar system, including financing charges, must be deducted from this total to determine the net savings.

% Annual Increase in Fuel Cost

Year	2%	4%	6%	8%	10%	12%	14%	16%
1	1.02	1.04	1.06	1.08	1.10	1.12	1.14	1.16
2	1.04	1.08	1.12	1.17	1.21	1.25	1.30	1.35
3	1.06	1.12	1.19	1.26	1.33	1.40	1.48	1.56
4	1.08	1.17	1.26	1.36	1.46	1.57	1.69	1.81
5	1.10	1.22	1.34	1.47	1.61	1.76	1.93	2.10
6	1.13	1.27	1.42	1.59	1.77	1.97	2.19	2.44
7	1.15	1.32	1.50	1.71	1.95	2.21	2.50	2.83
8	1.17	1.37	1.59	1.85	2.14	2.48	2.85	3.28
9	1.20	1.42	1.69	2.00	2.36	2.77	3.25	3.80
10	1.22	1.48	1.79	2.16	2.59	3.10	3.71	4.41
11	1.24	1.54	1.90	2.33	2.85	3.47	4.23	5.12
12	1.27	1.60	2.01	2.52	3.14	3.89	4.82	5.94
13	1.29	1.67	2.13	2.72	2.45	4.36	5.49	6.89
14	1.32	1.73	2.26	2.94	3.80	4.88	6.26	7.99
15	1.35	1.80	2.40	3.17	4.18	5.47	7.14	9.27
16	1.37	1.87	2.54	3.43	4.59	6.12	8.14	10.75
17	1.40	1.95	2.69	3.70	5.05	6.85	9.28	12.47
18	1.43	2.03	2.85	4.00	5.56	7.68	10.58	14.46
19	1.46	2.11	3.03	4.23	6.12	8.60	12.06	16.78
20	1.49	2.19	3.21	4.66	6.73	9.63	13.74	19.46
20-Year total	24.79	30.98	38.98	49.44	61.99	80.58	103.78	133.87
20-Year average	1.23	1.54	1.95	2.47	3.10	4.03	5.19	6.69

Table II.12. *Monthly payment and twenty-year total of $1.00 borrowed at various rates of interest. To determine total principal and interest of a given loan, multiply by figures in right hand column.*

% Annual Interest Rate	Monthly Principal and interest of $1.00 borrowed	Twenty Year Total Principal and interest of $1.00 borrowed
6	0.007165	1.7196
7	0.007753	1.8607
8	0.008365	2.0076
8.25	0.008521	2.0450
8.5	0.008679	2.0830
8.75	0.008838	2.1211
9	0.008998	2.1595
9.25	0.009159	2.1982
9.5	0.009322	2.2373
9.75	0.009486	2.2766
10	0.009551	2.2922
11	0.01322	2.4773
12	0.011011	2.6426

total financing cost over 20 years at 8½ percent annual interest = $5000 x 2.083 or $10,415. The monthly payment on the mortgage = $5000 x 0.008679 or $43.40.

The net savings resulting from the solar installation would thus be the monthly fuel savings minus the monthly finance charge, $77.49–$43.40 = $34.09.

Form 1.6 is shown on the next page completed for the Denver Alternate E example. The identical method can be used for mortgage periods other than the 20-years shown in Table II.12, with principal plus interest multiples obtainable from banking finance tables. As shown in Chapter 7, such calculations provide the best basis for comparing different solar alternatives, and can be used with any given set of solar cost, fuel cost and finance rate assumptions. Blank forms are provided on pages 273-278. The monthly calculations are aligned to the numbers given in the various tables for easy notation.

Length:	1 in.	= 0.08333 ft.
	1 cm.	= 0.03281 ft.
	1 mile	= 5280 ft.
Mass:	1 kg. (kilogram)	= 2.205 lb_m
	1 g. (gram)	= 2.205 x 10^{-3} lb_m
Energy:	1 ft-lb_f	= 0.001285 Btu
	1 kw-hr (kilowatt-hour)	= 3413 Btu
	1 hp. (horsepower)	= 2544 Btu
	1 kcal. (kilocalorie)	= 3.968 Btu
	1 joule	= 9.478 x 10^{-4} Btu
Heat flow rate per unit area:	1 cal/sec sq. cm.	= 13,272 Btu/hr sq. ft.
	1 watt/sq. cm.	= 3171 Btu/hr sq. ft.
	1 cal/hr. sq. cm.	= 3.687 Btu/hr sq. ft.
Pressure:	1 dyne/sq. cm.	= 0.00209 psf
	1 cm. Hg.	= 27.85 psf
	1 in. Hg.	= 70.73 psf
	1 in. water	= 5.20 psf
	1 ft. water	= 62.43 psf
Density:	1 gm/cu cm.	= 62.43 lb_m/cu ft.
	1 lb_m/gallon	= 7.481 lb_m/cu ft.
	1 lb_m/cu in.	= 1728 lb_m/cu ft.
Temperature:	1 R. (degree Rankine)	= 1 F. (degree Fahrenheit)
	1 C. (degree Celsius)	= 1.8 F.
	1 K. (degree Kelvin)	= 1.8 F.

Table II.13. *Metric Conversion Factors. To convert a given quantity from one set of units to another:*

1. *Write after the magnitude of the quantity the names of the units in which it is measured.*
2. *Replace each name by its equivalent in the new units, and arithmetically combine all numbers in the new expression.*
3. *To convert °F. to °C.:*
   $°F. = 1.8 \times °C. + 32$

   To convert °C. to °F.:
   $°C. = °F. - 32 \div 1.8.$

PROJECT: *DENVER ALTERNATE E*
PROJECT SUMMARY

1 Annual space heating requirement (Qr_1) — 72.88×10^6 Btus/yr.

2 Annual domestic water heating requirement (Qr_2) — 13.25 Btus/yr.

3 Auxiliary fuel requirement   space heating ($Qaux_1$) — 21.9 Btus/yr.

4 Auxiliary fuel requirement   domestic water heating ($Qaux_2$) — $.39$ Btus/yr.

5 Heating energy available from windows (Qw^*) ⎫
6 Heating energy available from collectors (Qc^*) ⎭ $72.88 - 21.9 = 50.98 \times 10^6$ ⎰ _____ Btus/yr. / _____ Btus/yr.

7 % Solar capacity = $\dfrac{Qr - Qaux}{Qr}$ = $\dfrac{72.88 - 21.9}{72.88}$ + $\dfrac{13.25 - .39}{13.25}$ = — 74 %

8 Carryover capacity of storage — — hours

9 Current unit cost of conventional space heating fuel — $.42$ $/gal.

10 Equivalent cost per million Btus — 4.29 $/$10^6$ Btus

11 Current unit cost of conventional *DHW* fuel — $.045$ $/kWh

12 Equivalent cost per million Btus — 13.88 $/$10^6$ Btus

13 Annual fuel cost saving (current fuel cost) space heating ⎫ $397.20 ⎰ $ 218.70
14 Annual fuel cost saving (current fuel cost) *DHW* ⎭ ⎱ $ 178.50

15 Estimated installed cost: solar heating system — $ —

16 Estimated installed cost: conventional heating system — $ —

17 Solar cost differential (line 15 minus line 16) — $ 5,800

18 Total cost of solar differential, financed at $8\frac{1}{2}$ % over 20 years 5800×2.083 — $ 12,081

19 Monthly financing cost of solar differential (principal plus interest) — $ 50.30

20 Total fuel savings, assumed fuel cost escalation of 8 %, over 20 year mortgage period — $ 19,638.

21 Monthly fuel savings (mortgage period in months) — $ 81.80

22   Net monthly savings (or loss) from solar heating
     (line 21 minus line 19) — $ 31.50   ~ $32

Form 1.6. Project Summary, *completed for the Denver example, Alternate E. Items 1 through 7 are taken from previous forms. Items 9 through 12 represent the local fuel costs assumed in the Chapter 7 example, converted into equivalent Cost Per Million Btus, as shown in Table II.10. Items 15 through 17 require a* *specific cost estimate of the individual solar system that is considered. The remaining calculations can be completed using the multiplying factors given in Tables II.11 and II.12. The net result (line 22) of this Denver Alternate E calculation is compared with other solar alternatives in Figure 7.5.*

	DHL/Delta T $\times$ 24	X	DDM	=	Qr Btus/mo.
JANUARY		X		=	
FEBRUARY	''	X		=	
MARCH	''	X		=	
APRIL	''	X		=	
MAY	''	X		=	
JUNE	''	X		=	
JULY	''	X		=	
AUGUST	''	X		=	
SEPTEMBER	''	X		=	
OCTOBER	''	X		=	
NOVEMBER	''	X		=	
DECEMBER	''	X		=	

TOTAL Qr =   Btus/yr.

Qr = heating energy required

DHL/Delta T = design heat loss divided by design temperature differential (t_i – t_o) in Btus/° F./hour. (Table II.1)

DDM = monthly degree days (Table II.2)

| | PROJECT: | | | | | | | | | | FORM 1.2 |
| SOLAR HEAT GAIN THRU WINDOWS (Qw) | | | | | | | | | | | |

	WHG	X	PA	X	DM	X	WA	X	SC	=	Qw Btus/mo.
JANUARY		X		X	31	X		X		=	
FEBRUARY		X		X	28	X		X		=	
MARCH		X		X	31	X		X		=	
APRIL		X		X	30	X		X		=	
MAY		X		X	31	X		X		=	
JUNE		X		X	30	X		X		=	
JULY		X		X	31	X		X		=	
AUGUST		X		X	31	X		X		=	
SEPTEMBER		X		X	30	X		X		=	
OCTOBER		X		X	31	X		X		=	
NOVEMBER		X		X	30	X		X		=	
DECEMBER		X		X	31	X		X		=	

TOTAL Q_w =   Btus/year

Designing & Building a Solar House

Q_w = heating available thru windows (*before* System Losses)

WHG = clear day heat gain thru vertical glass (Table II.3)
corrected for sky clearness factor of _____ (Table II.3A)

PA = percentage of possible sunshine (Table II.4)

DM = days per month

WA = glass area (ft^2)

SC = shading coefficient of window glazing (Table II.6)

	Ic	X	PA	X	DM	X	CA	X	E	=	Qc Btus/mo.
JANUARY		X		X	31	X		X		=	
FEBRUARY		X		X	28	X		X		=	
MARCH		X		X	31	X		X		=	
APRIL		X		X	30	X		X		=	
MAY		X		X	31	X		X		=	
JUNE		X		X	30	X		X		=	
JULY		X		X	31	X		X		=	
AUGUST		X		X	31	X		X		=	
SEPTEMBER		X		X	30	X		X		=	
OCTOBER		X		X	31	X		X		=	
NOVEMBER		X		X	30	X		X		=	
DECEMBER		X		X	31	X		X		=	

TOTAL Qc =   **Btus/year**

Qc = energy available from collectors (*before* System Losses)

Ic = clear day insolation Btus/day/ft.^{2} (Table II.7) collector tilt = _____
clearness factor = _____ (Table II.3A)
collector orientation = _____ (If off-True South, see Table II.8)

PA = percentage of possible sunshine (Table II.4)

DM = days per month

CA = net usable collector absorber area

E = overall collection efficiency at Delta T of _____ ° F. (Table II.9)

PROJECT:
AUXILIARY FUEL REQUIREMENT ($Qaux$)

	Qr	−	Qw^*	+	Qc^*	=	$Qaux$ Btus/mo.
JANUARY		−		+		=	
FEBRUARY		−		+		=	
MARCH		−		+		=	
APRIL		−		+		=	
MAY		−		+		=	
JUNE		−		+		=	
JULY		−		+		=	
AUGUST		−		+		=	
SEPTEMBER		−		+		=	
OCTOBER		−		+		=	
NOVEMBER		−		+		=	
DECEMBER		−		+		=	

TOTAL $Qaux$ =   Btus/year

Qr = heating energy required
Qw = energy available from windows. Assure _____% System efficiency
Qc = energy available from collectors. Assume _____% System losses

* The totals from Forms 1.2 and 1.3 must be adjusted to reflect assumed System
   efficiency and losses.

% Solar Capacity = $\dfrac{Qr - Qaux}{Qr}$

| PROJECT: | | | FORM 1.5 |
| SOLAR INSTALLATION COST ESTIMATE | | | |

ITEM	Material	Labor	Subtotal
01 Collector Mounting	$	$	$
02 Solar Collectors			
03 Liquid Collector Piping			
04 Air Collector Ducting			
05 Collector Manifold Insulation			
06 Manifold Flashing			
07 Storage Container Support			
08 Domestic Hot Water Storage			
09 Storage Container-Liquid			
10 Storage Container-Air			
11 Storage Container Lining			
12 Storage Container Insulation			
13 Liquid Storage Expansion Tank			
14 Rock Storage			
15 Liquid Collector Coolant (antifreeze)			
16 Heat Exchangers			
17 Circulating Pumps			
18 Valves and Fittings			
19 Dampers and Fans			
20 Special Equipment:			
21 Special Equipment:			
22 Storage to House Distribution System			
23 Controls			
24 Electrical			
25 Auxiliary (back-up) System			
26 Miscellaneous			
SUBTOTAL			$
Contingency			
Overhead and Profit			
Fees (Engineering, Brokerage)			

Total All Items This Page   = $_____
Assumed Conventional System Cost   = $_____
Solar Cost Differential = Total — Conventional System Cost   = $_____

1 Annual space heating requirement (Qr_1) _____ Btus/yr.

2 Annual domestic water heating requirement (Qr_2) _____ Btus/yr.

3 Auxiliary fuel requirement   space heating ($Qaux_1$) _____ Btus/yr.

4 Auxiliary fuel requirement   domestic water heating ($Qaux_2$) _____ Btus/yr.

5 Heating energy available from windows (Qw^*) _____ Btus/yr.

6 Heating energy available from collectors (Qc^*) _____ Btus/yr.

7 % Solar capacity $= \dfrac{Qr - Qaux}{Qr} =$ _____ %

8 Carryover capacity of storage _____ hours

9 Current unit cost of conventional space heating fuel _____ $/

10 Equivalent cost per million Btus _____ $/$10^6$ Btus

11 Current unit cost of conventional *DHW* fuel _____ $/

12 Equivalent cost per million Btus _____ $/$10^6$ Btus

13 Annual fuel cost saving (current fuel cost) space heating $ _____

14 Annual fuel cost saving (current fuel cost) *DHW* $ _____

15 Estimated installed cost: solar heating system $ _____

16 Estimated installed cost: conventional heating system $ _____

17 Solar cost differential (line 15 minus line 16) $ _____

18 Total cost of solar differential, financed at____% over ____years $ _____

19 Monthly financing cost of solar differential (principal plus interest) $ _____

20 Total fuel savings, assumed fuel cost escalation of ____%, over ____year mortgage period $ _____

21 Monthly fuel savings (mortgage period in months) $ _____

22   Net monthly savings (or loss) from solar heating
     (line 21 minus line 19) $ _____

INDEX

Other Garden Way Books You Will Enjoy

The owner/builder and the home-owner concerned about energy conservation and alternate construction methods will find an up-to-date library essential. Here are some excellent books in these areas from the publisher of **Designing & Building a Solar House.**

Low-Cost Pole Building Construction, by Douglas Merrilees and Evelyn Loveday. 118 pp., deluxe paperback, $4.95. This will save you money, labor, time and materials.

Build Your Own Stone House, by Karl and Sue Schwenke. 156 pp., quality paperback, $4.95; hardback, $8.95. With their help, you can build your own beautiful stone home.

New Low-Cost Sources of Energy for the Home, by Peter Clegg. 250 pp., quality paperback, $5.95; hardback, $8.95. Covers solar heating and cooling, wind and water power, wood heat and methane digestion. Packed with information.

Wood Stove Know-how, by Peter Coleman. 24 pp., illustrated paperback, $1.50. Installation, cleaning and maintenance instructions, plus much more.

The Complete Book of Heating with Wood, by Larry Gay. 128 pp., quality paperback, $3.95. Fight rising home heating costs and still keep very warm.

The Complete Homesteading Book, by David Robinson, 256 pp., quality paperback, $5.95; hardback, $8.95. How to live a simpler, more self-sufficient life.

Buying Country Property, by Herb Moral. 128 pp., quality paperback, $3.50. Sure to be your "best friend" when considering country property.

Methanol & Other Ways Around the Gas Pump, by John Ware Lincoln. 144 pages; quality paperback, $4.95. How to "drive without gas"—using methanol—and a look at the past experiments and future politics of our gasoline supply.

These Garden Way books are available at your bookstore, or may be ordered directly from Garden Way Publishing, Dept. SH, Charlotte, Vermont 05445. If your order is less than $10, please add 60¢ postage and handling.